The Ethnic Question

Note to the Reader from the UNU

It was with a view to shedding new light on the relationships between minority cultures and development processes that the United Nations University launched a project in 1983 on ethnic minorities and social and human development. Professor Rodolfo Stavenhagen of El Colegio de México acted as the project co-ordinator between 1984 and 1988. This book represents the main research findings and syntheses of activities undertaken during the project, including such issues as ethnicity in nation-building, ethnic rights in the international system, ethnic conflict, ethnodevelopment, immigration, and national policies in different world regions. The reader will be introduced to the complex ethnic problems that are attracting increasing attention throughout the world today.

The Ethnic Question
Conflicts, Development, and Human Rights

Rodolfo Stavenhagen

 UNITED NATIONS UNIVERSITY PRESS

The views expressed in this publication are those of the author and do not necessarily reflect the views of the United Nations University.

United Nations University Press
The United Nations University, Toho Seimei Building, 15-1 Shibuya 2-chome, Shibuya-ku, Tokyo 150, Japan
Tel.: (03) 499-2811   Fax: (03) 499-2828
Telex: J25442   Cable: UNATUNIV Tokyo

Typeset by Asco Trade Typesetting Limited, Hong Kong
Printed by Permanent Typesetting and Printing Co., Ltd., Hong Kong
Cover design by Tsuneo Taniuchi

EM-3/UNUP-752
ISBN 92-808-0752-8
United Nations Sales No. E. 90.III.A.9
03000 P

10881

3.27.92

Contents

Introduction   vii

1 The Ethnic Question Today   1
   Ethnies, Peoples, Nations, and States   1
   Ethnies and Culture   2
   Ethnies and the International System   4
   Nation-States and Nationalism   5
   The Ethnic Question and the Social Sciences   6
   Modernization Theory   11
   Ethnie and Class   12
   The Ethnic Question and Development   16

2 State and Nation: Some Theoretical Considerations   19
   Introduction   19
   The Origin of the Modern State   20
   The Rise of the Nation-State   20
   Statist Ideologies, Nationalism, and Ethnies   21
   Conclusions   29

3 Nations and Ethnies: Framework for the Ethnic Question   30
   Nation-States and Multinational States   30
   Ethnic Communities within Modern States   36

4 Culture and Society in Latin America   43

5 Ethnic Rights in the International System   52
   Introduction   52
   Individual and Collective Human Rights   54
   Group Rights and Nation-States   55
   Ethnic Groups Become Minorities   59
   Human Rights and Minority Rights   60

The Right to Self-determination   65
The Rights of Indigenous Peoples   70
Conclusions   71

6 Ethnic Conflicts   74

7 Ethnocide and Ethnodevelopment   85

8 Indigenous and Tribal Peoples: A Special Case   93
Definition, Membership, and Legal Status   96
Land, Territory, and Resources   100
Economic Development   105
Language, Education, and Culture   107
Indigenous Law and Social Organization   114
Self-government, Autonomy, and Self-determination   115
Conclusions   118

9 Immigration and Racism in Western Europe   120
Immigrants in Europe   120
The New Racism in Europe   122

10 Ethnic Rights and National Policies   129
Latin America   130
North America   130
Africa   131
Asia   135
Western Europe   136
Socialist Countries   139
Conclusion   140

11 Educational and Cultural Issues   142

Epilogue   157

Notes   160

References   174

Introduction

Whereas the international system is made up of about 160 nation-states, the world's cultures and ethnic groups number several thousands. Most countries are in fact polyethnic nations (or, in some cases, multinational States). The processes of social development and modernization are based on the assumption that ethnic and cultural differences within nation-states will tend to disappear, and the broad literature on economic and social development has paid relatively little attention to the ethnic question. It is assumed that social cleavages and mobilization focus around functional groups (social classes, occupational categories, urban-rural settings, political parties, and interest groups), and policies are devised for the solution of eminently "developmental" problems such as capital accumulation, savings, investments, rates of growth, employment, wages, intersectoral relations, etc.

However, it is becoming increasingly recognized that many of the developmental "failures" of recent years cannot be traced merely to technical, financial, or economic shortcomings but must also be linked to the cultural and ethnic complexities involved in "nation-building." A number of countries have attempted to deal squarely with these problems, others have ignored or neglected them. Yet all over the world in recent years, there has been a resurgence of ethnic and cultural demands by minority peoples who do not control the power of the State, and we witness the increasing militancy of social movements that wield such demands. Indeed, many of the major political (including violent) conflicts that the world has witnessed in recent years have a clear-cut ethnic dimension.

A few examples may suffice to illustrate the above and to bring out the difficulties of the problems involved. In the early eighties ethnic violence broke out in two Asian countries. In Sri Lanka, the conflict between the Tamil minority and the Singhalese majority brought into focus some basic structural cleavages in Sri Lankan society that had been overlooked or ignored by statesmen and scholars alike. In India, the conflict between the Sikh minority and the Indian State, leading to political violence, terrorism, and murder, shocked Indian society and world public opinion. In Indonesia and the Philippines, the central State faces resistance and rebellion by ethnic and religious minorities. In other Asian countries, relations between ethnic communities range from cordial to tense. In Africa, recent history witnessed, among other ethnic problems, a bloody civil war in Nigeria between ethnically differentiated regions and segments of the population; massacres and persecution of one ethnic group by another in Rwanda and Burundi; mass expulsion of Asians from Uganda and of Ghanaians from Nigeria; ethnic-political struggles in countries such as Mozambique, Zimbabwe, Zaire, Chad, and Angola. No mention need be made of the simmering and destructive conflicts in the Horn of Africa.

In the Arab world and western Asia, religious and ethnic minorities (such as the Druse, the Copts, the Baluchi, and the Berbers) attempt accommodation with the dominant culture, others struggle for self-determination (such as the Kurds, the Saharauis, and the Palestinians), and still others seek historical redress for ancient grievances (the Armenians). In Western Europe, recent years have witnessed a renewed militancy by territorial and national minorities in States that considered such problems as having been solved long ago. Examples are the Bretons and Corsicans in France, the Scottish and Welsh in Great Britain, the simmering linguistic conflict between the Flemish and Walloons in Belgium, and the well-known conflict in Ulster between Catholics and Protestants. In Spain, after the long Franco dictatorship during which ethnic and regional sentiments were suppressed, Basques and Catalans, as well as other groups, have demanded (and have achieved, to a certain extent) the recognition of their ethnic demands.

Ethnicity as a major focus for political action has come into the foreground in the United States, particularly since the sixties, in what used to be optimistically termed a "melting-pot." Ethnic voting is one of the principal aspects of the American political system, at both the local and the national levels. In Canada, similarly, linguisitc and ethnic demands by the francophone population and the native Canadians have become controversial political issues in recent years, leading to constitutional changes.

Not every multi-ethnic situation is conflictive, to be sure. In a number of South-East Asian, African, Caribbean, and Pacific countries, ethnic communities, in what have been termed "plural" societies, have found mechanisms for constructive association, coexistence, interest articulation, and potential-conflict management. In many countries, certain ethnic, linguistic, or religious communities have played leading roles in economic and political development. In the Soviet Union, Yugoslavia, and other Eastern European countries, as well as in China, the question of "nationalities" has been dealt with in law and policies; however, major problems remain unresolved and have surfaced into open political conflict in the eighties. Observers had for some time pointed out the "restiveness" of the Muslim populations of Soviet Central Asia, which did indeed erupt into violence by the end of the decade. Latent Baltic and Ukrainian nationalism became more open after *glasnost* and *perestroika*, and early in 1990, Lithuania unilaterally declared its independence from the Soviet Union. Complaints from disadvantaged minorities are heard in Eastern Europe: Turks in Bulgaria, Hungarians in Romania, Albanians in Yugoslavia. In China, despite numerous legal and institutional safeguards, many minority nationalities feel the cultural and political dominance of the Han majority, and during the eighties, nationalist sentiment in Tibet has been openly expressed.

In Latin America, indigenous populations, discriminated against for centuries, are the object of assimilationist State policies. Recent Indian ethnic movements in this part of the world have posed new cultural and political demands and "indigenist" policies are being revised in many countries of the area. Also in other parts of the world, such as Australia and some countries in Asia, "tribal" peoples that may also be considered as indigenous have suffered from economic development strategies that affect their habitat and ways of life. The international community has begun to take notice of the plight of these peoples, and new strategies are being devised to cope with the problem.

Massive human migrations across international borders, oceans, and continents contribute to changing the ethnic and cultural profiles of many countries, and they have affected cultural values and life-styles. These are no longer isolated phenomena: international labour migrations and the millions of refugees in many parts of the world have far-reaching ethnic implications, in terms of social structures, education, cultural values, attitudes, interpersonal relations, political action, and human rights. Asian workers have been migrating to the Gulf states; Africans, Asians, and Caribbeans to Europe; Asians, Caribbeans, and Latin Americans to the United States. Asian, African, and Latin American refugees have sought haven in other countries. In some cases, the return of the migrants to their homelands has produced unexpected cultural effects. In others, migrants have become concentrated in veritable cultural enclaves and ghettos. In certain industrialized countries there has occurred a chauvinistic backlash, and one can speak of a new kind of racism directed against foreign workers and refugees from other continents and cultures. Particular problems are faced by second-generation migrants, i.e. the children of migrants, born and bred in a host country yet culturally distinct and often discriminated against.

The international system took notice of national minorities in central Europe between the two world wars (the League of Nations developed special protection mechanisms). Yet within the United Nations system at present, there is relatively little concern with minorities as such. Emphasis is placed on universal human rights and fundamental freedoms and the struggle against discrimination and racism (particularly as regards apartheid in South Africa). Still, the special question of the protection of ethnic, religious, and linguistic minorities keeps cropping up within the United Nations system; for example, in the Human Rights Commission as well as in specialized bodies such as Unesco and the International Labour Organization. It is likely that in the coming years, greater attention will be paid to the international aspects of minority questions.

The present volume is a synthesis statement of comparative research undertaken within the framework of the United Nations University project on ethnic minorities and social and human development. The project involved a number of research institutions and individuals around the world who contributed reports and studies at different stages of the project. Under United Nations University auspices, a number of international meetings were held, the results of which have been published elsewhere. At El Colegio de México, a computerized world guide of ethnic minorities has been established on the basis of a common format that may be accessed by interested persons.

In chapter 1, a general overview of the ethnic question today is presented. Chapter 2 deals with some theoretical approaches to the issues of the State and the nation as a framework for the understanding of ethnic issues. Chapter 3 develops some propositions regarding the relationship between ethnic minorities and States. In chapter 4, the case of Latin America is presented as an illustration of statist and national ideologies. Chapter 5 deals with the problem of human and ethnic rights in the international system, and chapter 6 considers the problem of ethnic conflict, with a number of examples from the current scene. Chapter 7 looks at some ethnic issues within the framework of contemporary development concerns. In chapter 8, the special problems of indigenous and tribal peoples are dealt with, an issue which has become of major significance in recent years. Chapter 9 is concerned with immigrants and the phenomenon of rising racism in Western Europe. Chapter 10 looks at the way different national legislations deal with ethnic minorities, and chapter 11 attempts an overview of cultural and educational policies of governments in relation to ethnic minorities in various parts of the world.

Some of the material in this book has been presented previously at scholarly meetings or has been published under various forms. Due references are given in each case.

I wish to express my thanks to Vice-Rector Kinhide Mushakoji and to Janusz Golebiowski and Takeo Uchida of the United Nations University for their continuous support of this project. I would also like to acknowledge the cooperation, during various phases of the project, of Marie-Chantal Barre, Tania Carrasco, Kingsley de Silva, Susana de Valle, Laura Donnadieu, Deborah Dorotinsky, Asbjorn Eide, Martin Ennals, Natividad Gutierrez Chong, Michael Howard, Jane Margolis, Luis Arturo Rodriguez, Kumar Rupesinghe, Martha Judith Sánchez, Javier Tellez, Patrick Thornberry, and thank particularly Elia Aguilar for her untiring and efficient technical and secretarial help. To El Colegio de México, I would like to express my appreciation for the permanent institutional support which enabled this project to be carried out.

Finally, to my wife Elia my deepest affection and gratitude for her unwavering support and understanding during these years; and for Gabriel and Yara, may they live in a world where ethnic pluralism is respected and cherished.

1

The Ethnic Question Today

ETHNIES, PEOPLES, NATIONS, AND STATES

The opening phrase of the preamble of the United Nations Charter refers to the "peoples of the United Nations." Yet the United Nations is an association of States, not of nations or peoples. With due recognition of the conceptual confusion that exists in the social sciences regarding these terms, let us simply say, for a start, that States are political and legal entities that exercise sovereignty over a specific territory and wield power over its inhabitants. Nations are sociological collectivities based on ethnic and cultural affinities as well as shared perceptions of these affinities that may or may not be constituted into States, but which, in any case, become politically relevant under certain historical circumstances when they acquire political (national) consciousness. Peoples are ethnic groups, or *ethnies*, that may not have achieved, or at least expressed, such national consciousness but are nevertheless united through racial, linguistic, cultural, or national links that likewise distinguish them from other similar groups and through which their members are aware of sharing a common identity.

The world system today is made up of roughly 160 politically independent States, and it is probable that in the next few years a small number of additional countries will gain their independence. Still, there is a logical limit to the number of independent States that the international system will be able to recognize. While some of these countries are truly nation-states or national States in the sense that they are made up of only one nation, most of them are multinational or polyethnic States. Only a few States formally recognize their multinational or polyethnic nature; most of them maintain the fiction of appearing to be monoethnic or uninational States, or at best they give only lip-service to the ethnic pluralism within their borders. The number of nations and peoples that exist in the world is not easy to determine because there are few systematic treatises dealing with these matters, and the United Nations system, which

1

produces statistical information on numerous other subjects, does not carry detailed information on such questions. Educated estimates, based mainly on anthropological and linguistic criteria, would place the number of nations, peoples, or ethnic groups at around five to eight thousand, the real figure probably being closer to the latter.[1]

Frequently, peoples who share the territory of a State with other ethnic groups are referred to as minorities when they are either less numerous than the other group or groups or when they occupy a subordinate economic, political, or social position in the State, or both. Therefore, it is possible to speak of numerical and of sociological minorities. There are numerous criteria used in the definition and classification of minorities, most of which are similar to the criteria that refer to the definition of a "people," the distinguishing factor being precisely the relationship to the majority or to the dominant ethnic group.[2]

ETHNIES AND CULTURE

Ethnic groups or ethnies (I use the terms indistinguishably) are more often than not identified in cultural terms (language, religion, national origin, social organization). The relations between ethnic groups (interethnic relations) and the relations between such groups and the State constitute a primary element in political, social, and economic development in the modern world. Usually, however, development theory and practice have neglected the ethnic question, and this has led to some costly "development failures" in many parts of the world that have occurred because not enough attention was given to cultural or ethnic issues. Moreover, many social and political conflicts since 1945 (including a number of wars) throughout the world have taken the form of ethnic conflict, that is, conflict between groups and communities that identify themselves and each other in cultural terms.

To clarify, when I speak of culture I mean the broad spectrum of human activities, symbols, values, and artifacts that identify a human group and distinguish it from others: thus, we may speak in general terms of Indian culture or Chinese culture, Arab, Latin American, or European culture, and in more concrete terms, of French or English or Mexican culture. Even more specifically, there may be numerous cultures within a certain country, such as the French-Canadian, Anglo-Canadian, native Indian, and other cultures in Canada or the Tamil and Singhalese cultures in Sri Lanka.

Ethnic groups, or ethnies, then, may be thought of as collectivities that identify themselves or are identified by others precisely in such cultural terms. The most common elements that have been used to distinguish ethnic groups are language, religion, tribe, nationality, and race. Race may at first glance appear not to be cultural at all but biological. After all, are not the physiological features of individuals so often used to identify the members of different "races" inherited and thus may be considered as permanent personal attributes? This is of course true, but it is also true that certain biological features such as skin colour or eye shape are quite unimportant by themselves and only become important in human relationships when a given society attributes cultural and social significance to them. That is why race also serves to denote an ethnic group, and some authors speak of "social races" in contrast to the usually perceived "biological races."

Unesco has brought together scientists from all parts of the world to seek agreement on the question of race and racism. One group of experts produced a "Statement on Race" in 1950. This statement was updated by another group of experts in the "Statement on the Nature of Race and Race Differences" in 1951. A third group of experts produced a document entitled "Proposals on the Biological Aspects of Race" in 1964. The "Moscow Declaration," as this document is known, affirms that all men living today belong to a single species, *Homo sapiens*, and are derived from a common stock. Furthermore, biological differences among human beings are due to differences in hereditary constitution and to the influence of the environment on this genetic potential. Many anthropologists, the statement says, while stressing the importance of human variation, believe that the scientific interest of these classifications is limited and even that they carry the risk of inviting abusive generalizations. In 1967, yet another group of experts produced, in Paris, a "Statement on Race and Race Prejudice." Finally, the Unesco General Conference in 1978 adopted a "Declaration on Race and Racial Prejudice," of which Article 2, Paragraph 1 affirms

Any theory which involves the claim that racial or ethnic groups are inherently superior or inferior, thus implying that some would be entitled to dominate or eliminate others, presumed to be inferior, or which bases value judgements on racial differentiation, has no scientific foundation and is contrary to the moral and ethical principles of humanity.

While the Unesco statements seem to accept the existence of races, without, however, defining them, other scholars deny any scientific validity whatsoever to the concept of "race." [3]

At this point it is irrelevant whether an ethnic group is identical or not with a State, or whether it has legal or political existence. This is of course a most important matter for the nature and dynamics of such groups, and I shall return to these issues in later chapters, but it is not essential for their definition. Let me offer some examples. In many Latin American countries, there is officially only one nationality and one citizenship (e.g. Mexican, Peruvian, Bolivian, etc). Yet in these countries, a large proportion of the population is made up of native American Indians who are identified as distinct ethnic groups. Their social and economic problems and the potential for their development are in large measure shaped by the fact that they are ethnically native American Indians with a particular history that has determined the nature of their relations as groups to the rest of society and are not only citizens of this or that country. In western Asia, the Kurds, who number many millions and do not have a State of their own, are scattered amongst five different countries, in each of which they make up a distinct ethnic minority, even though at least one of these States (Turkey) denies their existence *qua* ethnic minority. In China, the majority population is Han, but the government officially recognizes the existence of 56 different minority nationalities. A final example refers to the Basques, who live astride France and Spain and who maintain a distinct ethnic profile, particularly because of their language, one of the oldest in Europe.

ETHNIES AND THE INTERNATIONAL SYSTEM

Let us look at some revealing facts. Most independent countries today achieved statehood after 1945. They each have a name, one or more official languages, a system of government and public administration, and all the symbols inherent to political sovereignty. Moreover, they proclaim a nationality or citizenship to which all subjects of the State are bound to express their loyalty and through which they are linked to each other and are distinguished from other nationals. The symbol of this system is the nation-state, as it has evolved in Western Europe since the seventeenth century and where it crystallized after the French Revolution. Some students hold that the nation-state and the development of industrial capitalism are inseparable, that the victorious bourgeoisie required the nation-state as the necessary expression of its economic interests. Others maintain that the nation-state is the result of the secular struggle for political democracy, the necessary successor to the failing absolutist and dynastic States of post-feudal Europe. The nation-state in Europe, as it achieved its greatest glory after the First World War, is the embodiment of the nationality principle, the romantic idea that each nationality should have its own State, and each State should incorporate but one nationality.

Much blood was shed in Europe over this idea, and yet when we look at the existing States in the international system, only a handful in fact embody the nationality principle. Most States today (including some in Europe) are multinational; that is, within their borders there exist more than one nationality, more than one ethnic group, more than one culture. This is not surprising in view of the fact that, according to some estimates, there are between five and eight thousand different ethnic groups in the world, each one of them identified by one or more of the cultural criteria mentioned earlier.[4] On the other hand, modern post-industrial capitalism and the contemporary transnational bourgeoisie have little use for the nation-state, which, as a matter of fact, has become more of an obstacle than an adjunct to the modern world economic system.[5]

Nevertheless, the idea of the nation-state has prospered. Europe only provided the example that other continents imitated assiduously. The breakup of the Spanish-American empire in the early nineteenth century, despite the common cultural heritage of the local ruling élites, led to the creation of more than 15 new States, which only much later were able to coalesce into nations (see chap. 4). The new independent States of Africa inherited the strait-jacket of the old colonial borders, most of which correspond to nothing more than the imperial strategy of "divide and rule." [6] Yet, because of the explosive nature of the issue of the nation-state, the so-called national question, the Organization of African Unity declared at an early stage that these borders and State structures would have to be respected. And so Africa embarked upon a conscious process of nation-building after the newly independent States had been established. That is why some observers maintain that the process should rather be called "State-building," for the true African nations are not the ones that the colonial empires created as administrative and legal units.

Thus, the world is made up of a relatively small number of States and a large number of ethnic groups distinguished by their cultural characteristics. Most contemporary States are polyethnic, and the nationality principle on which the nation-state is based only applies to a small number of them. Yet the idea of the nation-state has become the driving force of the modern political and economic system. The State is not only a legal framework designed to keep order amongst the population and guarantee the sovereignty of a given territory. Nowadays it has become the locus of economic and social development, the distributor of goods and services, the necessary link between the national and the international markets; it has to care for the basic needs of the population, promote growth and employment, redistribute wealth, take responsibility for the environment, and serve as the focus for societal integration, for what sociologists call "system maintenance." How the State goes about carrying out this task is always a matter for debate and the subject of political action. For our purposes, what is particularly relevant among the functions of State power is the articulation of cultural and political values that go under the name of "nationalism."

NATION-STATES AND NATIONALISM

The modern nation-state would hardly exist without the ideology of nationalism to sustain it, a doctrine that was born early in the nineteenth century and that, by the middle of the twentieth century, had become one of the most powerful and dynamic social forces in history. There are many variants and facets of nationalism;[7] suffice it at this point simply to make an elementary distinction between nationalist ideology that precedes the establishment of an independent nation-state and the State nationalism of governments that wield power. This distinction is relevant to the dynamics of ethnic groups and nation-states.

In the anticolonial struggles of the third world, nationalist ideologies have been more powerful weapons than military organizations.[8] In countries such as India and Indonesia, Nigeria, Ghana, and Zaire, among many others, the early nationalist ideologies attempted to gloss over the existing ethnic differences and to unite a host of religious, linguistic, regional, or tribal communities under the banner of a single national idea, that, as has been well documented in many cases, was often invented by an intellectual élite that had been nurtured in the colonial European tradition. Whereas in many instances such nationalist movements did indeed lead to political independence, and their leaders were duly baptized "fathers of their nations," to what extent the nationalist appeal has succeeded or not in breaking down ethnic divisions is one of the principal issues facing many post-colonial States. Among the leaders of the African independence movements, Amilcar Cabral was one of the few to underline the importance of culture and to draw attention to the need for respect of ethnic diversity within the wider framework of national liberation. India is still trying to cope with the opposing tendencies of a unifying secular Indian nationalism, which was so dear to Jawaharlal Nehru and many of the leaders of the Indian independence movement, and the centrifugal tendencies of regional, ethnic, linguistic, religious, and communal identities that command the loyalties of many hundreds of millions of citizens of that nation.

The second phase of nationalism is as an instrument of State power and a guide to relations between States. At this stage, nationalism usually denies all subnational ethnic loyalties and requires unconditional allegiance to the State, considered as the embodiment of the nation. This is the nationalism of the post-colonial States, of the period of nation-building as it is often called in which the concept of the nation, as expressed in the ideology of the State, encompasses and subsumes all prior and partial identities. However, as a number of authors have shown, if the integration of the new nation requires the demise of the pre-existing ethnic groups as such, then the process should be called State-building and nation-destroying, rather than nation-building.[9]

THE ETHNIC QUESTION AND THE SOCIAL SCIENCES

Concern with the problems of ethnies, particularly with minority groups, is of course not new. Politicians have to deal with them frequently. Two world wars began over these issues. Civil wars are fought over them. Millions of people the world over have been killed because of the way other people thought about them in ethnic terms. Yet in general, the so-called "development sciences" have practically ignored the ethnic question and have not yet been able to integrate it meaningfully into their analytical frameworks.

A likely reason for this, in my opinion, is that the paradigms of modern social theory have not included the ethnic factor as relevant to the questions they have asked of reality. Let us take a few examples. Economic theory, for instance, deals with supply and demand, the market, prices, interest rates, the factors of production, etc., in their "pure" state, that is, unpolluted by social and cultural, that is to say, by the so-called non-economic factors. Not all branches of economics are equally blind to non-economic factors, however. Development economics is more "institutional" or structural in its approach; still, the unit of analysis is usually the individual, the firm, or perhaps the State. It is not the social group, not the community, except insofar as cultural values are said to influence the economic behaviour of individuals; for example, as regards consumer spending or entrepreneurial behaviour or labour commitment. But then, most economists tend to consider these as exogenous variables.

Anthropologists have described numerous cases of prestige economy in peasant societies; that is, of expenditures on feasts and ceremonies for prestige purposes. But many economists tend to dismiss this kind of behaviour as simply non-rational and therefore unworthy of their attention. However, when we look at economic history, we find numerous references to cultural, religious, and ethnic factors. Tawney and Weber, for instance, each in his own manner, linked the rise of capitalism to religious factors, namely the Protestant ethic.[10] Max Weber also suggested that Hindu religious values would be inimical to capitalist development.[11] Some contemporary authors, following the Weberian tradition, recognize similar factors at work elsewhere, for example, the role of religion in the modernization of Tokugawa Japan.[12] Werner Sombart, a German economist, linked the Jews to the development of capitalism in Europe,[13] and other authors (following both Marx and Weber) have spoken of the Jews as an "ethnic class."[14] Sikhs and Parsis have played a particular economic role in India and so have Asians in East Africa and the Chinese in South-East Asia. The role of the Levantine merchants in some sub-Saharan African countries is frequently underlined. Despite so many references to ethnic and religious factors in economic development, it is surprising that most economic theory (and particularly development theory) does not integrate such factors as relevant to its purposes.[15]

A similar situation prevails regarding political science. Liberal political theory is based essentially on the relation between the individual and the polity: and here the individual is shorn of his various social and ethnic attributes. Liberty, equality, fraternity; one man, one vote; these are the watchwords (and catchwords) of the modern liberal democratic political systems. Indeed, these watchwords represent a major achievement in human history; they are the result of endless struggles, conflict, and sacrifice by many generations.

The struggle for, and the achievement of, equal rights, as against earlier forms of exclusion and discrimination of different kinds of social groups has, in a way, inoculated modern political theory against dealing with such groups *qua* groups and has placed the individual citizen squarely in the centre of the limelight. Contemporary political science, to be sure, does not ignore groups. On the contrary, it has developed important theories concerning political parties, interest articulation, coalition behaviour, political culture, and so forth. But these are more related to functional aggregates such as occupational groups, consumers, or class-based parties than to ethnic, racial, or religious communities. In some countries, political parties based on racial or religious criteria are not legally recognized. Various theories of social and political development specifically stress the evolution from groupings and loyalties based on consanguinity, affinity, religion, and so forth to more functionally oriented and instrumental groups; from ascription- to achievement-orientation. Tönnies, Maine, Durkheim, Weber, Parsons, and their followers have all produced important work along these lines. Within this functionalist-structuralist viewpoint of development, there is little place for the role of ethnic groups. They are dismissed as primordial, traditional, obstacles to modernization. Here again, ethnic attachments would be considered as non-rational, traditional, even conservative.[16]

The "ethnic question," as we call this problématique, which includes issues such as "ethnic identity," "interethnic relations," "ethnic conflict," and so forth, has been the object of much theorizing in the social sciences over the last few decades. Despite all the literature, however, there is little consensus among social scientists regarding the nature and characteristics of the problem and its relation to other problems of the social sciences. Various theoretical approaches compete with each other, and the field is clearly divided into several "schools." This situation should not be seen as discouraging, insofar as the sciences (including the social sciences) advance knowledge by the competition between paradigms and the eventual replacement of one paradigm by another. The problem becomes more complicated, however, when we see, as is so often the case, that public policy and social action in specific cases tend to be the acknowledged or implicit consequences of the use and/or application of different paradigms.

Such is the case of the ethnic question. For example, in country A, the majority and dominant ethnic group B, having thrown off the yoke of colonialism, is engaged in national integration, which means creating an "A identity and unity." On the other hand, minority ethnic group C, not having been consulted, is not particularly interested in the concept of country A (which it considers an imposition by ethnic group B) but would like to exercise self-determination among C. The problem here is not only the possible conflict between B and C but the different perceptions of what country A is all about. Or suppose that political movement X is trying to unite the labouring masses (no matter what their ethnic identity) against an exploitative bourgeoisie mainly belonging to ethnic group Z, whereas ethnic movement Y (including a cross-section of social classes) resents the privileges of ethnic group Z and struggles for greater equality and opportunity. Here again the main problem is not the apparent "rivalry" between the two ethnic groups Y and Z but the perceptions that different groups may have about concepts such as "the State," "the nation," "the people," "class interests," and so forth. Each one of these terms may be taken as a central concept around which a theory of social and political action may be constructed. When different theories are utilized as instruments of political action, then these concepts are not neutral but highly value-laden and they in turn become weapons in the political and social struggle.

A relevant example of this, as will be shown later, is the use of the terms "people" and "minority." In the usage of international law, a "people" has the right to self-determination, but a "minority" does not. Consequently, certain population groups claim for themselves the right to be deemed a "people" and reject the label "minority" that others apply to them.

While it is generally agreed that ethnic groups may be defined by a number of common and shared characteristics, more often than not such defining traits stand out as a result of the nature of the relationship linking a specific ethnic group to others and to the State. Various theories in the social sciences attempt to explain the nature of interethnic relations, and such theories have made important contributions to the understanding of these complex phenomena, each from its own particular perspective. Some of the approaches underline the subjective, psychological elements in ethnic identification and confrontation. Here emphasis is placed on so-called primordial affiliations: the in-group feeling that characterizes every human group, the hostility felt for all "others," the rejection of "them" by "us." Ethnic conflict, according to this viewpoint, is simply the open expression of latent, permanent attitudes.

When social norms that keep intergroup hostility in check break down, due to any number of possible causes, then conflict and often violence tend to break out. This perspective would have us believe that ethnic rivalry or hostility is a natural phenomenon, the expression of human nature, that when different ethnic groups or ethnies live side by side within a given society, the likelihood of conflict is always present. Only the legal and political institutions of the State can regulate the behaviour of the opposing groups; and when these institutions fail, then ethnic conflict becomes the order of the day.

Other theories emphasize the social organizational aspects of the ethnic group and the maintenance of ethnic boundaries. Within this theoretical perspective, the ethnic identity of a group is not so much the result of deeply ingrained primordial sentiments as, rather, the expression of a type of social organization within which individuals situate themselves and relate to others. Ethnic conflict, when it occurs, is then a specific kind of conflict between two different types of social organization. It is the society that defines the ethnicity of the individual, of the member as well as of the outsider, and not the individuals who crystallize the ethnic identity of a society. According to this viewpoint, there can be no "ethnic" individual, only ethnic groups.

Still others pay attention to political power and its distribution within the wider society. Ethnies relate to each other unequally and struggle over political power; ethnic conflict is then a purely political struggle to be solved only by political means. Ethnic politics, or ethnopolitics, is simply an instance of how politics in general is played within the polity. An ethnie may activate its ethnicity when it considers this politically useful, as it will downplay or ignore its ethnicity when this is not deemed useful. Conversely, political actors may impute ethnicity to their political opponents for purely instrumental ends.

A widely accepted approach to ethnic relations places them within the framework of segmented, plural societies resulting from the imposition of colonial exploitation. Within such plural societies, ethnic groups and communities maintain a separate, parallel existence. They are united only by an overarching, integrating (usually colonial) political system and tend to meet only in the "market place." Ethnic conflict within the plural society is then the result of inequalities instituted by colonialism.

Marxist analysis relates the ethnic problématique to the dynamics of class struggle on the one hand and the "national question" on the other, but the former seems to have received more attention in post-Leninist Marxism. Some contemporary Marxists would deny any reality whatsoever to ethnicity, labelling it merely an ideological ploy used to distract attention from the more serious matter of the class struggle. They tend to point out that in Africa, for example, the concepts of "tribe" and "ethnie" have been widely manipulated by colonialists to divide and rule the African labouring masses.

Whereas most earlier approaches take ethnies as something given and permanent, new Marxist analysis recognizes that ethnic groups are in constant flux. They may arise, crystallize, decay, and even disappear as identifiable units under certain historical conditions. There is nothing final nor fatal about ethnicity. Most certainly the causes of ethnic conflict are not to be sought within the ethnic groups themselves, but rather within the contradictions of the wider society in which ethnies may or may not happen to be significant actors, as a result of other forces with little if anything to do with ethnicity as such.

Few of the theoretical approaches mentioned here, however, pay much attention to the nature of the ethnic State and its relations with ethnic groups. Why so many theories on ethnicity and ethnic relations simply ignore the State is not quite clear, but this may be due to the characteristics of the two major traditions in political science that have dealt with questions of the State. On the one hand, the *liberal tradition* regards the State as the confluence of individual wills and places it above the particular interest of any specific group. In a rationally organized polity, ethnic affiliations, when not based on objectively measurable interests, are dysfunctional to the tasks of the State and therefore of little concern to the theorist. On the other hand, the *political economy approach* to the study of the State sees in it a reflection of the economic power of different social classes; again, the ethnic factor seems of little concern here.

If theories of the State have not dealt much with problems of ethnic conflict, the theorists of ethnic relations have tended to deal with their subject matter mostly outside of the sphere of the State. Yet it is precisely the State-ethnie relationship that must be explored if we are to gain a better understanding of the nature, causes, and dynamic of ethnic conflict around the world.

MODERNIZATION THEORY

The 1950s and 1960s witnessed an explosion of studies and theories on the process of development in the third world. A major feature of this collective effort to understand and guide the process of change that the less-developed countries were undergoing focused on the theory of modernization. Succinctly, this theory states that in order to achieve economic well being, the "backward" countries would have to change their traditional institutions and values and conform to a modern, Western model of market relationships, urbanization, industrial production, and political bureaucracy. They would have to shift their loyalties from village and tribe and religious community and ethnic group to the nation and the State and its attendant institutions. In order to obtain this change, widely hailed as progress, it was not sufficient to build roads and take produce to market; it was also necessary to establish a unified school system, a workable public administration, a national language, and all the trappings of a legitimate State that could command the allegiance of individuals and groups that had formerly been fragmented into isolated, rival, and sometimes conflictive communities.

If the West had shown that it could embark upon industrial development, it was because certain basic changes had occurred in Western societies in conjunction with the Industrial Revolution: changes that affected the values, outlook, attitudes, and social relations of the individuals caught up in the economic turmoil of the times. Thus it was held that if the third world countries wanted to "catch up" with the West, they too would have to undergo similar changes and adopt the cultural values that had proven to be so successful in Western economic development. If this premiss was accepted, then it was easy to conclude that the new States would have to Westernize or modernize by turning their backs on their own cultural values and traditions that, by these standards, were considered to be inimical to progress and development. Economic growth, industrial manufacture, production for exchange, capital accumulation for further investment, in short, all the elements of a modern economy (whether free enterprise or State planned) were attributed to certain cultural traits that had been historically identified with the West. And so it was concluded that in order to achieve these ends (deemed to be desirable and incorporated into so many national and international development plans), the traditional non-Western cultures would have to either change profoundly or else disappear entirely.

Interestingly enough, the theory of modernization – tomes on the subject soon filled the library shelves of academic institutions – was taken up enthusiastically by many of the governing élites of the third world countries. In the name of progress, development, and nationalism, these mostly Western-educated professionals or military men rejected traditional culture and attempted to reduce the cultural and ethnic diversity of their countries to a single, homogeneous "national culture." Frequently, however, it has turned out that a new national culture is not a synthesis of the diverse ethnic strands that exist within a given

State but rather the generalization of the cultural model of a single ethnic group that is either the majority or, if a minority, then the dominant group in the country as the controller of the power of the State.

In fact, the "ethnocratic" State, as it is sometimes called, is not a recent phenomenon at all.[17] In Western Europe, for example, Spain, France, and the United Kingdom attempted for a long time to build monoethnic nations by denying cultural and linguistic rights to the non-dominant ethnic groups or nationalities within their borders.[18] (On the question of ethnic and minority rights, see chap. 8). They have been variously successful at this, and the process has generated resistance, conflict, violence, and more recently, clear-cut changes in government policies. In the United Kingdom the word is devolution, in France regional decentralization, and in Spain, regional autonomy.[19]

In the post-colonial States of the third world, the situation is more complex. The modernization paradigm had shown its ineffectiveness by the early seventies. To be sure, the governing élites had modernized rapidly, but the large masses of the population remained, generally speaking, in a state of poverty. In fact, post-colonial capitalist development produced large-scale poverty by breaking up pre-capitalist modes of production and forms of social organization, furthering the market economy and one-crop agriculture, uprooting people from their traditional villages, creating urban squalor and a growing landless proletariat. As the third world economies became increasingly incorporated into, and subordinated to, transnational capitalism, internal polarization and inequalities increased between social classes and regions.[20]

ETHNIE AND CLASS

When economic polarization occurs in an ethnically homogeneous environment, then we may simply speak of the workings of the class structure, and the ensuing problems may be dealt with in class terms. For example, a land reform may break the power of a landholding élite and distribute resources and political power to the peasantry. Or the organized industrial working class may obtain a fairer share of the national wealth through collective bargaining. A social revolution may bring a completely new class to political and economic power or, conversely, a ruling class may hold on to its privileges by hook or by crook and deny the exploited classes their rightful due.

In ethnically homogeneous societies, social and class conflict may almost become identical, and because in the West over the last 150 years class conflict has been at the forefront of all social conflict, it was almost inevitable that the concept of class conflict, together with that of the nation-state, should also have become a major feature of the dominant ideologies in third world countries.

However, the transposition of class analysis and ideology from the Western industrialized countries to the third world has run into some serious problems precisely because most third world societies are ethnically heterogeneous. Just what do we mean when we speak of ethnic heterogeneity or of multi- or poly-ethnic societies? This is delicate ground that must be treaded on carefully, for it is easy to fall into absurd simplifications or caricatures of reality. There is a growing debate among scholars as to the meaning of "ethnicity" and its relation to social and political process in concrete societies.[21]

Let us look first at some simple types of ethnic situations in modern societies.

Type A is the *conquest situation*, in which a conquering group imposes its sovereignty over an aboriginal population. The ensuing "colonial situation" maintains a rigid hierarchy between a ruling class of colonizers and their descendants on the one hand and a mass of subordinate "natives" on the other.[22] In time, the situation may evolve in different ways. For example, the conquering group may exterminate the natives (or almost) and take over the country altogether. This is what happened in the United States, Canada, Australia, Argentina, Uruguay, Brazil, and other Latin American countries. Or else it may maintain a rigid system of ethnic and racial stratification (apartheid in South Africa). Or, as in some Latin American countries, the conquering group mixes with the native population and attempts to create a synchretic national culture, even though in fact an ethnic stratification system continues to exist (as in Mexico, Peru, Guatemala, Bolivia, and other States). This has also been called *internal colonialism*.[23] Finally, the colonial situation may terminate by independence, the colonizers go home, but the new society that rests in place bears the mark of colonization and the relations between ethnic groups cannot be understood unless it is in reference to colonialism. This is what happened in most African and Asian countries.

Type B situations arise after the breakup of a multinational empire when the *multi-ethnic successor States* consist of a majority nation and a number of national, linguistic, or religious minorities. This happened in Eastern Europe and the Middle East after the dismemberment of the Hapsburg and Ottoman empires.[24] Such situations have frequently led to serious internal and sometimes international conflicts and have been the subject of much political and diplomatic activity for many years. In fact our current concept of "ethnic minorities" stems to a great degree from this experience during the years between the two world wars.[25]

We may describe as *type C* those situations in which the modern State is based upon the process of *integration and amalgamation* of different ethnic groups (or nationalities as they are called in some countries) and in which one of these may be in fact an absolute majority, but not necessarily so. The State is neither the result of foreign conquest and decolonization nor of the breakup of empire, but rather of internal consolidation. Here the modern history of the State reflects the changing relationships between these ethnic communities and policies of accomodation and political integration. As in type B, it may or may not be an ethnocratic State. Such has been the case in a number of Western European countries.

Finally, let us refer briefly to *type D*, settler or immigrant societies, in which individuals from many countries and different ethnic groups take up residence and citizenship and by their presence contribute to transforming the earlier ethnic homogeneity of the country. Immigration may lead either to assimilation or to segregation and discrimination, or a sequence of both. This is the classic case of the United States and Canada since the nineteenth century and more recently of a number of Western European countries.

These different types of ethnic situations are simply very general outlines of possible combinations, and there may not be a clear-cut difference between them. Historically, countries of one type may change into another, and of course there are other ethnic situations in the world that fit into none of these types.[26]

What becomes clear from a comparative analysis is that ethnicity cannot be understood in isolation from concrete historical process. An ethnic group does not exist by itself anywhere in the world. Even the most remote and isolated Amazonian Indian tribe is only an "ethnic group" in relation to the wider society by which it was either rejected in earlier times or into which it becomes integrated at present. Thus, if we may speak of ethnic groups at all, we must consider them in the framework of a system of ethnic relations. We cannot take as our object this or that isolated ethnic group (even though for many years ethnographers have been doing just that), but we must consider the political and economic framework in which relations between ethnic groups take place. Comparative analysis shows that relations between ethnic groups within the wider society (generally the so-called nation-state) are frequently of a hierarchical or stratified nature. Rarely do ethnic groups within a given society relate to each other, and to the State, on a completely equal footing. Scholars disagree as to whether ethnically plural systems are necessarily stratified according to ethnic categories, whether ethnic stratification cross-cuts other kinds of social stratification (occupational, wealth, class), or whether ethnic groups can coexist in a plural society without any kind of stratification.[27]

We may now return to a consideration of a society divided into social classes that is at the same time ethnically heterogeneous. I would say that the majority of the world's countries fit into this category, and certainly most of the third world countries do. What we find here is that our traditional analyses of class dynamics (whether functionalist or Marxist) are usually of little relevance to an understanding of social and political process involving systems of interethnic stratification.

Contrary to earlier and, to a certain extent, still common usage of concepts such as "tribalism" or "ethnic rivalry" that pretended to be self-explanatory, contemporary analysis seeks to find behind the appearance of purely ethnic relations the economic and political forces that shape them. In ethnically stratified social systems, members of ethnic groups – or the groups as such – show differential access to political power and economic resources and benefits; frequently also to the educational system and other socially sanctioned privileges and rewards. Thus ethnic stratification often coincides with class stratification.

If there were complete equality between ethnic groups in a given open and mobile society, then the members of such groups would be randomly distributed among the different social and economic statuses of the society; that is, in the professions and occupations, in the different social classes and income strata, in the various levels of the educational system, the political bureaucracy, the military hierarchy, etc. When random distribution is not the case, then ethnic inequality exists. The historical causes of such inequality, of course, may vary from country to country, and the social, psychological, and political implications of this situation also differ according to circumstances.

Let us look at some examples. In the Indo-American countries, the native Amerindians are concentrated mainly among the peasantry and the lower strata of the working class, even though a small number may have attained professional status and become members of the upper strata of society. The ruling élites and the dominant classes are mainly of Spanish origin. In fact, Indians who do enter the upper strata of society are considered to have lost their Indian ethnic characteristics. Thus Indian ethnicity is usually identified with lower class status (see chaps. 4 and 7). In the United States, blacks continue to occupy the lowest rungs of the social hierarchy, and incomes and educational levels are lower and unemployment rates higher among blacks than among the rest of the population. In these circumstances, it is relatively easy to correlate ethnic and class characteristics.[28]

In certain parts of the world, ethnic groups have a territorial base, they are identified with a particular region that they may consider their "homeland" and that may be recognized as their traditional historical habitat. According to the circumstances under which such regions have been incorporated into a larger economic and political space, it is frequently the case that peripheral regions are economically exploited by outside power centres, and their ethnically distinct populations are subordinated to the will of the power-holders. When this occurs, we may speak of *internal colonialism*, because the relation between the centre and the periphery within the State resembles the classic colonial relationship between metropolis and colony. This is also the case among the Amerindian populations in Latin America. The situation of the Mexican-Americans, or Chicanos, in the United States, the French-speaking Québecois in Canada, and the so-called Celtic fringe in Great Britain has likewise been described in terms of internal colonialism.[29]

In the history of many peoples, certain ethnic groups have played at times the role of an ethnic class, that is, the group as such occupies a specific function in the class structure. This is the case of the ethnic group as middleman in the economic system. For example, the Jews in medieval Europe, the Chinese merchants in South-East Asia, the Lebanese and East Indians in some African countries.[30] Sometimes, certain ruling classes display specific ethnic characteristics that distinguish them from their subjects: feudal lords, aristocrats, landowners, and even financial and industrial entrepreneurs have been known under differing circumstances to stress their ethnic distinctiveness (through race, language, customs, or religion) in order to maintain their power and control over the subordinate classes and to bar access to their class by the underlings or by rash outsiders.[31] And when social revolution occurs, these upper classes are sometimes persecuted or liquidated because of their ethnic appurtenance rather than on purely political or economic grounds. A singularly bloody case in point occurred in the sixties and seventies in Rwanda, where the neo-feudal Tutsi aristocracy, whose claim to ethnic superiority had been bolstered if not fashioned outright by the Belgian colonialists, was overthrown and massacred by the Hutu peasantry. And an analogous, but inverse, situation, the dominant Tutsi group massacring the Hutu peasantry, took place in the eighties in neighbouring Burundi.[32]

Here we find an important feature of ethnic dynamics; namely, that ethnicity is not some abstract, eternal attribute of a specific social group. In many cases it becomes a cultural invention to serve the political and economic needs of a ruling class; in other words, it is consciously fashioned into an ideology to justify crass economic exploitation. The most dramatic example of this use of ethnic symbols is the system of apartheid in South Africa: the white Afrikaaners' attempt to justify their rule by reference to godly missions and inherent racial superiority, which was of course also the European pretext for colonization.[33] And in the United States, the whites have used the same arguments against the blacks, the Hispanics, and other "coloured" minorities.[34]

Thus we are led to conclude that ethnic stratification systems are very often the expression of political and economic forces that can only be understood in concrete historical terms. In other words, ethnic relations may be seen as power relations and frequently (but certainly not always) as economic class relations.[35] We should be careful, however, not to oversimplify this analysis or to fall into some kind of untenable economic determinism.[36]

THE ETHNIC QUESTION AND DEVELOPMENT

By the middle of the seventies it became obvious that the modernization paradigm that had held sway for the previous 25 years was not really very useful for understanding the complex realities of the third world countries. It became fashionable to speak of alternative development strategies, the basic-needs approach, self-reliant development, ecodevelopment, endogenous development, and so forth. Nobody seemed to question the development aim itself, however, except perhaps during the singular and dramatic episode of the Pol Pot regime in Kampuchea. Most everybody would agree that some sort of economic modernization was necessary, but it was no longer accepted that the social institutions and the cultural values of a changing multi-ethnic third world society would necessarily have to adapt to the Western urban industrial model. Tradition was no longer considered to be an archaic, unchanging, eternal obstacle to development, but rather as the result of decades or centuries of interaction between the third world countries and the West, ever since European colonial expansion, and was to be seen as a dynamic, potential resource for development. The simple opposition of tradition and modernity, so dear to the expounders of modernization theory, turned out to be an illusion. Nowhere was there a single, unchanging tradition, but rather a multiplicity of traditions and cultural strands that were now considered to be mobilizable in the service of endogenous development.

Yet, while it was fairly easy to reject the exogenous, Western cultural models, it is not so simple to define what should be understood by endogenous or inward-oriented development. In fact, very often the most vociferous proponents of tradition and endogenous development are the representatives of dominant ethnic groups and classes who see that their power may fade under the changes of modernization: landlords, upper castes, religious leaders, tribal chiefs, hereditary aristocrats, and others.

Contrary to what had been expected within the framework of the theory of modernization, ethnic identity, ethnic consciousness, ethnic conflicts did not disappear during the years of post-colonial nation-building. On the contrary, in many cases they became stronger, and the so-called ethnic revival occurs not only in the third world countries but also in Western and Eastern Europe as well as in North America. Ethnic mobilization can no longer be considered some sort of archaic, pre-modern, primordial, non-rational form of social action.[37] It is, rather, a legitimate social and political force on par with, and closely linked to, class and national organization. Ethnic groups are not eternal entities, but changing, dynamic social units that may emerge, metamorphose, and disappear over time according to historical circumstances.

Still, many authors as well as politicians and statesmen frequently consider that there exist "ethnic barriers" in the process of nation-building that must be broken down. One practical way to do this, according to some, is through the multiplication of associations and organizations whose membership cross-cuts ethnic boundaries, such as polyethnic political parties, professional and occupational groups, youth associations; and of course, the army is said to play an important role in this process. Others maintain, however, that frequently multiethnic participation in such associations tends to underline ethnic distinctiveness and make people more conscious of their particular ethnic identity when it stands in contrast to that of other individuals. The two arguments are not necessarily contradictory but may be complementary. Cross-cutting membership may indeed contribute to forging supra-ethnic links and create a national consciousness. At the same time, it may underline the ethnic diversity of a population and strengthen so-called primordial attachments. This will depend upon the particular circumstances under which ethnic groups come into contact and interact.

Given the number and variety of ethnic conflicts around the world, development strategies can ignore them only at their own peril. The prospect for peace
and war, the maintenance of national unity, and the enjoyment of fundamental
human rights in many parts of the world depend on the adequate solution to
ethnic tensions. To ignore the problem is to neglect an important aspect of
contemporary reality; to stress this issue at the expense of other problems is to
see only one side of a complex problématique. The task for social scientists,
development planners, and nation-builders is to understand the dynamics of
ethnicity in relation to other social forces and to forge futures in which the basic
human rights and the right to self-determination of ethnic collectivities may be
safeguarded within the framework of national and international society.

2

State and Nation: Some Theoretical Considerations

INTRODUCTION

One of the major unresolved contradictions of our time is that the world is divided into a set number of political units (independent States or dependent territories) that are thus assured of international legal recognition, and a large number of peoples, nations, or ethnies that are not constituted as States. This may at first glance seem to be quite normal; in fact it is well known that most contemporary States are polyethnic or multinational. The problem arises because most modern States are built on the conception of the nation-state; that is, a conception that posits an equivalence between the State and the nation, the former being a political and the latter essentially a sociological concept. The model of the nation-state developed in Europe in the eighteenth and nineteenth centuries, and hence spread to other parts of the world. Many newer, post-colonial States in Latin America, Asia, and Africa adopted the European model uncritically with slight regard to completely different historical and cultural circumstances. This fact has led to many of the difficulties that third world countries encounter in the task of "nation-building"; it has led to conflicts between States and peoples and to international conflicts, which should rather be acknowledged as being interstate conflicts. The lack of congruence between States and nations has led to unexpected difficulties in the implementation of economic and social development models; it has contributed to instability in the international system; and it has influenced some prevailing political ideologies and their impact on political and social processes.

The sources of this situation are to be found in the origin and history of the modern State.

THE ORIGIN OF THE MODERN STATE

The modern State, by the accounts of historians, arose in the nineteenth century in Western Europe out of the transformations of previously existing political units. After the fall of the Roman Empire, the prevailing system of rule was feudalism, whereby a personal hierarchical bond linked a lord to his vassals and these in turn with the subordinate classes (peasants, serfs). This relationship was repeated innumerable times and tended to fragment any kind of unified control or system of rule. Thus it is not possible to speak of a "feudal State" in the modern sense (there simply was no such thing), but rather one must speak of a loosely interconnected system of similar hierarchical relationships.

However, by the thirteenth century, the development of towns and their attendant economy required another type of political arrangement. This turned out to be the *Ständestaat*, or "the polity of the Estates," in which the estate, a specific kind of corporate stratification unit, related through constituted assemblies, parliaments, and other kinds of bodies to the ruler of the land (king, emperor, prince, duke), and each one defended rights and privileges against the other.[1] According to Poggi, the *Ständestaat* consisted basically of three elements: the territorial ruler, the feudal element, and the town-based groups. Their cross-cutting interrelationships defined the political process and characterized the *Ständestaat* as a transitory phenomenon.

By the seventeenth century, the *Ständestaat* was in decline, and a number of larger, sovereign political units became the prevailing pattern. In these units, the ruler and his court became the key to economic and military activity; power was concentrated at the top, with the support of a growing State bureaucracy. Lower-level aristocrats were displaced, the power of the estates was diminished. The absolutist State emerged. It based its strength on the tax system, the imposition of impersonal law, the management of the mercantilist economy, the development of a body of officials and functionaries. A rising bourgeoisie took the place of the previous estates and began developing a counterweight to the centralizing tendencies of the absolutist monarchy. The absolutist State first developed what has become the political standard of modern times: a centralized administration and a civil society. The relation between these two elements of the polity has been at the centre of the political process during the last three centuries.

THE RISE OF THE NATION-STATE

The Peace of Westphalia in 1648, which put an end to the Thirty Years' War, set the framework of the modern interstate system in which State sovereignty and autonomy was first formally acknowledged, if not always respected. Within its recognized borders, the State wielded sole sovereignty, to be defended by military means, if need be, against any possible aggressor. Sovereignty implied administrative, fiscal, and legal unity, and this led to the identification of a distinct population belonging to a particular State. The "people," who were later to become the sole depositories of State sovereignty, after the French and American revolutions, also distinguished each other increasingly as "nations" belonging to different States. The modern State also required a sense of "national unity," a common language, an educational system, and other sundry symbols whereby the State strengthened itself. Thus arose the "nationality principle," which identified State and nation and which led to the current world system of so-called nation-states. When the absolutist State gave way to the nineteenth-century constitutional State (still the basic model of today's State system), the idea of "nation" had been definitely welded to it.

The only hitch in this ideal model of political organization was that in the end only a few "nations" were able to carve out their "nation-states" through political unification: France, Germany, Italy, and, to a lesser extent, England and Spain. Others did so through separation from larger entities: Norway, Belgium, Poland – sometimes by war and violence. Most peoples in Europe remained "non-State nations" subordinated to multinational empires, such as the tsarist, Austro-Hungarian, and Ottoman empires, that did not finally break up until after the First World War. At the same time, the leading States of Europe had built their own overseas multinational colonial empires in which the "nationality principle" did not apply and that in turn did not break up until after the Second World War. Moreover, in a number of European countries, ethnic minorities and non-dominant nationalities subsisted and frequently resisted incorporation and assimilation into the dominant "nation-state." After the Treaty of Versailles, which put an end to the First World War, the League of Nations concerned itself with a regime of "minority protection" in Europe, but the system was on the whole unsuccessful. The basic inconsistency, perhaps even contradiction, between the conception of the modern nation-state and the pervasive reality of multinational and polyethnic States remains to this day an unresolved issue in many parts of the world.

STATIST IDEOLOGIES, NATIONALISM, AND ETHNIES

The concept of a people being a "nation," identified by some objective criteria of commonness or distinctiveness and a subjective feeling of belonging and sharing, arose sporadically during the Middle Ages and in early modern times.[2] But it is only after the rise of the modern State, and particularly during the nineteenth century, that the idea of "nation" became a political notion, soon linked to the ideologies and the various political movements of nationalism and to the politics of State-building.[3] There are many theories of nations and nationalism, and I would like simply to review some of the major ones that are of particular relevance to the contemporary world.

The Nation as an Objective Fact

A widely held view is that a nation consists of a relatively large number of people who share a certain number of common objective traits: language, religion, customs, values, history, culture, economy, territory. For some authors, some of these traits in isolation (language, for example) are enough to define a nation. For others, a combination of several of these elements are required for a nation to exist. The question of scale is important: small, isolated tribal units are not usually identified as nations, whereas larger groups that have a historically grounded link with a specific territory or "homeland" would be so identified.

There are two ways in which the concept "nation" may be understood using such objective criteria. One is the concept of "territorial nation," that is, all the people occupying a certain territory and generally being members of a single State structure, whether this is an empire, a colony, a monarchy, or a republic. This would make nationhood practically synonymous with citizenship. The other concept refers to the "ethnic" or "cultural" nation, regardless of the particular territory or State structure to which its members happen to be attached. Here the criteria mentioned above would be essential (language, religion, ethnicity, and so forth). The distinction between territorial and ethnic nation becomes important when either one becomes the basis of a nationalist movement. The anti-colonial nationalisms of recent decades are usually based on the concept of the territorial nation, which was also the case of the independence movements of the United States and the Latin American countries early in the nineteenth century. In contrast, the nationalist movements of nineteenth-century Europe and a number of ethnonationalist movements in contemporary independent States take as their starting point the existence of ethnic or cultural nations.

By these criteria, a nation exists objectively whether all the people involved are aware or conscious of its existence or not and regardless of its particular political status. Thus, some nations do in fact constitute States or other political units, whereas other nations do not. The theory behind this view, however, is that nations tend historically to constitute themselves as States and that the ideal form of political organization is that in which nation and State do in fact coincide. It is held that the "nation" exists as an objective reality in history prior to the emergence of the nation-state and that the nation-state as we know it today is simply the political expression in its purest form of the nation. Thus, the French Republic is the embodiment of the French nation; the Italian State is the result of the drive towards unity embarked upon in the nineteenth century by the then politically fragmented units of the Italian nation. A similar process involved the German nation. The German romantics considered language the test by which a nation is known to exist. In discussing them, Kedourie states that "A nation, then, becomes a homogeneous linguistic mass which acts as a magnet for groups speaking the same language outside its boundaries. . . ."[4] The successor States that emerged from the disintegration of the Austro-Hungarian empire at the end of the First World War reflected the objective reality of the pre-existing but suppressed nations (Czechs, Hungarians, Bulgarians, Albanians, etc.), as did the Greeks earlier when they achieved independence from the Ottoman Empire.[5]

It is more difficult to sustain these arguments as regards the new States that achieved independence in the process of decolonization following the Second World War or, for that matter, the Latin American States that proclaimed their independence early in the nineteenth century. The prior existence of a nation in many of these cases is hard to document, even taking into account such loose definitions as simply common language or culture. Still, in some cases, the idea of a nation existing prior to accession to independence is strongly sustained by nationalist scholars and statesmen alike, as in the cases of Egypt, India, and Indonesia.

Many a nationalist movement and ideology finds its inspiration and driving force in this conception of the nation. Here nationalism is recognized as being the spiritual, ideological, and/or political expression of an objective, underlying reality, the national consciousness of the nation. Nations, within this perspective, are singular, unique, specific units that are clearly distinguishable from other, similar units. "In nationalist doctrine," states Kedourie in summing up this position,

language, race, culture, and sometimes even religion, constitute different aspects of the same primordial entity, the nation. The theory admits here of no great precision, and it is misplaced ingenuity to try and classify nationalisms according to the particular aspect which they choose to emphasize. What is beyond doubt is that the doctrine divides humanity into separate and distinct nations, claims that such nations must constitute sovereign states, and asserts that the members of a nation reach freedom and fulfilment by cultivating the peculiar identity of their own nation and by sinking their own persons in the greater whole of the nation.[6]

The Nation as Subjective Consciousness

Not all theories of the nation and nationalism begin with the idea of a pre-existing, objectively identifiable nation. An alternative approach holds that it is not essentially a series of objective traits that define a nation so much as the subjective awareness of it by its presumed members. A nation thus becomes the expression of a common consciousness; a common *will* to be a nation, and not the other way around. In a famous address in 1882, the French philosopher Renan defined a nation as a daily plebiscite, and, significantly, added that in the process much of history should better be forgotten. He referred of course to the violence done upon the non-French peoples by the French kings in the process of nation-building, which the French would rather forget. Gellner defines nations as "groups which *will* themselves to persist as communities."[7] This *will* to become a nation is one aspect of nationalism, and Gellner states categorically that "it is nationalism which engenders nations, and not the other way around."[8] A recent author puts this approach in a nutshell. "A nation," he argues,

is an imagined political community—and imagined as both inherently limited and sovereign. It is *imagined* because the members of even the smallest nation will never know most of their fellow-members, meet them or even hear of them, yet in the minds of each lives the image of their communion.[9]

If nations are no more than subjective perceptions of certain objectively existing facts or indeed of "invented" facts (such as the invention or rediscovery of a glorious common history by a number of post-colonial States in the third world or the rebirth of long-forgotten or -neglected vernacular languages during the nineteenth-century surge of nationalism in Europe), then the question arises as to the circumstances under which such national consciousness comes about, and particularly, the identity of the social groups that promote it. Though scholars differ as to the details and the particular approaches, there seems to be general agreement that "national consciousness" (and attendant nationalisms) arise during the period of transformation from an agrarian, village society to an urban-industrial society, when local loyalties and social organization break down and larger political units (the modern State) take over; when the individual somehow loses his links with the smaller, local primary units of social organization and faces, *qua* individual, the bureaucratic apparatus of what one author calls the "scientific state."[10]

Not all the people achieve "national consciousness" of course. Only certain strata of the population become so enlightened. Gellner underlines the importance of literacy and a higher culture to the emergence of nationalism. He argues:

Nationalism is *not* the awakening of an old, latent, dormant force, though that is how it does indeed present itself. It is in reality the consequence of a new form of social organization, based on deeply internalized, education-dependent high cultures, each protected by its own state.[11]

Another scholar points to the pivotal role of the intelligentsia in what he terms the "ethnic revival" that has taken place in the world since the eighteenth century. He pinpoints the central meaning of 'nationhood' for the intelligentsia: a project which must be realised by transforming the components of the ethnic community they have rediscovered and seek to regenerate. It is not the community as such which draws the zeal and activity of the intelligentsia, but the community transformed according to a political blueprint, in short, the 'nation'.[12]

But Smith sees in the motives of the intelligentsia little else than their own petty bureaucratic self-interest for advancement in the scientific state.[13] For Anderson also it was the "print languages" and their "printmen," including the lexicographers, philologists, grammarians, folklorists, publicists, and composers, as well as other professional intellectuals, who furthered the imagined communities that were to become the nation-states of the modern world.[14]

The Functionalist Approach

The salience of the educators and the intellectuals, as well as the printed page, in promoting the idea of "nation" leads us to yet another theoretical approach to the question of nationalism, namely the role played by communications in general. Deutsch, for example, argues that the communications revolution that began in the nineteenth century with railroads, telegraph, widespread book publishing, secular, state-supported educational systems, and other aspects related to the industrial transformation of the world helped bring people together, broke down ancient divisions and isolations, and enabled the concept of nationhood to spread well beyond the yearnings of a few romantic historicists.[15] Here the nation is more than a list of discrete traits or the subjective consciousness of the members of a community; it is a functional requirement of the modern State. In the process of nation-building, argues Deutsch, people will lose their local, parochial identities and loyalties in order to identify themselves with the larger economic and political unit, the nation. Here again, the role of a leading group or ruling class is underlined, as is the process of modernization and social mobilization that is conducive to the emergence of nationalism. National consciousness, argues Deutsch, is a matter of communication and a "nationality" is characterized functionally by its ability to communicate more effectively with members of one large group than with outsiders.

This functionalist approach to nationalism is in line with the vast literature on social and political modernization that has been produced mainly in the West over the last few decades. Modernization theory posits the transformation of an agrarian, pre-industrial society into an industrial, market-oriented economy, the process of change from local, village loyalties and solidarities to an individual's identification with larger, bureaucratic, impersonal structures; the breaking down of kinship and other small-scale, bounded corporate bodies and the increasing importance of complex, functionally specific institutions; the change from religious to secular world outlooks, from particularistic to universalistic values; from primary-group focus to secondary-group participation. All this, it is held, takes place within the framework of the development of the modern State and the process of nation-building. The nation and sometimes the State (hopefully the two together) replace the family, the clan, the tribe, the village, the ethnic group as a focus for the individual's loyalty and as a claim on the individual's social and political, as well as ideological, commitment. Thus, the nation is an essential ingredient in the process of modernization and the ideology of nationalism is its necessary concomitant.

Nationalism as a Form of Politics

We have seen that some authors consider nationalist ideologies to be the logical expression of the collective national consciousness of objectively existing nations. Other scholars argue that nationalist ideologies are the result of certain specific social forces or interests (the capitalists, the intellectuals, for example) and that the concept, the idea of the nation, is but the result of their various efforts, no more than an "imagined community" that, at times but not always, becomes objectified in the modern State.

A somewhat different approach has been developed by the historian Breuilly, for whom nationalism is neither the expression of a nation nor an abstract idea, nor a particular political doctrine, but rather a specific form of politics that groups make use of under certain historical circumstances in opposition to the State.[16] He does not deny that human groups may share certain common cultural characteristics, nor that the nationalist ideology has been developed and put together by certain inspired intellectuals, but he argues that the historical significance of nationalism as a movement arises only when it is used for political ends (usually the control or possession of the power of the State), which cannot be achieved, or can be achieved only much less efficiently, by other means. Nationalism thus understood may be of three kinds and has three major functions. Breuilly speaks of "separatist" nationalism when he refers to groups that wish to break away from an existing State in order to form their own State, including of course the anti-colonialist variety. He speaks of "reform" nationalism when the nationalist political groups wish to change the policies and/or nature of the existing State (as, for example, the Turks under Ataturk or Japan during the Meiji Restoration); and he speaks of "unification" nationalism when politically fragmented but ethnically similar groups struggle to create States or supra-State units (e.g. Pan-Africanism or Arab nationalism).

On another level, Breuilly attaches three important functions to nationalism as a form of politics: the mobilization function, which brings people into the political movement; the co-ordination function, which links local and national politics together (both of which are internal to the State); and finally the legitimacy function, which is designed to garner external support for the political movement (which turns out to be particularly important in the anti-colonial

nationalist movements). Breuilly does not consider in his analysis the nationalist policies of governments in power.

From the angle of political science, another scholar, J. Rothschild, develops a
framework for the analysis of politicized ethnicity, or *ethnopolitics*.[17] For Rothschild, politicized ethnicity is not the expression of some form of primordial
attachments, but rather an instrument in the struggle for power, directly linked
to the process of modernization. In certain societies, "politicized ethnicity has
become the crucial principle of political legitimation and delegitimation of
systems, states, regimes and governments. . . ."[18] Politicized ethnicity is not
absolutist, it is a variable, it is invented, it is utilitarian and may be used
or discarded by an ethnic group in accordance with the group's economic and
political interests.

The Marxist Approach

Controversial debates regarding the so-called "national question" have taken
place among Marxist scholars and ideologists ever since the time of Marx and
Engels. The founders of Marxism were of course more interested in the class
struggle under capitalism than in the national question, and to the extent that
capitalism became a world system, the class struggle, for Marx and Engels, was
to become a world-wide phenomenon, irrespective of national borders. Thus, in
principle, Marx and Engels considered that the issues related to nationalism
were subordinate to the class struggle. They argued, as is well known, that
whereas the bourgeoisie is nationalist, the proletariat is by nature and instinct
internationalist, or at least it should be.

In practice, however, Marx and Engels did develop specific proposals regarding national issues in the nineteenth century. An interesting, if controversial,
position was developed by Engels and more or less accepted by Marx regarding
the concept of nations with history and nations without history. The former,
such as the Germans, had developed State structures that enabled them to
progress economically and expand their territory. The latter were doomed to
disappear, not having been able to become "nations with history." Engels, following Hegel, referred to them as "ruins of nations" and he had in mind particularly the Slavs. These smaller "nations without history" were also referred to
as counter-revolutionary in distinction to revolutionary or potentially revolutionary nations. Based on such arguments, which appeared mainly in news-
paper articles, Marx and Engels are sometimes accused of having been German
nationalists.

In other circumstances, however, Marx and Engels did support the national
struggle of oppressed peoples of their time, particularly as regards Poland and
Ireland. Still, in their earlier writings, they approved of the colonial and imperial expansion of Europe and the United States as being "historically progressive," even though later they did indeed recognize the brutal and destructive

impact of colonialism on native peoples or weaker nations and justified the resistance of the latter to imperialism.[19]

Before the First World War, European Marxists engaged in passionate polemics regarding the national question.[20] The nation was seen as a result of capitalist development and nationalism as a specific bourgeois, and therefore reactionary, ideology. National struggles were supported only insofar as they advanced the revolutionary struggle of the proletariat. Rosa Luxemburg and Lenin did not see eye to eye on this question, for whereas the former disapproved of Polish nationalism, the latter found it necessary to support it in the name of the socialist revolution.[21] Kautsky argued that the nation was basically a linguistic community, whereas Otto Bauer of Austria defined it as a community of character and of fate.[22] Both were later chastized by Lenin as reformist or revisionist. Stalin, at the behest of Lenin, wrote the official thesis on the "national question" in 1913, which for many decades was considered by Communists as the only authoritative Marxist text on the issue.[23]

The First World War shattered many illusions, for the European proletariat and its revolutionary parties split up into as many national factions as there were States at war, and much to the displeasure of revolutionary Marxists, the European labour movement, or at least its official leaders, developed more of a nationalist than a revolutionary socialist ideology. Still, Lenin developed the principle of the self-determination of nations, but in practice he subordinated it to the struggle for socialism.[24] Whereas some authors, such as Connor, consider the Leninist position on the self-determination of nations only a stratagem to further the fortunes of the Bolshevik party, it must be remembered that the Marxists developed arguments in favour of national self-determination long before the notion became acceptable in the West as a result of President Wilson's commitment to the idea during the First World War.[25] For many decades, however, nationalism was considered by most Marxists as a purely bourgeois ideology, and to the extent that it appeared occasionally in the labour movement or in socialist and Communist parties, it was decried as deviationist. This was particularly so in the thirties and forties when nationalist ideologies were expounded by extreme right-wing or outright Fascist political movements in Europe and Japan.

In later years Marxists, especially in the third world, became actively engaged in the anti-colonialist struggle, and nationalism again became respectable, even though it has always remained somewhat suspect by most Marxists. Oppressed peoples, to the extent that they waged a revolutionary struggle for independence, were recognized as a progressive historical force, even in those quite common cases in which the leadership of the anti-colonialist movement was in the hands, not of the proletariat, but of the bourgeoisie or the middle classes.[26]

In the multinational federation of the Soviet Union, it was expected that national differences would coexist harmoniously within the socialist economic and political structure, to the extent that all objective reasons for national oppression and separatism – as may exist in capitalist countries – would have disappeared. In recent years, Soviet authors have stressed that the various nationalities that are officially recognized as such by the Soviet legal system are becoming amalgamated into a new historical community, the "Soviet people."[27] Events in 1989–1990 in the Soviet Union have shattered this illusion. As a result of *perestroika*, nationalist movements are on the rise within the USSR (for example, the conflict over the Armenian enclave Nagorno-Karabakh in Azerbaijan; nationalist demands in Moldavia and several Central Asian republics, and in early 1990, the attempt by Lithuania to secede from the Union).[28]

CONCLUSIONS

The modern State provides the necessary environment for the ideology and politics of nationalism. States may adopt nationalist policies that tend to identify "nation" with State, thus relegating claims to "nationhood" made by other people within the State structure who do not identify themselves with the prevailing notion of "nation." Or else, people engage in nationalist politics and adopt nationalist ideologies, thus effectively pressing claims for recognition of their own "nationhood" and struggle for State power. Nations, as sociological collectivities, are identified by both objective and subjective criteria. Shared objective traits (such as language and culture) become meaningful within the framework of subjective consciousness, and this in turn may become a powerful force in shaping the common objective features, particularly within the context of determined State policies of "nation-building."

The nation-state is characteristic of the epoch of industrial capitalism, but certain ethnic features of modern nations (myths, symbols, historical consciousness) have their origins in antiquity. In the nineteenth and early twentieth century, the rising industrial bourgeoisie wielded powerful nationalist ideologies, usually produced by an "intelligentsia," to further its own ends; but today "narrow" nationalism seems to be a strait-jacket for the expansion of transnational capitalism. Still, national State structures and policies continue to be the principal vehicle for capital accumulation.

In the third world, nationalism became a potent weapon in the struggle for independence, and most third world countries have adopted the Western model of the nation-state. But given the unique historical circumstances in which this model developed in the West itself, and the very different conditions under which modern States have arisen in the colonial countries, the model of the nation-state is subject to strong tensions in Asia and Africa, and even in some parts of Latin America. Essentially, it embodies the contradiction between the so-called "nationality principle" on which it is based and the multiplicity of ethnies and peoples who vie for status, resources, dignity, and power within the boundaries of today's State territories.

3

Nations and Ethnies: Framework for the Ethnic Question

NATION-STATES AND MULTINATIONAL STATES

In the literature about the relationship between nations and States, two principal approaches may be recognized. On the one hand we have the position that identifies nation and State on the old "nationality principle" that became the driving force in nineteenth-century Europe: every State should have its nation, every nation should have its State. Actually, there are only a few countries in the world to which this principle applies completely. These are the classic nation-states, in which the cultural and sociological community defined as a nation coincides with the political community bounded by the State and its structures.

Here the concept nation tends to overlap with that of all the citizens of the political community: nationhood and citizenship tend to be the same. Nationalist politicians and ideologists as well as political theorists assume that this is the normal situation of the modern nation-state, that this is the "model" to which nation-building and state-formation should aspire. When such is not the case, when not all citizens consider themselves in fact to be members of the same "nation" though they belong to the same State, then the nationalist doctrine of the nation-state attempts to invoke and sometimes impose policies and values tending to assimilate the non-national or the subnational elements into the dominant national mould. In extreme cases, social groups identified as "non-national" will be excluded, isolated, expelled, or eliminated. This extreme form of nationalism found its most notorious and sinister expression in German Fascism, which, linked to a virulent form of racism, led to the genocide of the European Jews and Gypsies. But even today, the "new right" in Western Europe takes up again some of the old nationalist arguments (see chap. 9)[1]

On the other hand, a more common situation, even when not always recognized as such, is that of modern States in which a number of ethnically distinct

30

groups or communities coexist within a single political structure. Such countries may be called multinational or polyethnic States. They have become what they are by various historical processes and they have quite different political arrangements to deal with their cultural diversity. Whereas in some cases government structures reflect the cultural, linguistic, religious, or simply regional diversity of the multinational State, in others they adhere to the traditional model of the nation-state, or rather the monoethnic State, and it is here that contemporary societies frequently have to face serious maladjustments or conflicts with deep political and social consequences as a result of the lack of congruence between the ethnic composition of the population and the nature of the political community.

Several distinct historical processes have intervened in the formation of multinational or polyethnic States. A summary overview provides us with the following cases.

European Nation-States

The classic Western European model followed a process of national integration or consolidation by a dominant and majority ethnic group that was able either to create for itself or to take control of the State apparatus and to subordinate other nations in the process. Some of these subordinate nations, or subnations as they are sometimes called, occupy the position of "ethnic minorities" and are treated as such, a subject to which we shall return below. In Britain, for example, the so-called Celtic fringe, composed of the Welsh, the Scots, and the Irish, was thus subordinated to the dominant and majority English. The French nation was able to establish its own dominance over the Bretons, the Occitans, the Corsicans, the Alsatians, and others who now occupy minority status in that country (though not recognized as such legally). In Spain, a similar process produced the political subordination of Basques, Catalans, and other regional and linguistic groups that are still today questioning the traditional Spanish-dominated model of the nation-state. These conflicts led to the adoption of regional autonomy in the post-Franco Spanish political constitution. In other Western European countries, similar situations pertain. Japan would be another example of such a process, in which the original Ainu population was almost completely absorbed into the majority Japanese ethnic group but still maintains a certain identity of its own even to this day.[2]

From Empire to Multinational State

Another variant is the multinational State that has the structure of the former multinational empire that preceded it. China and the Soviet Union may be cited as examples. Here a majority nation coexists with a number of minority nationalities within the framework of a federal or unitary political organization.

In both the Soviet Union and in the People's Republic of China, the particular arrangements governing relations between the State and the minority nationalities have changed over time, but the legal recognition of the rights of the minorities is incorporated into the State constitution and various national laws. Whereas the Soviet constitution recognizes the formal right of non-Russian peoples to secede from the Union, in fact Soviet practice strongly discourages any open espousal of separatist nationalism by the non-Russian nationalities. This position was challenged formally in early 1990 by the Lithuanian decision to withdraw from the Soviet Union, to which it had been illegally annexed, together with Latvia and Estonia, in 1940. Contemporary Chinese politics incorporates the territories and borders of the traditional Chinese empire, and secession or national separatism is not only not countenanced but considered as endangering territorial sovereignty (consider events in Tibet during 1986–1989).

In both China and the Soviet Union, however, official positions regarding relations between nationalities clearly draw distinctions between current policies and those that prevailed in pre-revolutionary times. During the imperial regimes, "national oppression" of minority nationalities was the rule, whereas the revolutionary governments have developed policies tending towards economic, social, and cultural development and the abolition of socio-economic inequalities between nations and peoples within the socialist States. As mentioned above, before the events of 1989–1990, the Soviet Union had foreseen an amalgamation of its different constituent nations and the emergence of a new "historical community," which suggests that national differences were thought to be diminishing or actually disappearing. Recent developments have proved otherwise. In China, by contrast, the majority Han nationality, representing over 90 per cent of the total population, is so predominant that the "cultural development" of the non-Han minority nationalities is seen as a progressive assimilation to the Han.[3]

The Successor States of Multinational Empires

A different set of problems arises in countries that have become the successor States to former multinational empires that became fragmented or disintegrated, particularly after the First World War. This has occurred mainly in the Balkans and the Middle East, where nation-states arose as the result of the dissolution of the Habsburg and Ottoman empires. Whereas a number of these relatively new States have been organized according to the "nationality principle," in fact some of them include sizeable national minorities, and others, such as Yugoslavia, are indeed structured as multinational States. The problem of "national minorities," particularly when such minorities identify with majority ethnic kin groups in neighbouring countries, was a major issue before the

League of Nations between the two world wars and has been considered by many observers as a permanent threat to peaceful coexistence between States. Here again, political arrangements vary from case to case (from full recognition of all minorities on an equal footing, such as in Yugoslavia, to the denial that minorities exist at all, such as the government's attitude towards the Kurds in Turkey, or Romania's treatment of its Hungarian minority and Bulgaria's treatment of its Turkish minority).[4] The conflict in Cyprus is of a particular nature insofar as both Greeks and Turks have powerful support in neighbouring kin States, and the Turkish military occupation of northern Cyprus has effectively frozen the internal political process in the country.

The Polyethnic Post-colonial States

Particularly significant in contemporary world affairs is the situation of numerous new States that have achieved independence since the Second World War, the post-colonial States. At the demise of the European world empires, numerous independent States arose in Asia, Africa, and the Caribbean that now constitute the majority of the third world countries. Some of them became structured as nation-states, particularly because even before their subordination to Western colonialism, they possessed some sort of national identity that they were able to recover in the post-colonial period. However, in the majority of cases, the new States were political units that simply took over the administrative divisions and territorial boundaries of colonial times, regardless of the ethnic, linguistic, or cultural composition of the population. Thus, most of the third world countries today constitute veritable polyethnic mosaics. Whereas in some there are clear-cut national majorities, in others the different ethnic groups are all, taken singly, merely minorities within the wider whole. At the risk of being excessively schematic, a number of different situations may be briefly described.

Multiethnic rivalry. There are multinational States with distinct, often regionally localized, sub-State national identities based on linguistic, religious, historical, or other factors (or a combination thereof) that juggle with each other and with the central State for political power, resources, and influence. Arrangements here go all the way from loose federalism to highly centralized political structures. These kinds of situations have been wrought with conflict and occasional violence and civil war, particularly when secession, irredentism, or separatism is the objective of the nationalist political movements. India, Pakistan, and Nigeria are examples of this. One of the principal tasks of statesmen and nationalist politicians in these situations is to attempt to build a national identity and consciousness (a real task of nation-building) out of the various ethnic and national traditions (some would prefer the term sub-national) that make up the State totality. Frequently in these countries, the different ethnic groups have regional power bases and, not being able to achieve full control of the State apparatus for themselves, negotiate and accept a *modus vivendi* with other, similar regional ethnies, thus achieving some sort of political balance or equilibrium that maintains State unity, albeit on a very shaky foundation. Moreover, the number of cases in which the State unit has been seriously challenged have been so costly in human and economic terms (e.g. Nigeria and Zaire in the sixties), that unless success is assured beforehand (which is unlikely in any case), few non-dominant ethnies will attempt either to break away or to concentrate power in their own hands. The exceptions to this latter assertion, of course, are the personalized military dictatorships based on force and highly repressive policies, third world regimes that Richard Falk, following Samuel Huntington, classifies under the label of "praetorianism."[5] A number of independent African States would fall into this category.[6] Most leaders of independent African States have sung the praises of "national unity" and have decried the evils of "tribalism" or "ethnism," yet as some authors have shown, many of these leaders have used politicized ethnicity for their own ends.[7]

Ethnic domination.   In some polyethnic States, an ethnic or linguistic majority holds a dominant position in the State structure and yet has to deal with the interests and demands of one or several minority ethnies that may feel slighted or marginalized by the dominant or majority nationality and that sometimes tend to question the latter's legitimacy. In Asia, Sri Lanka approaches this situation. At times, the minority ethnies are actually split nationalities, in the sense that the artificial boundaries created by the colonialists were taken over by the new post-colonial States and have been recognized as such by the international system. This process has divided what used to be relatively homogeneous cultural units into several "national" fragments. Many countries in Africa have this problem, and it is a constant source of friction and discontent between the dominant ethnie and the subordinate ethnic groups, as well as between neighbouring States.[8]

In order to prevent constant instability and threats to peace, at an early stage the Organization of African Unity decided to respect the territorial boundaries imposed by colonialism, despite many of their negative consequences. This decision may have prevented more war and bloodshed in Africa in the post-colonial period, though it has created other, as yet unresolved, problems of "nation-building."[9] As so many observers have pointed out, linguistic, religious, or ethnic-group identities do not necessarily constitute a basis for political action, except under certain specific circumstances. In many African and some Asian cases, authors do speak of "tribal" identities and "tribal" rivalries that, according to them, constitute challenges to national unity and in some cases, even to "national security." However, such tribal units are not necessarily communities rooted in a common historical identity that partake of a common tribal consciousness. There is nothing fixed or eternal about them. On the contrary, many of these tribes and ethnies were actually created by the colonial powers for their own purposes of domination and control, and at least during the colonial period, they were manipulated by the colonial government. Still, over the years, their identity in administrative and political terms has become established and currently some of these ethnies, whatever their origin or background, constitute power groups on their own terms and are able to challenge other similarly constituted groups and even the post-colonial State itself.[10]

Immigration States

Another set of polyethnic countries is the so-called "first new nations" that used to be European colonial settlements, yet obtained independent or autonomous political status much earlier than other post-colonial States. While they have many of the elements of the post-colonial State (basically a dominant core ethnie that identifies itself with the original metropolitan power), ethnically they are characterized by having become the object over the decades of numerous waves of immigration. While many of the migrant groups attempt to retain or sometimes even recover their ethnic identity, others have become assimilated in the larger national group that has been forming over the years. Typical of this situation is the United States, as well as Canada, Argentina, and Australia.

States with Indigenous Populations

Finally, we may mention those countries in which, through conquest and colonization, a pre-existing indigenous or native population has been subordinated to State structures that have been imposed on it from the outside but in which the indigenous peoples maintain a degree of separate identity and face the State on the issues of a certain number of demands and rights (see chap. 8). This situation prevails in some Latin American countries in which the post-colonial State has been traditionally controlled by the descendants of the European (in this case Iberian) settlers and where the indigenous ethnic groups (in some countries, such as Guatemala and Bolivia, in fact the majority of the country's population) have been kept in a position of economic, cultural, and political subordination for centuries. Most Latin American countries had traditionally applied a policy of assimilation, which has only been relatively successful, to their native Indian populations, and in fact in many of these countries, a mixed, or so-called *mestizo*, ethnic group constitutes a sizeable segment of the national population. Some immigrant or European settler countries also include indigenous populations, and their situation is quite different from that of the immigrant ethnic groups. A case in point is Canada, in which "ethnic minorities" and native peoples are dealt with separately in law and policy.[11] Other examples are Australia and New Zealand.

ETHNIC COMMUNITIES WITHIN MODERN STATES

The way polyethnic or multinational societies (at this point I use the two terms as equivalent, though there are evident analytical distinctions between them) deal with the question of pluralism has become one of the most important political issues in many contemporary States. An important fact to remember is that every multinational or polyethnic State is the result of very specific historical processes and political and economic structures. It is therefore risky to generalize about these phenomena. But precisely because of (a) historical process and (b) politics as a struggle for power, the different nations or ethnies that coexist within a given State structure are usually arranged within a hierarchical system of stratification. In other words, ethnic groups relate to each other asymmetrically, whether in terms of numbers, wealth, power, or status. In most countries, ethnic communities may be ranked according to a number of possible criteria, particularly as regards their relationship with the State. Thus, polyethnic States may be regarded as stratified systems in which ethnic characteristics tend to play different roles according to particular circumstances in addition to the usual variables of any socio-economic system of stratification. Two basic variants of an ethnic stratification system may be recognized:

(a) *Non-congruent overall ranking*, in which the position of a specific ethnic group in one scale does not necessarily correspond to a similar position in another scale. For example, in some South-East Asian countries, the Chinese are ranked highly on an economic scale but lower on a scale of political power.

(b) *Congruent ranking*, in which a given ethnic group in a society is ranked consistently in similar fashion in the various scales indicating the stratified system. This is the most common situation; a dominant ethnic group tends to occupy higher positions on all scales, whereas a subordinate ethnic group (for example, indigenous peoples in Latin American countries, Africans in South Africa, blacks in the United States) occupies low rank in all scales and thus in the system as a whole.

Again, a number of ideal types may be distinguished:

1. The Ethnocratic Polyethnic State

In polyethnic States, a common situation is that in which a dominant ethnic group (either numerical majority or minority) concentrates power, and often wealth and resources, in its own interest, at the same time attempting and frequently succeeding in keeping the other non-dominant ethnic group or groups in a subordinate or marginalized position. The dominant ethnie holds and keeps privileges for itself, whereas the subordinate ethnies either conform to the pattern or else challenge it by any number of possible political strategies. We may refer to such societies as *ethnocratic* States, and though many of them may have formal or legal guarantees for equality and against discrimination, in fact ethnic dominance in multinational States is a most common occurrence. An extreme example, of course, is South Africa and its apartheid system, in which the numerically small, white dominant group oppresses the majority Africans. Another example may be provided by some Latin American countries in which the majority (as in Bolivia and Guatemala) or minority native Indian populations are by all standards subordinated to the ruling white or *mestizo* ethnic groups. In the United States, even though in recent years acknowledgement has been given to minority ethnic demands, the dominant cultural model is still that of the so-called WASPS (White Anglo-Saxon Protestants), who dominate the government, the economy, and most of the social institutions of the country.[12] Israeli Arabs share citizenship with Jews, but most observers agree that they are in fact second-class citizens.

In many Arab or Islamic countries, in turn, non-Arab or non-Muslim ethnic groups occupy inferior positions in relation to the dominant Muslim or Arab majority (for example the Kurds in several western Asian countries, the Berbers in Algeria, the Christians in southern Sudan, the Jews in Iran and Syria, etc.). In France, certain regional ethnic communities (such as the Bretons, Occitans, and Corsicans) have long complained about the discrimination by the centralized bureaucratic State. Many other examples may be cited.

The competition for power and resources between ethnies, particularly when the object of the competition is the State apparatus itself, frequently generates tensions and conflicts, and if adequate mechanisms for the solution and management of such conflicts are not present, the situation may lead, as it has so often done, to communal or general violence and, on occasion, to civil war and external intervention (for example, the situation in Sri Lanka during the eighties; the conflicts that led to the creation of Bangladesh; the Biafra war in Nigeria; the conflict between the Nicaraguan government and the Miskito Indians of the Atlantic Coast in the eighties; the Moro rebellion in the Philippines, etc.)

Not all kinds of ethnic competition involve a struggle for the control of the central State, nor does it always result in violent conflict. Still, ethnically characterized conflict and rivalry is more widespread than is generally assumed. Even multinational countries that have elaborate legal and policy safeguards regarding the rights and interests of non-dominant nationalities or ethnic groups (such as the Soviet Union, China, and Yugoslavia) are not immune to ethnic conflicts, as events during the eighties in these countries have amply demonstrated. The ethnocratic State is not only a structure in which the dominant ethnie can exercise power and privilege at the expense of other national ethnies; what is most disturbing is that the dominant ethnie frequently appropriates for itself, and identifies itself with, the nation-state as a whole. In other words, in a world of nation-states where polyethnicity or cultural pluralism is frowned upon or frankly discouraged, the dominant ethnie is likely to present itself as the only true, real, or authentic nation, or at least as the model towards which other ethnies or nations within the State's limits must attempt to conform.[13]

2. *The Policy of Assimilation*

To the extent that the ethnocratic State recognizes ethnic and cultural plurality within its borders at all, its usual strategy is *assimilation*. The nation-state ideology proclaims national unity and homogeneity as a supreme value and frequently develops policies designed to rapidly assimilate, integrate, or incorporate the non-dominant ethnies and nationalities (the terms and concepts may vary) into the dominant mould. For decades, the governments in Latin America consciously practised (and some still do) an assimilationist policy towards their indigenous peoples. Many countries that receive major immigration flows from around the world hold up assimilation as the objective to be attained. Despite formal legal structures that recognize and even guarantee multinational diversity, a number of Marxist-Leninist countries in fact foster assimilation and integration, calling it the merging of nations or the emergence of a new national consciousness. In fact, the majority nations, such as the Russians in the USSR and the Han in China, are held to be the models towards which the other nationalities must tend.[14] In some central European countries, assimilationist policies have been cruder: before the dramatic changes in 1989, Bulgaria's policies towards its Turkish minority or Romania's policy regarding its Magyar ethnie were cases in point.

Assimilation as a national objective is sometimes desired by minority ethnies, particularly if they have been historically persecuted or oppressed by the State or the dominant ethnic groups. Thus, in nineteenth-century Europe, the Jews strove for emancipation from the ghetto and its attendant stigmas to which they had been relegated since the Middle Ages. Also in Europe, Gypsies desire acceptance and not rejection by the dominant society. In many countries, foreign immigrants wish to assimilate rapidly. The "American Dream" of yesteryear held up assimilation in the desired "melting pot" as the measure of an immigrant's success. Some still hold to this creed in the United States, others favour the approach of cultural pluralism as in Canada.[15]

Still, the objective of assimilation is generally proclaimed by the dominant ethnic group itself and frequently becomes official policy. However, assimilation is not always desired or accepted by the non-dominant ethnies. If such ethnies are territorially and historically identified communities with strong bonds and cultural and ethnic identity, then assimilationist policies may be perceived as aggression and they meet with passive or organized resistance. Under such circumstances, ethnic violence may arise.

3. *Internal Colonialism*

Ethnic stratification is sometimes attributed to subjective factors such as attitudes held by members of ethnies regarding the value or superiority of their own group and the supposed inferiority of other ethnic groups.[16] Ethnocentrism does of course play a role in shaping interethnic relations, and it is sometimes sharp-

ened by collective attitudes such as chauvinism, xenophobia, or racism. Such
attitudes, when they exist, determine social behaviour between groups and,
conversely, certain patterns of social relations between different ethnic groups in
turn shape and condition individual attitudes, thus conforming a mutually rein-
forcing pattern that may generate intergroup hostility and rivalry. This is a
common phenomenon when racial, linguistic, or religious groups coexist within
the framework of local communities, and it may lead to communal conflicts, as
have so often shaken India in pitting Muslims against Hindus, for example. Of
course, subjective attitudes and attendant group behaviour may be instigated or
manipulated by special interests within or outside the community itself. Again,
in India this seems to be the case of the separatist movement of a part of the
Sikh community.

   Generally, however, interethnic attitudes and group behaviour are not self-
generated and are certainly not to be attributed to some underlying, immutable
ethnic hostilities or rivalries. If and when ethnic hostility or rivalry occurs, there
is generally a specific historical reason for it that relates to political struggles
over resources and power. Thus, for example, when superficial observers attribute conflicts in, say Africa, to some abstract "tribal rivalries" as if rivalry and
conflict were something inherent in the concept "tribe" itself, they probably
miss the point and more often than not confuse the issues.[17]

   In fact, ethnic rivalries, hostilities, and conflicts are no more "natural" than
interethnic solidarity and co-operation. While ethnic identity and in-group solidarity are universal phenomena, they do not necessarily imply hostility and
rejection of other ethnic groups. Peaceful coexistence between different ethnic
groups within the limits of wider political units are at least as common and
persistent as interethnic conflicts. What seems to be a constant, however, is that
when interethnic rivalries, hostilities, or conflicts exist, these are usually the
result of underlying structural disparities and inequalities that result from historical grievances often related to conquest, colonization, economic exploitation, political oppression, and other processes of domination and subordination
associated with the ethnocratic State. In many parts of the world, a persistent
pattern of unequal development, regional disparities, economic exploitation,
political oppression, and social polarization has been historically associated
with European expansion and colonialism, which became the world capitalist
system and incorporated practically every region and society in the world,
either directly or indirectly.[18]

   The "centre-periphery" pattern so aptly described and analysed by the
"world-system" approach created the conditions for its own reproduction within a number of colonial and post-colonial societies. In fact, long before the
establishment of the international colonial system, a number of "central" countries, later to be identified with mercantile and industrial capitalism (Britain,
France, Spain, and later the United States), established patterns of internal
domination within their expanding territorial limits that foreshadowed the international colonial and imperialist relationships that came to characterize the

world system during the nineteenth and twentieth centuries. Thus the centralized monarchy of Castille first established its dominion over the Iberian penin-
sula before embarking upon its early colonial conquests in the Americas. Likewise for France and Britain in later centuries. Before it became a world power,
the United States incorporated vast territories and subordinated numerous native Indian and Mexican peoples to its dominion, in addition to the imported
slave labour from Africa.

Colonialism and imperialism are an integral part of the expansion of capitalism on a world scale. Indeed, they are part of its very nature.[19] Capitalist accumulation requires unequal development and social and economic polarization.
The underdeveloped countries of today, the so-called third world, are not simply the laggards in the race to development and modernization; they are the
necessary by-product of capitalist accumulation. And within each underdeveloped, dependent capitalist country the pattern repeats itself. The international bourgeoisie, the social class that is the historical instrument of capitalist
accumulation, is not only localized in today's capitalist centres (New York,
London, Tokyo . . .), it is also entrenched in the third world countries. Here it
is, to be sure, a dependent subordinate bourgeoisie, but it plays a crucial role in
keeping the network of capitalist accumulation within the centre-periphery
framework working smoothly.[20] And many a third world State also plays this
very same role within the new pattern of economic transnationalization.

Within this general framework, the system of stratified interethnic relations
plays a crucial role. Because more often than not, the pattern of capitalist
domination/subordination involves not only economic classes (landlords/
peasants; industrialists/workers) and geographic regions, but also ethnic
groups, particularly when in the post-colonial ethnocratic State social class
divisions happen to coincide or overlap with ethnic (linguistic, cultural, religious, racial) distinctions. Of course, this does not just "happen" accidentally
but is the outcome of a particular colonial and post-colonial history. Thus, the
pattern of ethnic stratification that we encounter in so many countries today is
the expression of a deeper structural relationship that we may call *internal colonialism*.

The relationship between the ethnocratic States in Latin America and the
native Indian populations may be understood in terms of internal colonialism.[21]
In other parts of the world where aboriginal populations have been subordinated to capitalist development, the term is an apt description of the situation. It
has also been used to characterize the oppression of blacks and Hispanics in the
United States and even that of the so-called Celtic fringe in Britain.[22] Some
authors criticize the use of the internal colonialism approach when applied to
first-world countries, but there is no doubt that it is a useful tool for the analysis
of asymmetrical ethnic relations in a number of post-colonial States in the third
world, where ethnic, regional, and class exploitation are closely linked within a
significant and recurrent pattern.[23]

4. The Problem of Ethnic Minorities

In the modern nation-state, the non-dominant ethnic groups or peoples become "minorities": ethnic, racial, linguistic, religious, national – whatever their specific characteristics, but usually numerical minorities, and when not numerical (as in the case of indigenous people in Bolivia and Guatemala, or the Indians in Fiji, or the situation in South Africa), they are sociological and political minorities. The term minority has become a specific sociological concept that has political and legal implications both in national and international law.

Most of the world's 5,000 to 8,000 ethnic groups are thus usually considered as "minorities" when they do not, in the guise of "nations," control the power of the nation-state. The United Nations system, and before that, the League of Nations, attempted to deal with the problem of minorities because of large-scale international concern about them. In the period between the two world wars, the problem of national minorities, if unresolved, was held to be a permanent danger to international peace, as it had been in the circumstances leading up to the First World War. In fact, the situation of the ethnic German minorities in neighbouring countries was used by Nazi Germany as a pretext for military aggression and expansion.

Since the Second World War, the issue of ethnic minorities has been downplayed within the UN system and it has mainly been reduced to a question of individual human rights. The international instruments for the protection of human rights, based on the principles of equality and non-discrimination, are held to be sufficient guarantee for the protection of ethnic minorities anywhere in the world. Universal individual human rights apply to these minorities just as to all other persons. For many years politicians and scholars felt that no special attention need be given to minorities as such, insofar as the new, modern universal concern with individual human rights could serve perfectly well as a protective umbrella against the human rights violations that might be perpetrated against members of ethnic minorities.

But before the era of universal human rights (ushered in by the Universal Declaration), minorities were indeed occasionally the object of special protective measures against discrimination, particularly when third parties, such as neighbouring governments or superpowers, became interested in their situation. Religious and national minorities have been the object of bilateral treaties and the League of Nations developed what became known as the "minorities regime."

5. Contradictions between Ethnic Minorities and Nation-States

Beyond the question of specific protective measures for minorities, it might be asked if there is not a more profound contradiction between the idea of the nation-state in an increasingly interdependent and transnational world system and the survival or preservation of minority ethnic cultures. States, particularly small and medium-sized, economically weak, third world States that have not yet been able to throw off the effects of colonial rule and its aftermath, are justifiably wary of potentially disruptive political demands by what they consider to be subnational groupings. Minority rights issues are often seen as nation-endangering demands that weaken the State and play into the hands of real or perceived external enemies. Many recent and current ethnic conflicts have shown that not only domestic interests but also external, third-party interventions play a role in their dynamics (India, Sri Lanka, Cyprus, Northern Ireland, Ethiopia, Chad, Nicaragua).

On the other hand, there is the prickly question of the relationship between ethnicity and class, a question that has sparked an impressive amount of writing (more ideological than scholarly, to be sure) in recent years. Very frequently, minority ethnic groups seem to concentrate or cluster around a specific class position within the class system. While numerous ethnic minorities are multi-class, often class and ethnic identity do overlap or are closely correlated. For numerous authors, particularly within the Marxist approach, ethnic discrimination is a function of the class system. Without going into a more careful discussion of this debate (see chap. 2), a widely held position within this approach is that the human rights of ethnic minorities are best protected through collective class rights (social, economic) rather than so-called ethnic rights. Consequently, the locus of the struggle for collective rights should be class, and not ethnicity.

An illustrative case of the way States, nations, and ethnic minorities have been conceived is provided by the countries of Latin America, which are the subject of the following chapter.

4

CULTURE AND SOCIETY IN LATIN AMERICA

What often strikes outside observers about Latin America is the apparent cultural unity of the dozen and a half countries in which Spanish is the official language. Indeed, except perhaps in the Arab culture area, there are few regions in the world in which such a large number of independent States share a common language and, to a certain extent, a common history, a common religion, a common set of values and ethos. For a number of valid reasons, Brazil is sometimes added to this list, though its differences with the hispanophone countries are many. For over a century now, Latin American intellectuals have consciously attempted to build a Latin American culture and identity. Understandably, this collective effort has not been alien to the politicians' attempts to forge a Latin American economic and political unity, but the two movements should not be confused because they do represent, after all, a different dynamic. Latin America has certainly been more successful in these efforts at the cultural level than at the economic and political one.

The concept "Latin America" itself, of course, is not original to the subcontinent. It was coined by a French apologist for the court of Napoleon III, who saw in "La Latinité" a good ideological argument to counteract Anglo-American expansionism on the continent and at the same time, favour France's own imperialist designs. Latin America's liberal intellectuals did not at first relish their French-inspired Latinity; many of them were more inclined to seek inspiration and salvation in the United States and its Monroe Doctrine, identified with progress and modernity. Nineteenth-century "thinkers" (*pensadores*), as they came to be called, looked towards the United States for a model to follow in the struggle for the "second emancipation," the cultural one, which was to take place after political independence.

In the Hispanic countries, the intellectual élite was usually split between the more traditional and conservative groups, strongly identified with the Spanish and Roman Catholic heritage, and the more modern and progressive elements

43

that rejected this tradition as feudal and backward and wanted to bring the French enlightenment, British rationalism, and American pragmatism and empiricism into Latin American culture.

Later generations of "Latin" intellectuals became more critical of the Anglo-American model, as the political and economic pressures associated with Yankee Manifest Destiny made their presence felt on the development of Latin America, beginning by the middle of last century. Mexico, for example, lost half of its territory to the United States in the war of 1847. There came a tendency to "look inward," to seek cultural roots and identity, not in foreign models, but in the Latin American societies themselves, in their ethnic and historical make-up.

The search for roots, for an identity of one's own as against the simple transposition and adaptation to national circumstances of the British, French, or American cultural models, became almost an obsession for generations of Latin American writers, artists, musicians, and philosophers, and it was closely related to the economic and political process of "nation-building." Obviously, there was a political choice involved. After the early failure in the nineteenth century of Bolivar's dream of a single "American" nation from California to the Straits of Magellan, which could become a counterweight to the then already perceived threat of North American hegemony on the continent, the newly independent States had to develop the forms and contents of their truly "national" cultures, and where these did not yet exist (as was the case everywhere, in fact), national culture would have to be invented and created. And this is a slow and painful process anywhere, which in Latin America has not yet been completed.

The first major contradiction, then, in this process of cultural evolution was between the search for a truly "American" identity and the almost desperate desire for "progress" and "modernity." The latter meant throwing off the shackles of a degrading colonial and feudal past and embracing imported European and North American values and institutions. But the former meant rejecting artificially imposed "foreign" models in order to enhance what might rightly be called "national" culture. This contradiction has characterized Latin America's cultural history for well over a century and is still at the very heart of the great cultural debates that take place in contemporary times.

The second principal contradiction is to be found in the competing demands between "national" culture and the "regional" or "continental" culture. Looking inward meant not only rejecting extra-continental models (though of course these were never really rejected but in fact actively courted, imbibed, and absorbed, and this is one of the permanent and persistent ambiguities in Latin America's cultural development). Looking inward also meant stressing the distinctiveness of the "national" as against the commonality of the cultural traits shared by the different countries. Such a situation was not the produce, by any means, of some arbitrary or subjective decision by the continent's cultural élites, but rather the result of the economic and political fragmentation that took place after the breakup of the Spanish empire.

Three centuries of colonial rule had created in Latin America an economic structure and political administration that was highly centralized in Spain but that had succeeded in incorporating the disparate regions of Latin America into an interlocking network of functionally interrelated units. There was more contact and exchange between the American provinces of the Spanish empire during colonial times than there was between the independent successor States during the nineteenth and early twentieth century. Contrary to what occurred in the Balkans a century later, where after the breakup of the Ottoman and the Austro-Hungarian empires each pre-existing nation was finally able to establish its own State, in Latin America, the new States were carved out to satisfy the ambitions of military and political leaders or small ruling cliques, and the task of forming a nation to give context and substance to the political and juridical shell of the young States came later. The building-up of a national culture became a primary objective of the new Latin American States after the political turmoil of the post-independence period had simmered out and a modicum of economic stability had been regained.

Three major reasons stand out in relation to the importance of this objective. In the first place, it was necessary to legitimize political power. The leaders of revolutionary factions, the military dictators, the regional strongmen propelled by circumstances into a national role, the spurious self-anointed "emperors," and the elected representatives of the handful of "notables" who controlled the political process during the independent period (i.e. more or less during the whole of the nineteenth century) needed more than the outside trappings of authority to make their mark on history. They spoke and acted in the name of the "nation" or the "people," that abstract entity that in fact did not yet exist. They needed a nation in whose name they could legitimately wield the power they had obtained, in whose name they could speak as equals to other States and for whose benefit and happiness – or so they wished people to believe – they had been elected, appointed, called by the people, or made a revolution. Thus, where there was a State, there had to be a nation, and where there is a nation, there has to be national culture. The intellectual élites picked it up from there.

In the second place, nation-building was important because after the dismemberment of the Spanish empire in America, the weak, fledgling States fell easy prey to the expanding imperialist ambitions of the British, French, and North Americans. If none of these rival empires was able to establish permanent formal sovereignty over any of the larger Latin American countries, it was mostly because of the rivalries between the imperialist powers themselves, which led to indirect economic and political controls over the new States rather than direct colonial administration (with a few exceptions such as Puerto Rico or the Falkland Islands). Nationalism and national culture became powerful instruments in strengthening the new States against ambitious foreign empires and unfriendly neighbours. There is no doubt that countries such as Paraguay, Peru, Colombia, Chile, Ecuador, Bolivia, Guatemala, Panama, and Mexico developed their national consciousness rather strongly as a result of resistance to foreign invasions or wars with neighbouring states or of simply their refusal to become attached or subordinated to a larger political unit.

Thirdly, the development of national consciousness, and hence of national culture, became an imperative for building up the State apparatus (public administration) and the national economy (economic development). And it is here that we find the third major contradiction in the cultural evolution of the Latin American countries.

This is the contradiction between the concept of national culture as espoused by the intellectual and political élites and the crude reality of fragmented, non-integrated, highly polarized economic and social structures as well as, in some countries, a highly differentiated ethnic and cultural composition of the country's population.

At times, a "national historical project" seemed to coalesce and bring together a "national" or "popular" will so dear to the romantic nationalists of the nineteenth century. More often than not, however, national culture turned out to be the more or less coherently articulated wishes of a small ruling class, inheritor of the colonial administration and that was desperately in need of legitimizing its power and of developing ways and means to exclude the popular masses (peasants, Indians, former Negro slaves who had taken part in the wars of independence) from the body politic. The fruits of independence were soon appropriated by the *criollos*, the native-born élites of Spanish stock, the land-owning oligarchy, who were separated by a profound cultural and social chasm from the *mestizos* (the biologically mixed population) and, of course, from the Indian peasant masses and, in some countries, the rather numerous black population of slave origin.

To many observers, the Latin American countries during the first half of the nineteenth century were not yet national States at all but rather a series of loosely knit regional units based on a partially self-sufficient agrarian economy that has been described as semi-feudal. Many of the conflicts among the different factions of the ruling class expressed the tensions between the need for a strong, centralized State (favoured by the urban middle classes and the emerging bourgeoisie) and the centrifugal, sometimes separatist, regional interests (mainly agrarian). The idea of a national culture became, in a way, an ideological weapon for the centralists, who were also, generally speaking, the liberals, the progressives, the modernizers of their day.

A deeper and much more persistent rift existed along class lines, between the small ruling groups, owners of the land and the mines, and the subordinate Indian peasantry. In fact, in most countries, the Indians made up the majority of the population and occupied the lowest rungs of the social and economic ladder. The Latin American countries have been described as "dual societies," and the highly polarized social and economic structures persisted in most countries up to the twentieth century.

Class cleavage was also a cultural cleavage. The subordinate Indian populations had been incorporated by the Spaniards as servile labour into the colonial economy, and a rigid system of stratification and segregation kept them effectively outside the political process. After independence, slavery and serfdom were abolished and legal equality of all citizens was proclaimed. But in fact, the subordination and exploitation of the Indians persisted, mainly through the operation of the landholding system.

The concept of the nation-state, and of national culture, was that of the upper classes, the white descendants of the European settlers, the landholding aristocracy, the urban bourgeois elements. The model of the modern nation that evolved together with the expanding capitalist economy was that of the Western liberal democracies on the French, British, and American patterns. In fact, Latin American political constitutions were almost exact copies of the American constitution, and Napoleonic legal systems were introduced. The educational system, though still influenced by the Spanish colonial élitist model, soon adopted European (mainly French) and later American concepts. The Latin American élites considered themselves as part and parcel of Western civilization; by religion (Roman Catholicism), language (Spanish and Portuguese), and cultural ethos. The fact that in most countries by the beginning of the twentieth century the majority of the population still spoke one of many hundreds of Indian languages and lived in closed, semi-isolated villages or tribal communities according to their ancestral customs (though most of them had become nominally Catholic as a result of the forced conversions practised by the colonial missionaries) did not basically alter the national self-perception of the dominant classes.

In fact, the Indian populations were considered an obstacle to national integration and therefore a threat to the rightful place that the national élites considered to be theirs among the civilized nations of the world. The principal intellectual leaders of the nineteenth century were openly contemptuous of the Indian cultures and considered them to be inferior to the dominant culture of the times. To be sure, much of the earlier greatness and brilliance of the pre-Hispanic Indian civilizations had long since disappeared, and the remaining Indian populations were but a weak shadow of their ancestors. But the blame for this could not be placed on the Indian cultures themselves (as did the intellectual leaders of the times) but on the system of colonial exploitation that had dismembered and disorganized the Indian civilizations, reducing them to little more than a mass of exploitable labour. To this was now added the destructive impact of the expanding capitalist economy.

The prevailing ideology (based on liberalism and positivism) considered that the Indian element had no place in the new national cultures that were being built. The State and the ruling classes used a number of mechanisms to try to do away with this "blemish" that they considered imperiled their chances to become truly modern nations. In a number of countries, State violence and mili-

tary expeditions "cleared the land" for the cattle ranchers and the new entrepreneurs of the agricultural frontier, and the Indian peoples were physically exterminated. This happened in Uruguay, Argentina, and southern Chile, as well
as in parts of Brazil and elsewhere. The pattern resembled the process of "set-
tling the frontier" that had worked so effectively in the early history of the
United States.

A good deal of racism was involved in this process. According to the racist
ideology in vogue during the latter part of the nineteenth and the first half of the
twentieth century, which was eagerly accepted by many members of the Latin
American cultural élite, the indigenous people were to be considered racially
inferior to the whites of European stock and thus incapable of acceding to the
higher levels of civilized life. This same appraisal was often extended to the
growing numbers of mestizos, the biologically mixed population that was to
become the majority ethnic element in most Latin American countries by the
twentieth century. But as regards the Indians, the racist ideology suggested that
the only possible way out for the Latin American countries was to proceed
towards an improvement of the "biological stock" of the population (like so
many cattle) through massive European immigration. A number of countries,
such as Argentina, Uruguay, Chile, Brazil, Venezuela, Costa Rica, and to a
lesser extent some others, embarked upon a systematic policy of attracting
European immigrants, who were to provide technology, capital, know-how, and
entrepreneurship to the backward countries and who would eventually contribute to a racial "whitening" of the population and thus to improvement and
progress (the concept of "development" had not yet been coined) of these nations.

The racial ideology has by no means disappeared from the élite culture in
Latin America, but for obvious reasons of recent history, it has been largely
discredited. What many of the home-grown racists preferred to forget was that
in the view of the North European racial pseudo-theorists, the "Latin" races
themselves (to which of course these ideologues belonged) were to be considered
as inferior by Anglo-Saxon, Celtic, Aryan, or Teutonic standards (to mention
but a few of the racial categories that became politically charged value judgements). It has sometimes been stated that racism was absent from Latin American history (in contrast to the situation in the United States) and that the
mixing of the races began early in colonial history. While the latter is of course
true, the former is not. A strong undercurrent of racist thinking characterized
the cultural evolution of the nineteenth and twentieth centuries and contributed
to a cultural profile, effectively wielded by the ruling classes, from which the
subordinate Indian peoples (with their languages, customs, and traditions,
world-view and social organizaation, as well as artistic achievements) were
practically excluded.

The major ethnic fact of the twentieth century, in the countries where the
Indians had not been completely exterminated, was the rapid growth of the

mestizo population. The "pure" whites (if there ever was such a category at all, and of course the concept of white race itself corresponds to no known scientifically established fact) were rapidly diminishing in numbers, as was the relative proportion in the total population of the "pure" Indians. The mestizo population also occupied the middle rungs of the social and economic stratification system and has been increasingly identified in recent years with the growing Latin American "middle classes." It did not take long for the intellectuals to discover formerly unknown virtues in the mestizos. Soon they were considered to have incorporated the best features of the two original races (the white and the Indian) that had intervened in their make-up. They became the bearers of the new concept of nationality that evolved together with the strengthening of the nation-state. The rise of the mestizo, now extolled in literature, social science, and political discourse, coincided with the growing political presence of middle class parties and social movements that, by the middle of the twentieth century, had practically displaced the more traditional oligarchic parties from the centre of the stage. José Vasconcelos, a Mexican philosopher and educator of the twentieth century, called the mestizos a "cosmic race" that promised a major role for Latin America in world history.

"Mestizo-America" was a concept that anthropologists liked to use in order to distinguish those countries with large Indian populations from the mainly southern-cone countries from which the Indians had practically disappeared. The term mestizo nowadays refers not only to the process of racial mixture, but rather to the process of cultural syncretism or acculturation, whereby the two great cultural traditions that clashed in the sixteenth century have become meshed in a single emerging global culture that, in each one of the countries concerned, is now considered to be the "national" culture. At least so goes the argument wielded by those who see in the figure of the mestizo the kernel of nationalism and national unity.

To the extent that the "racial" (or rather, racist) solution to the problem of ethnic and cultural diversity (as considered by the ruling élites) has fallen out of favour, emphasis has increasingly come to be placed upon cultural issues. Indigenous peoples are no longer considered to be racially inferior to whites and mestizos, but Indian cultures are thought to be backward, traditional, and not conducive to progress and modernity. Furthermore, the existence of a diversity of Indian cultures, distinct from the dominant, Western, urban culture of the wielders of political and economic power, has been considered as undermining efforts towards national unity and development. Thus, the "solution" found by governments and social scientists in the twentieth century has been to further what has variously been called acculturation, assimilation, incorporation, or integration. For this purpose, governments have set up specialized institutions and have followed specific policies in the educational, cultural, economic, and social fields designed to "integrate" the Indian populations into the so-called national mainstream.

In modern Latin America, the concept of national culture has been predicated upon the idea that Indian cultures do not exist, that if they do, they have nothing or little to do with "national" culture, that, at any rate, they have nothing or very little to contribute to national culture (their greatness, if any, lies in the historical past); that such cultures, if they still exist at all, are but vestiges of their former splendour and are naturally tending to disappear anyway and therefore the best that an enlightened government can do is to hasten their demise. In this fashion, not only are national culture and unity strengthened but the indigenous peoples themselves will greatly benefit in terms of material and spiritual development, modernization, and progress.

Thus, in cultural and political terms, the idea of the nation in contemporary Latin America is based on the denial of the Indian cultures. Development projects aimed at improving the conditions and standards of living of the Indian rural communities (most Indians are in fact peasants), and there are many such projects, actually contribute to the disappearance of the Indians *qua* Indians. This is, in fact, the objective of the so-called Indianist policies (*indigenismo*) that most countries adopted in line with the recommendations periodically made by the Inter-American Indianist congresses that have been held ever since 1940. Only in recent years have these policies begun to change (see chap. 8).

Except in museums, handicrafts, and folkore, and as tourist attractions, Indians have been denied a cultural collective existence in Latin America. In the UN Commission on Human Rights, as in the League of Nations before that, Latin American delegates would regularly deny that there were any "minorities" in their countries and that they had any "minority" problems. This has changed in the last 15 years since a new awareness has arisen in Latin America regarding the so-called "indigenous problématique."

Whereas in some countries Indians do represent relatively small and regionally isolated minorities, in others they make up fully half if not more of the population. Here, the Indians are "sociological" but not numerical minorities. In all of Latin America, there are over 400 different Indian ethnic groups, each with its own language and distinctive culture and way of life. They range from small bands of isolated jungle dwellers whose physical survival is constantly threatened by the advancing frontier of the national society to the several-million-strong Indian peasant societies of the Andean highlands. While estimates vary and census returns are unreliable, it is safe to state that Indian populations today might well represent around 30 million people on the subcontinent (about 10 per cent of the total population of Latin America), and their numbers are growing.

Assimilationist policies by governments, churches, international organizations, and private associations have been fairly successful over the years and have tended to reinforce the natural integrative tendencies of the expanding market economy, means of transport and communications, the school system, and other such mechanisms. Some observers during the fifties and sixties predicted the complete disappearance of Latin America's Indians by the end of the twentieth century. However, things have not turned out exactly that way.

By the early seventies, a number of militant Indian organizations had sprung up in several parts of Latin America that in one way or another demanded a change in official policies as well as respect for their cultures and recognition of their own Indian identities. Indigenous intellectuals, who had gone through the official school systems, developed arguments for alternative cultural policies. Social scientists, many of whom had worked in the service of national governments or international organizations in the field of "indigenous affairs," had become critical of the official assimilationist ideology and posed important new issues concerning the "national question" in Latin America. It was obvious that the whole issue of "national culture" and, conversely, of cultural nationalism had to be raised anew.

These new cultural and ideological currents did not arise in a vacuum. In the first place, they coincided with similar movements elsewhere in the world, and which have been termed an "ethnic revival" by some observers. Secondly, they emerged in Latin America at a time when dissatisfaction with traditional models of economic growth and social development, which had been followed by most governments in the region over the past 25 years or so, was great. So-called "developmentalism" (desarrollismo) had not provided the easy way out of poverty and backwardness that it had promised earlier, and the social, cultural, and political costs of purely growth-oriented strategies was particularly high in some countries. Military coups and repressive authoritarian governments on the one hand, and revolutionary guerrilla movements and populist political parties seeking inspiration from the grass-roots on the other, were instrumental in the search for alternative models and strategies of development. In this process, it became necessary to reject the prevailing, dominant concept of national culture and to reconsider the role of the multiple Indian ethnic groups in the process of national development.

Suddenly governments and public opinion became aware that the Indian ethnic groups were not really only living vestiges of some historical past to be thrown in the dustbin of history, but dynamic social forces that were demanding their rightful place in contemporary society on their own terms and not only on those decided for them by élitist intellectuals, political ideologues, government bureaucrats, or foreign missionaries.

5

Ethnic Rights in the International System

INTRODUCTION

The ethnic question has long been a subject of concern to the international community. The League of Nations dealt with the problem of national minorities, but on the whole, the system of minority protection that it tried to establish turned out to be a failure. After the Second World War, the United Nations again took up the issue, but only half-heartedly. The majority countries of the West maintained the position that if only the human rights provisions of the Charter, the Universal Declaration, the International Covenants, and other instruments were complied with by governments, there was no need for special international legislation concerning ethnic minorities. This position has been found to be faulty, and efforts have long been underway in the specialized UN bodies to develop standards and norms pertaining to the collective human rights of ethnic minorities and indigenous and tribal peoples.

The Sub-Commission on Prevention of Discrimination and Protection of Minorities has for many years debated the possibility of a declaration of minority rights and has argued during many of its sessions about an adequate definition of minorities. The debates in the Sub-Commission reflect, of course, the differing and sometimes opposing views of its individual members, the countries they represent, and the ideologies they wield. Despite all its efforts, the Sub-Commission has not been able to agree either on a satisfactory definition of minorities or on a declaration of minority rights. It did, however, produce a first draft of what finally became Article 27 of the International Covenant on Civil and Political Rights, which refers specifically though briefly to minority rights. Nevertheless, most observers and minority organizations consider this article wholly unsatisfactory to ensure adequate protection and promotion of minority rights. There is general agreement that much remains to be done in the UN in this field.

One difficulty that has arisen in the task of international standard-setting is the question of the self-determination of peoples as a human right. International law, as developed by the UN, denies that the right of self-determination applies to ethnic minorities (thus denying such groups the right to be identified as "peoples"). But certain ethnic groups, particularly indigenous peoples, reject this position and claim for themselves the term "peoples" and thus the right of self-determination. This continues to be a bone of contention in the debates of the UN, and it has serious implications for political action and conflict at the national level.

Some specialized UN organizations, such as Unesco and ILO, have dealt with certain aspects of minority rights in their particular fields. Regional international bodies have also become concerned. The Organization of American States has done some work regarding the indigenous peoples of the American continent. The Organization of African Unity has had to deal with rival claims between States whose borders were drawn by the colonialists, and ethnically defined groups or peoples who, as one author states, have become "partitioned Africans."[1] Early in its history, the OAU determined that existing borders be respected, thus perhaps wisely avoiding what might have become an era of major conflicts on the continent. The African Charter of Human and Peoples' Rights does not refer to the rights of ethnic minorities and tends to identify the term people with that of the inhabitants of existing States or at best, the few anti-colonial national liberation movements existing on the continent. Still, within the framework of "the rights of peoples," Africa cannot ignore the fate of ethnic minorities, some of which in various parts of the continent have been actively struggling for what they see as their legitimate collective rights. The European Community has concerned itself with regional or territorial minorities in Europe and of course with certain questions relating to immigrant labourers, many of whom have become racial and/or cultural minorities in some European States. The European Court of Human Rights has had the opportunity to deal with claims of ethnic minorities on that continent. The Helsinki agreements also refer to the human rights of ethnic minorities in Europe.

The time is long past when the international community could smugly consider that ethnic conflicts were a purely internal domestic matter of States. Recent history has shown that the ethnic question usually has international ramifications. The relationship between internal ethnic conflict and international relations has not yet been sufficiently analysed, though it appears to be an issue whose significance will probably increase in the future.

Over the years, the idea took hold that minorities have group or collective rights, without which their individual human rights cannot be adequately safeguarded. The collective rights that ethnic minorities around the world have been demanding have to do with the survival of the ethnic group as such, the preservation of ethnic cultures, the reproduction of the group as a distinct entity, the cultural identity attached to group life and social organization. This is much more than expecting non-discrimination and equality before the law. It relates to the use of language, schooling, and educational and cultural institutions, including religious institutions; frequently, with self-government and political autonomy. In a world of polyethnic nation-states, these rights can only be guaranteed by the active involvement of States in their implementation, just as in the case of the more universally recognized and accepted social and economic rights.

Many countries have already adopted some such policies; others refuse to do so in the name of "national unity," "integration," and other concepts linked to the sovereign national State. Most States consider, in any case, that the way they deal with minorities within their borders is solely a domestic matter. This is one of the reasons why the UN has been unable to make much headway in this field. And this is also the reason why some observers consider the need for collective minority rights to be recognized by the international community as human rights.[2]

INDIVIDUAL AND COLLECTIVE HUMAN RIGHTS

The world-wide struggle for human rights in our time has been based fundamentally on two premisses: equality and non-discrimination. The former premiss contains two elements: on the one hand, in terms of civil and political rights, it implies the formal, legal equality of all human beings before the law (with well-known exceptions regarding minors, mentally ill, and other noncitizens), and secondly, in terms of social, economic, and cultural rights, it means equality of opportunity for all individuals. The non-discrimination aspect of human rights implies that no specific or particular human group may be excluded from the enjoyment of universal human rights. Both the United Nations Charter and the Universal Declaration of Human Rights stipulate that member States promote human rights without distinction as to race, sex, language, or religion. But as one author wisely puts it, does "no distinction" mean that all social groups must be dealt with alike? The problem, as he sees it, is "whether differentiating measures are to be justified in the name of a group right or interest or whether they are to be condemned as violating the right of individuals to equal treatment."[3]

The question arises because over the last few decades it has become evident that a distinction must be made between individual rights and collective rights. Universal individual human rights, even when fully effective, do not necessarily ensure the full enjoyment of rights by collectivities. Moreover, at times the promotion of individual human rights in disregard of collectivities may lead to the violation of collective rights, just as the priority of collective rights over individual rights may lead to violations of the latter.

The problem is not simply a legal one, it is ideological and political. The idea of universal individual human rights rested on the concept of a direct, unmediated link between the individual and the State; the individual has rights, and the State has the obligation either to abstain from infringing on these rights or else to ensure and provide them. This is the classic liberal position; it emerged in Europe and spread to the rest of the world.[4] In this perspective, not only the individual but also the State has rights, but the latter are not human rights; only the individual has human rights.

Upon closer inspection, the classic liberal model does not actually exclude collectivities other than the State from enjoying specified rights under certain conditions, usually spelled out in law. Thus, children, workers in dangerous occupations, pregnant women, refugees, religious and national minorities, among others, have at one time or another been singled out for special protection in national and international legislation. Generally, however, the rights thus protected pertain to individuals who belong to said collectivities, rather than to the group as such. Authors often point out that human rights are only to be enjoyed by individuals, that groups *qua* groups can enjoy privileges or special treatment, but not human rights. This is still an open and controversial issue to which we will devote some attention in this chapter, as it relates directly to the question of ethnic minorities.

GROUP RIGHTS AND NATION-STATES

The last two centuries of Western political thought have included a strong "Statist" bias; the State is the only legitimate political unit over and above the individual; the State is the only or principal unit in the international system; the State is the guarantor of sovereignty, freedom, and human rights; the State is the only legitimate depository of power and the only actor that can legally wield violence and use force to impose its will. Statist ideology ranges from *laissez-faire* liberalism (liberal economics can only be guaranteed by a strong political State) to welfare States, socialism, and Fascist totalitarianism. Pure Statist ideology does not recognize collective rights to groups other than itself, but in practice of course, States have had to deal with demands put forward by collectivities within their territories to which some collective human rights attach. States have dealt with such problems in different fashion and by doing so or refraining to do so, they have become involved in situations of tension, stress, conflict, and violence.

Not all sub-State collectivities are the possessors of human rights; some lay claim to corporate rights or privileges of a legal or moral nature, but they should not be confused with human rights. For example, the situation of the church or other religious bodies in a number of countries; the army in some cases, or certain occupational guilds or crafts. Formerly, it may have been the nobility.

But the collective human rights referred to in this chapter pertain to collectivities that some would call "natural social groupings" and that claim for themselves certain rights that cannot be subsumed under the generally accepted universal individual rights. Rights that can only be guaranteed, and sometimes only provided, by the State but that some existing States may consider as competitive with their own prerogatives *qua* States.

These social groupings are ethnic groups or ethnies. Anthropologists tend to consider them as "natural" social groupings because next to the family as a basic human institution, ethnies – whatever their particular definition – are universal phenomena and are very, very ancient: antedating nations, empires, and of course, States and social classes. They are not of course natural in the biological sense; that is, there is no empirical evidence that ethnic identity and integration is biologically or genetically determined, or that it is the result of anything else but linguistic and cultural affinity between a group of people who share certain historical, environmental, economic, and political characteristics and interact with each other within the limits of certain types of social organization.[5] When I say that ethnies are very ancient, I refer to ethnicity as an integrating principle, not to any single or particular ethnic grop. Ethnies have come and gone and have changed over time, but ethnicity as a principle of social integration has remained, even while it has achieved a new importance in recent times. One author, who studies the ethnic revival in the modern world, shows that the liberal view that "as mankind moved from a primitive, tribal stage of social organisation towards large-scale industrial societies, the various primordial ties of religion, language, ethnicity and race which divided it would gradually but inexorably lose their hold and disappear" has not stood up well to the facts of historical development in the last century or more.[6]

To substantiate the above, let us briefly look at what some students of these issues have to say about the matter. Glazer and Moynihan refer to ethnic groups as "all the groups of a society characterized by a distinct sense of difference owing to culture and descent. . . *forms* of social life that are capable of renewing and transforming themselves."[7]

Another American sociologist contends, with a number of other specialists, that "ethnic identities implicate a 'primordial' relationship between people. . . . Ethnicity. . . derives from a cultural interpretation of descent."[8] In Soviet scholarship,"*ethnoses* are social phenomena. . . . The term 'ethnos' has always denoted not only 'small' peoples, but also multi-million communities. . . . Along with the view, widespread in modern Soviet scientific literature, that this term can be used to denote not only a tribe or nationality but also a nation, there is the opinion that its use should be confined to pre-nation formations."[9]

Social scientists generally agree that ethnic groups are not biological, but social and cultural constructs. In this sense, the concept of ethnicity must be distinguished from that of "race," even though the two concepts are closely related. "Race" of course is also a sociological construct, but based on the perception of biological distinctions and similarities, whereas "ethnies" or ethnic groups do not necessarily relate to biological characteristics.

Ethnic groups are frequently assimilated to other kinds of social groupings and categories, such as social classes. And if social classes have interests, it is said, ethnic groups are also interest groups. Several scholars, however, take issue with such a position. Brass, for example, is categorical when he states:

> ethnic groups are centrally concerned with cultural matters, symbols, and values and with issues of self-definition that distinguish them from other types of interest associations. . . . The interest group approach pays attention only to groups formally organized to press demands upon the state, whereas the organizations of many ethnic groups are internal to the community. Many ethnic groups of potential political significance would thus be ignored in a strict interest group analysis.[10]

Whatever the definition – and there are many – and whatever the meanings attached to the term ethnie or ethnos (or its derivatives) by different scholars, it is clear that we are dealing with a generic concept related to other terms, such as "peoples" and "nations." Thus, Bromley writes of ethnos "that we should remember that what we have in mind is the meaning when we speak about the 'people of the world'. And by that we usually have in mind such communities as 'tribe', 'nationality' and 'nation.' Accordingly, the main task of the term 'ethnos' is to define the common, generic name of these formations."[11] Again, the British scholar A. D. Smith writes: "Ethnic nationalism has striven to turn the ethnic group into that more abstract and politicised category, the 'nation', and then to establish the latter as the sole criterion of statehood."[12] Another current scholar who writes about nationalism and who is, like many others, awed by the fact that contrary to so many predictions, nationalism has not withered away, writes that "nationality, or, as one might prefer to put it in view of that word's multiple significations, nation-ness, as well as nationalism, are cultural artefacts of a particular kind." And he goes on to define the nation as an "imagined political community – and imagined as both inherently limited and sovereign."[13]

If I have quoted selectively from a number of current scholars, it is simply to underline that, on the one hand, no clear unequivocal definition of terms related to ethnicity exists and that, on the other, the phenomena we are dealing with are almost indistinguishable from other sociological and political terms such as "people," "nations," and "nationalities."

It is within this framework that the issues of collective human rights arise. The criteria used to define such groups, to identify and distinguish them from others and to attribute membership to them, may vary from case to case, but generally they have to do with language, religion, territory, history, social and political organization, shared myths, and, of course, the feeling of identity and belonging that Anderson labels the imagined community.[14] Aside from such common internal characteristics of the group, a crucial distinguishing factor is the relational element, that is, the way in which the group as such relates to other similarly defined groups and particularly, the way it relates to the State. Most modern States like to see themselves as national or monoethnic States. The widely used concept of nation-state or national State in contemporary politics makes the two terms almost coterminous, but it has also created a great deal of confusion. Hugh Seton-Watson puts it very clearly:

> States can exist without a nation, or with several nations, among their subjects; and a nation can be coterminous with the population of one state, or be included together with other nations within one state, or be divided between several states. There were states long before there were nations, and there are some nations that are much older than most states which exist today. The belief that every state is a nation, or that all sovereign states are national states, has done much to obfuscate human understanding of political realities. A state is a legal and political organisation, with the power to require obedience and loyalty from its citizens. A nation is a community of people, whose members are bound together by a sense of solidarity, a common culture, a national consciousness. Yet in the common usage of English and of other modern languages these two distinct relationships are frequently confused.[15]

In fact, whereas the ideology of the nation-state prevails in modern times, most countries are multinational States or, as some would have it, polyethnic states.[16] However, only a relatively small number of States make constitutional or other legal provisions for their multiple ethnicity. Most national legislations ignore their multiple ethnicity altogether, while others provide for it in such a fashion that it provokes misunderstandings, rivalries, tensions, friction, conflicts, and sometimes violence between different ethnies or between the State and specific ethnies. It is in the framework of such a dynamic that collective human rights issues of ethnic groups within the State arise.

This is so because almost invariably in situations of polyethnicity, a hierarchical ranking of ethnies occurs as a result of numerous historical, economic, and political processes, in which a majority or dominant ethnic group controls the power of the State and/or the economy and is frequently able to subordinate the other ethnie or ethnies to its own interests. In the ethnocratic State, the dominant and/or majority ethnie identifies only itself with the nation and with the State and tends to exclude the minority and subordinate ethnies from this identification. Many contemporary authors see the State, not as an autonomous entity above the units it encompasses nor as simply a neutral arena where political interests and conflicts are played out, but as a differentiating force that distributes resources selectively among regions, classes, interest groups, or ethnies.[17] State policies may equalize or compensate the unequal distribution of resources among ethnies (e.g. affirmative action, preferential policies, regional development projects, tribal or indigenous development), but it may also, through specific policies or most often the lack of any specific policy in this regard, foster or strengthen inequality among ethnies.

ETHNIC GROUPS BECOME MINORITIES

As a result of the processes outlined above, in the modern nation-state, the non-dominant ethnic groups or peoples are treated as "minorities." But who and what are minorities in formal and legal terms? This question is not a purely academic matter, because upon the definition of "minority" hinges a whole international system of minorities protection that took form after the First World War, and in many countries national legal structure and policies may reflect, and in turn may have an impact upon, the existence and recognition of minorities. The United Nations has occupied itself with the minorities question for some decades since its founding, but it is no closer to a satisfactory definition of "minorities" than it was in the early fifties when it began to tackle the problem. The most generally currently accepted definition of minorities is the one given by Francesco Capotorti, special rapporteur of the UN Sub-Commission on Prevention of Discrimination and Protection of Minorities, to wit:

A group numerically inferior to the rest of the population of a State, in a non-dominant position, whose members – being nationals of the State – possess ethnic, religious or linguistic characteristics differing from those of the rest of the population, and show, if only implicitly, a sense of solidarity, directed towards preserving their culture, traditions, religion or language.[18]

This definition has not satisfied all the experts (who sit in their individual capacity and not as official representatives of member States) of the Sub-Commission, and this UN body is still groping for a definition that it might formally adopt.[19] Regardless of international efforts, States have sometimes defined minorities to suit their own interests, calling them everything from national minorities to minority nationalities, or else they have neglected to define, that is to say, to recognize them. As has been mentioned before, States have usually been unwilling to accept the existence of ethnic minorities in their midst, particularly when they live by the myth of a single, unified national being identical with the State. As one author put it,

The lack of a binding general definition of minority is a lacuna but not a fatal obstacle to progress. States will doubtless continue to be as evasive as previously on the existence of groups. . . . While it is possible to deny the existence of minorities, this may only deflect the operation of particular treaties for a time; the definitions have a rationality which is cumulative. The failure to define and recognize is normative, not cognitive. It may be felt that "recognition" fuels demands: minorities are always likely to want more than States will concede.[20]

As can be seen, the question of the definition of minorities has serious policy implications for the well-being of the members of ethnic groups and the nature of the State itself. Let us take an example. In some Latin American countries, there exist legal definitions as to who is and who is not an Indian. In other Latin

American States, the definition is merely administrative, to be taken at the time of a national census, for example. In both cases, Indians themselves are affected because special government policies, educational opportunities, or land rights depend on such definitions. In earlier years, Latin American delegates to the United Nations refused to admit that Indians were minorities in their countries and denied having any minorities at all, at least in the sense that the term was being used in United Nations debates.[21] Lately, Indians have demanded the right to self-definition; they deny government bureaucrats the right to determine who is and who is not an Indian. The right to "self-definition" has become a major claim of indigenous rights in the world (see chap. 8).

In China, for a people to be labelled a minority nationality is a long process that involves the participation of teams of linguists, anthropologists, folklorists, as well as government officials and members of the ethnic groups themselves.[22] In Africa, it is now claimed that some of the ethnic groups are simply inventions of former colonial administrators or European ethnographers but that the ethnic "label" has stuck and in fact does at present serve to condition interpersonal relations between such groups in terms of sometimes conflicting political interests.[23]

Thus, the very definition of an ethnic group frequently becomes a political act, and whether an ethnic group should be called an ethnic group at all, or rather a nation, a nationality, a minority, a tribe, a community, a culture, a society, or a people, or be denied any of these labels, has become a political issue more than a simple procedure of scientific inquiry.

HUMAN RIGHTS AND MINORITY RIGHTS

The non-discrimination component of universal individual human rights is considered by many specialists to be sufficient guarantee for the protection of the rights of minorities. When these rights are not adequately implemented, minorities may rightly invoke the non-discrimination clauses of human rights legislation in their defence. Discrimination against ethnic minorities may be a stated or unstated government policy, or it may simply be a pervasive, subtle condition that prevails despite human rights legislation and government policies. As Van Dyke points out, non-discrimination against minorities may sometimes entail special treatment by governments (as in language or educational policies) that others may decry as being "discriminatory."[24]

The United Nations has been involved through the work of its Sub-Commission on Prevention of Discrimination and Protection of Minorities in developing international standards regarding the protection of minorities. To date, contrary to what many had hoped for, a universal declaration, let alone a convention, on minority rights has not yet been produced by the UN. The only tangible result of 40 years of labour by the Sub-Commission has been the inclusion of Article 27 in the International Covenant on Civil and Political Rights, which states:

Article 27. In those States in which ethnic, religious or linguistic minorities exist, persons belonging to such minorities shall not be denied the right, in community with the other members of their group, to enjoy their own culture, to profess and practise their own religion, or to use their own language.

Minority peoples around the world who had hoped that the United Nations would come up with a strong and clear-cut statement on the rights of minorities have understandably felt cheated over the language of this lone article in the whole of the International Bill of Rights, which deals with minority rights. Critics argue that this article does not constitute an effective basis for a system of protection of minority rights.

In the first place, by introducing the text with the phrase "In those States in which. . .minorities exist," Article 27 leaves the entire question of definition wide open, and we have already seen that a number of States deny having any minorities at all (even when the opposite can easily be established). Who, and under what circumstances, is to decide whether minorities exist within a certain State? This important question is either left entirely up to the States themselves or else it should be decided by the competent organs of the United Nations. Up to now, no such action by the United Nations is envisaged in Article 27 or any other instrument. The Human Rights Committee of the UN, which has been established under the International Covenant of Civil and Political Rights, has not been able to prepare a "general comment" on Article 27 (as it has on other articles of the Covenant) because of the complexities involved.

Secondly, the article clearly refers to individual rights ("persons belonging to such minorities. . .") and not to collective rights, even though the article admits that these rights are to be enjoyed by individuals "in community with the other members of their group." Minorities as groups, however, are not considered. This is a major failing of Article 27, because certain collective social and cultural rights can only be enjoyed by organized communities that are recognized as such. By phrasing Article 27 the way it stands, the General Assembly obviously avoided dealing with the issue of the legal or political status of minorities in order to placate those governments that opposed any formal recognition of such groups. In line with other international instruments of human rights, Article 27 includes the protection of minorities within the general framework of the protection of individual human rights and freedoms. As one author put it:

Concerning the holders of the rights under article 27, no doubts can exist. Protection is not afforded to minority groups as such, but rather to persons belonging to minorities. This formulation cannot be viewed just as an accident of drafting. To conceive of minority protection in individualistic terms fits well into the general pattern of the International Covenant on Civil and Political Rights.[25]

Thirdly, the rights of minorities are protected negatively ("persons belonging to such minorities shall not be denied . . ."), and the text does not impose on States any obligation to enhance actively the rights of minorities to enjoy their own cultures and languages or practise their own religion. Even when such rights are not denied by a State, it is clear that minorities will have a difficult time preserving their culture and identity unless they are able to obtain such support that nowadays is generally only provided by governments. States may carry out assimilationist policies detrimental to the cultural survival of minorities even without an outright denial of minority rights as set forth in Article 27. That is why minority peoples have argued that Article 27 does not guarantee their rights and in no way obligates States that may have ratified the Covenant to carry out policies in favour of the rights of minority groups.

Fourthly, the article makes no mention of national minorities nor of indigenous peoples. Given the experience of the League of Nations between the two world wars, it may be understandable that the General Assembly did not wish to include national minorities under the purview of Article 27. If national minorities were to be given special protection in the International Covenant on Civil and Political Rights, this might lead to constant bickering between States regarding the situation of one nation's minority in the territory of another, just as had occurred during the time of the League. The United Nations considered that this was to be avoided by all means. Still, it is little solace to millions of members of national minorities around the globe that their rights and aspirations are not envisaged by Article 27. In contrast, indigenous peoples, if they were considered at all, would be included within the framework of minority peoples as dealt with in Article 27. But, as is more carefully discussed in chapter 8, this is not the case at present, and the rights of indigenous peoples are being discussed not only within the framework of this article. However, notwithstanding its limitations, Article 27 does represent a step forward in comparison with the Universal Declaration and its emphasis on individual freedoms. In truth, Article 27 may be considered as a step in the transition from individual to collective rights in the work of the United Nations.

The main argument that has been used against widening the scope of clauses dealing with minorities in the United Nations human rights instruments is that the general provisions on human rights provide enough protection to all persons regardless of their ethnic status, and that no special protective measures for minorities should be required if these general human rights provisions are adequately implemented. Minorities argue that, on the contrary, universal human rights are not enough and that, without specific provisos obligating States not only to abstain from interfering with the collective rights of minorities but also to provide active support for the enjoyment of such rights, minority groups will always be disadvantaged within the wider society. Above all, they hold, the existing instruments do not establish the obligation of States to "recognize" minorities legally, and this seems to be a basic point of contention in any system for the protection of minorities.

Behind such formal arguments there are, of course, a number of sociological and political factors involved. As pointed out before, States like to think of themselves as nation-states, that is, as monoethnic collectivities, and they have always been uneasy with minorities within their borders. In case of national minorities that may have majority kin in neighbouring States, the threat of irredentist demands is always present and the European experience between the two world wars is there to remind us of the dangers involved. Then there is the possibility that if minorities are given too much leeway, collective rights may lead to demands for autonomy, self-government, self-determination, and even political secession or independence, which may threaten the territorial sovereignty or even the very survival of a State. Furthermore, one of the great tasks of our time, particularly in the third world countries, is the struggle for economic and political viability of the new States, that is, the task of nation-building. For the groups in power, this means integrating and assimilating the minority peoples who do not share the dominant or majority culture, whether these are tribes, immigrants, territorial minorities, linguistic enclaves, or indigenous or aboriginal peoples.

Frequently, the smaller and weaker States feel especially vulnerable to external pressures from neighbouring and rival States or colonial or neo-colonial powers through problems and conflicts arising out of demands made by minorities. And, of course, there is no lack of evidence that shows that minority demands are quite often used or manipulated by outside powers or third parties for their own geopolitical purposes.

Whatever the position taken by States or by the dominant ethnic groups within such States, minority peoples are increasingly looking towards the international community for protection when they feel that their basic human rights *qua* collectivities are being threatened. Recent world history provides plenty of evidence that minority peoples are indeed under constant pressure from the dominant society, so that not only their cultural survival but sometimes even their physical existence is endangered.

Whereas genocide has been declared an international crime by the United Nations, the cultural destruction of an ethnic group, also termed ethnocide, has not been considered in any international protective instrument.[26] Article II of the Convention on the Prevention and Punishment of the Crime of Genocide defines the crime of genocide as meaning

any of the following acts committed with intent to destroy, in whole or in part, a national, ethnical, racial or religious group, as such: (*a*) killing members of the group; (*b*) causing serious bodily or mental harm to members of the group; (*c*) deliberately inflicting on the group conditions of life calculated to bring about its physical destruction in whole or in part; (*d*) imposing measures designed to prevent births within the group; or (*e*) forcibly transferring children of the group to another group.

At the time of the drafting of the Convention, there was talk about including an article on "cultural genocide," but this was finally not taken up. The Genocide Convention refers exclusively to the physical destruction of ethnic groups.

Whereas individual members of minority groups may wish to assimilate into the dominant society, and other minorities may be indifferent to their own continued existence, experience shows that most ethnic minorities (except perhaps immigrant minorities) in the world resist forced assimilation and integration and prefer to maintain and live by the values of their own cultures. Against the arguments of the ethnocratic State, minorities argue that demands for secession or independence are only raised when the State or the dominant ethnic group denies a minority its basic collective human rights. In the historical process of State formation, ethnic groups are frequently incorporated into the larger society against their will or, at least, without their explicit consent, sometimes in a most brutal fashion. In this way, many peoples and nations have disappeared, others have amalgamated into new social and cultural formations, and yet others, once free and sovereign, have been reduced to a "minority" status of discrimination and marginalization by the dominant ethnic groups. Indeed, what for some is "nation-building," for many minority peoples around the world is in fact "nation-destroying."[27] This is the basic contradiction that Article 27 of the ICCPR has not been able to solve and that crops up again with increasing frequency in the debates of the Sub-Commission.

To be sure, the United Nations has adopted other international instruments that have bearing on the rights of minorities even though they do not directly refer to them. The many activities that the organization has carried out with the purpose of eliminating discrimination, prejudice, and intolerance are, of course, also designed to protect the basic human rights of ethnic, linguistic, racial, and religious minorities. In this respect, it is important to mention the International Convention on the Elimination of All Forms of Racial Discrimination (1965), the Committee on the Elimination of Racial Discimination, established by the Convention, the Decade for Action to Combat Racism and Racial Discrimination (1973–1983), and the two World Conferences to Combat Racism and Racial Discrimination, held in Geneva in 1978 and in 1983, as well as the Declaration on the Elimination of All Forms of Intolerance and of Discrimination Based on Religion or Belief (1972).[28]

A detailed analysis of these instruments and activities designed to combat racial discrimination would show that they are true to the principles of the International Bill of Rights, particularly as regards the full enjoyment of the universal individual human rights that are the backbone of the Universal Declaration and the International Covenants. As regards the specific rights that minorities are always claiming, especially insofar as these would require affirmative action by the States in which these minorities live, the international instruments relating to racism and racial discrimination are widely regarded as being insufficient.

The collective rights that ethnic minorities around the world have been demanding have to do with the survival of the ethnic group as such, the preservation of ethnic cultures, the reproduction of the group as a distinct entity, the cultural identity attached to group life and social organization. This is much more than expecting non-discrimination and equality before the law. It relates to the use of language, schooling and educational and cultural institutions, including religious institutions; frequently, with self-government and political autonomy. When Article 27 of the ICCPR states that persons belonging to minorities shall not be denied certain rights, it does not go far enough. If the preservation of minority cultures and ethnic identity is to be considered a universal collective human right, then the simple statement that such rights shall not be denied is insufficient. In a world of polyethnic nation-states, these rights can only be guaranteed by the active involvement of governments in their implementation, just as in the case of the more universally recognized and accepted social and economic rights of the so-called "second generation" of human rights.[29]

THE RIGHT TO SELF-DETERMINATION

Another set of international norms developed by the United Nations that has a direct bearing on the question of minorities is the principle of the self-determination of peoples. While this principle is mentioned in the Charter, it was not included in the Universal Declaration, perhaps because at that time it was not yet considered a "human right." Still, the right of peoples to self-determination developed rather rapidly in the United Nations. In 1952, the General Assembly recognized that "the right of peoples and nations to self-determination is a prerequisite to the full enjoyment of all fundamental human rights."[30]

A historic further step was taken in 1960 when the General Assembly adopted resolution 1514 (XV), the Declaration on the Granting of Independence to Colonial Countries and Peoples, which solemnly states that "All peoples have the right to self-determination; by virtue of that right they freely determine their political status and freely pursue their economic, social and cultural development." Furthermore, the Declaration states that the subjection of peoples to alien subjugation, domination, and exploitation constitutes a denial of fundamental human rights. Commenting on the scope and impact of the Declaration, a special rapporteur of the UN Sub-Commission states:

The Declaration and the principles proclaimed in it were interpreted as calling for the immediate abolition of the domination of any people by an alien people in any form or manifestation; it was held that the abolition of domination by the granting of independence should be complete and should prevent forever any attempt to revive any alien influence on peoples which had achieved independence; that independence should not mean only political independence, but also economic and cultural independence, free from any direct or indirect influence or exercise of pressure of any kind on peoples or nations, in any form or on any pretext; that the principles of the Declaration should be universally applicable to all the peoples of the world, without limitation of time or geography, or limitation as to race, creed or colour, not only for the achievement, but also for the preservation of their full and absolute independence; and that independence should depend solely on the free will and determination of the peoples themselves and not on any other influence.[31]

A further step in the development of the right of peoples to self-determination was taken in 1966 when the General Assembly adopted the two International Covenants on Human Rights. Article 1 of both the International Covenant on Civil and Political Rights and the International Covenant on Economic, Social, and Cultural Rights proclaims again that "All peoples have the right to self-determination. By virtue of that right they freely determine their political status and freely pursue their economic, social and cultural development."

In the Declaration of 1960, the right to self-determination was to be applied exclusively to peoples subject to alien occupation, that is, to colonies, and it has been interpreted as such for a long time. Yet, by virtue of its inclusion as Article 1 in the International Covenants on Human Rights, it is now understood that this right applies to all peoples, regardless of whether they live in colonies or not. The right of peoples to self-determination is considered a right belonging to the human person, as a pre-condition or a necessary prerequisite for the real existence and enjoyment of all other human rights and fundamental freedoms.[32]

Aurelio Cristescu, special rapporteur of the Sub-Commission, holds that

the principle of equal rights and self-determination should be understood in its widest sense. It signifies the inalienable right of all peoples to choose their own political, economic and social system and their own international status. The principle of equal rights and self-determination of peoples thus possesses a universal character, recognized by the Charter, as a right of all peoples whether or not they have attained independence and the status of a State. Consequently, the right of peoples to self-determination has the same universal validity as other human rights.[33]

It is clear from the United Nations texts that there is a distinction to be made between "peoples," "nations," and "States." That the right of self-determination applies to existing States is obvious and is indeed one of the principles of the Charter of the United Nations. It has been proclaimed many times, among them, in the Declaration on the Rights and Duties of States, adopted by the General Assembly in 1974. In its 1952 Declaration quoted above, the General Assembly distinguishes between "peoples" and "nations." By the time the principle of self-determination had been included as a human right in Article 1 of the International Covenants, the word "nation" had been deleted, since "peoples" was considered to be the more comprehensive term and was used in the Preamble to the Charter.[34]

The right to self-determination has now become an integral part of international law, if we are to judge by the resolutions of the General Assembly.[35] The Declaration on Principles of International Law concerning Friendly Relations and Co-operation among States in accordance with the Charter of the United Nations (resolution 2625 [XXV] of 1970) affirms:

By virtue of the principle of equal rights and self-determination of peoples enshrined in the Charter of the United Nations, all peoples have the right to freely determine, without external interference, their political status and to pursue their economic, social and cultural development, and every State has the duty to respect this right in accordance with the provisions of the Charter.

Here again, it is clear that the resolution refers to the territory of a colony or other non-self-governing territory that has a status separate and distinct from the territory of the State administering it. The Declaration states strongly that

nothing in the foregoing paragraphs shall be construed as authorizing or encouraging any action which would dismember or impair, totally or in part, the territorial integrity or political unity of sovereign and independent States conducting themselves in compliance with the principle of equal rights and self-determination of peoples as described above and thus possessed of a Government representing the whole people belonging to the territory without distinction as to race, creed or colour.

The General Assembly went on to declare that "the principles of the Charter which are embodied in this Declaration constitute basic principles of international law. . . ." The special rapporteur concludes: "Hence, it is clear that self-determination, having been classified as a right by the Charter, is a legal concept which finds expression both as a principle of international law and as a subjective right."[36]

The question remains, however, What happens when a specific government does not "represent the whole people . . . without distinction as to race, creed or colour."? Such is certainly the case in South Africa, and the General Assembly, as is well known, has taken a firm stance on the policy of apartheid, which has been declared an international crime. But in other cases, the situation is not nearly as clear-cut. Minorities in different parts of the world may claim that the governments of the States in which they live do not represent them and that distinctions as to race, creed, or colour are indeed practised, by virtue of which such minorities are disadvantaged. Might this not be the case of the Kurds in

Western Asia, the Tamils in Sri Lanka, the Moros in the Philippines, the Indians in Canada or in Colombia, the Aborigines in Australia, and many other similar situations? In such cases, do the minorities in question possess the right to self-determination according to international law? Most international lawyers would dispute this, arguing, as I have pointed out above, that the right of self-determination is intended to apply only to colonial peoples or, rather, territories. Some scholars, however, taking the wording of this and other resolutions literally, argue that racial and religious minorities, living in the territory of independent and internationally recognized States, may, under certain circumstances, claim the right to self-determination.[37] The debate is by no means closed.

From the foregoing discussion, it is clear that a pivotal question regarding the right of peoples to self-determination is that of the definition of a people: who are the peoples who enjoy the human right of self-determination?

This is precisely where we encounter serious theoretical and practical difficulties. There is no legal definition of *a* people. There is not even a generally accepted sociological or political definition of *a* people. The United Nations has carefully avoided to define "people," even as it has conceded all peoples the right to self-determination. The 1960 declaration on decolonization referred to peoples under alien domination (that is, colonies), but it rejected explicitly any attempt to undermine the national unity or the territorial integrity of a country. Some of the governments consulted by the special rapporteur, Hector Gros Espiell, for his study on the right to self-determination, made a distinction between "people" and "minorities," and the special rapporteur himself holds that international law applies to peoples and not to minorities.[38] Thornberry considers that the UN never defined the term "peoples" in an ethnic sense, but referred it to the inhabitants of a colonial territory. People, then, is a territorial concept, and the territorial integrity of the colonies was to be maintained until and beyond independence. Thus, he concludes, self-determination in the modern incarnation has little to do with minorities. If "peoples" applies within States, it is to majorities: there is little in the UN definition for minorities. "It seems that minorities, whatever depredations are inflicted upon them, must attempt to find justice within the boundaries of existing states and be reconciled with them. Self-determination is not a right of minorities. They must look instead to human rights: those which are not the rights of 'peoples.'"[39]

If this is indeed the case, then ethnic minorities the world over can expect very little from the United Nations. There are very few outright colonies left, and soon the Special Committee on Decolonization – created in 1961 with regard to the Declaration on the Granting of Independence to Colonial Countries and Peoples – may have to close its doors. At that time, the concept "peoples" will become synonymous with "nations" and "States." And minorities will have to accept that the international community does not consider them to be peoples.

Many minority peoples, however, and I use the term advisedly, do not accept happily the way the United Nations has disposed of their human rights. A close look at today's world shows that many independent States – as has been pointed out before – are made up of a number of ethnically distinct peoples. The "people" who, according to the United Nations, have a right to self-determination are not only ethnically and culturally distinct from those of the colonial metropolis, but are usually geographically distant from the metropolis. Is the criterion for self-determination, then, a geographical one, the old "salt-water" principle?[40] That would indeed be a *reductio ad absurdum* of the whole question. In fact, many minorities in independent States consider themselves to be the historical victims of earlier colonizations or simply the result of the way a modern post-colonial State has been artificially carved out of the old colonial administrative units. This might be the case in dozens of the new States of Africa and Asia that have achieved independence since the Second World War. Take the struggles of the Kurds in western Asia, of the Saharauis in the Maghreb. Consider the Basques in France and Spain, the Catholic Irish in Ulster, the Québecois in Canada, the Hawaiians, the populations of West Papua, or the original Hispanics in the south-western United States or, for that matter, the Puerto Ricans. And what about the Tibetans? Or the Latvians, Lithuanians, and Estonians, who have always resisted their forcible annexation by Stalin in 1940? Should these ethnies be considered peoples or not? In terms of the United Nations resolutions, all these groups would not be considered peoples, even if in domestic legislation they may be considered as "nationalities" or even as "peoples." Still, many of them look to the UN as a forum where their claims and demands can be ventilated.

Many of the ethnic, religious, or linguistic conflicts that are taking place in so many countries all over the world these days relate to the question of self-determination. It is unfortunate that in the various United Nations instruments relating to the decolonization process, the concept of self-determination is generally considered to mean only accession to political independence by colonial territories or else the free and sovereign decisions of independent States and the non-interference of one State in the affairs of another. That is why the United Nations finds it so difficult to deal with the problems of minorities within the framework of the right to self-determination.

However, according to numerous scholars, as well as the internal practice of a number of States, self-determination has many facets, only one of which implies political independence or secession. Self-determination may be internal and external and its components range from simple self-identification at one extreme to full self-government at the other. Between the extremes, different forms of self-determination may be identified, the applicability of which will depend in each case on particular historical circumstances.[41] Until now, the United Nations has preferred not to move into the finer complexities of the problem of self-determination. That is why there exists an obvious contradiction between the proclamation of the right to self-determination of "all peoples" on the one hand and its restrictive application to the specific field of decolonization on the other. From the study of some recent cases of ethnic and national conflict, it would seem that only when a "minority" adopts a strategy of armed struggle and becomes a "national liberation movement" will it be recognized as a "people" by the United Nations. But this is certainly a self-defeating attitude of the United Nations and stands in open contradiction to the universal principles proclaimed in the International Bill of Rights.[42]

THE RIGHTS OF INDIGENOUS PEOPLES

A particularly illuminating issue regarding these questions refers to the way the problem of indigenous peoples has been dealt with in the United Nations (see chap. 8). At an earlier stage, when the human rights of indigenous populations were discussed, these generally referred to all of the inhabitants of the colonial non-self-governing territories (designated as indigenous or natives). Upon attaining independence, these populations ceased to be "indigenous" and became citizens of their respective independent States. But the question did not end there, for indigenous peoples existed also in a number of independent States.

During the earlier discussions in the United Nations on the rights and the protection of minorities, the Latin American delegations denied that any minorities existed in their countries and, if at all, these were foreign immigrants whose task was to assimilate or integrate into their adopted new nations. No mention was made of the Indian populations in Latin America. Many countries in fact deny the existence of "indigenous" peoples within their territories, arguing that the majority and ethnically distinct population is itself indigenous to the country. This is the stance most commonly taken by a number of Asian countries with respect to their tribal populations. Others, however, maintain that tribals are the indigenous peoples of Asia, akin to the Indians of the Americas, and that their situation should be dealt with in the same fashion.

Indigenous peoples themselves, whose non-governmental organizations have in the last few years been able to expound their views in a number of United Nations fora, hold that their situation is different from that of minorities in general and must be given special attention. For one, in some Latin American countries, the indigenous are not a minority at all but a numerical majority. Secondly, the indigenous are the descendants of the original inhabitants of a country settled or colonized by immigrants or conquered by force. Thirdly, they have been the victims of certain processes of economic and political development that have placed them in a situation of subordination and dependence with respect to the dominant society in their own lands. The indigenous peoples argue that they are the original or first nations and that their human rights have been systematically violated by the dominant states, the legitimacy of which they do not recognize in some cases. In Canada and the United States, for example, the indigenous peoples were originally dealt with as sovereign nations by the settler societies and signed treaties as equals with the newly independent States. These treaties, they now claim, have been broken unilaterally by the governments. Based on these and other arguments, the indigenous claim the status of "peoples" and not minorities or simply populations, as they are sometimes described, and they demand the right to self-determination in accordance with international law.[43]

The claim of "prior occupancy" as giving rise to special collective rights is the object of much discussion. Not only the indigenous peoples in conquest societies base their demands on this claim, but also the traditional inhabitants of countries that, over the years, have received successive waves of immigrants. In some south Asian countries, for example the *bumiputera*, or "sons of the soil," demand special rights or recognition against more recent settlers (even if these are the majority), and in turn, the more ancient aboriginals may hold similar claims against them. Such situations have arisen in Assam and Bihar in India, in Malaysia, in Sri Lanka, and other countries.[44]

CONCLUSIONS

From the foregoing, we may conclude that the problem of human rights and peoples' rights with respect to ethnic minorities and to peoples who are ethnically distinct from a dominant ethnic group (which may or may not be a numerical majority) within the framework of an independent State is far from solved within the United Nations system.

The traditional concept of human rights (both the civil and political rights, as well as the social, cultural, and economic rights) applies predominantly to individuals. On the other hand, collective rights apply primarily to States and in some exceptional cases to peoples struggling for national liberation and recognized as such by the international community. However, between individual rights and States' rights there are millions of human beings in dozens of countries in every part of the world who claim their own identity, their own right to an existence according to their own values and forms of social organization and, in many cases, their right to self-determination.

States deal with these questions in various ways, as will be seen in chapter 10. Some States have elaborate mechanisms for the protection of the rights of ethnic groups and minorities, others refuse to do so in the name of "national unity," "integration," and other concepts linked to the sovereign national State. Most States consider, in any case, that the way they deal with minorities within their borders is a purely domestic matter. This is one of the reasons why the UN has been unable to make much headway in this field. And this is why it is important that collective minority rights become recognized by the international community as human rights.

One of the reasons this has not been the case is that an important segment of

the international community still considers that only individuals, and not col-
lectivites or communities, are the true bearers or subjects of human rights. It is
held that if only the already established individual human rights were fully
respected and implemented in every country – including, of course, the polyethnic States – then ethnic minorities would be free to preserve their cultures
and identities if they so wished, without government interference. Others, however, consider that this is more illusion than reality. Only if collective ethnic minority rights are recognized as such, and specifically as human rights, can such
communities survive in environments that are often hostile to their very existence
and survival. At any rate, a rapidly changing world, where nation-state ideologies are political imperatives, where the mass media and world-wide communication systems can penetrate even the most isolated village or the most
closely knit community, minority cultures are frequently undermined by social
and economic forces beyond their control and beyond the control of even the
most sympathetic of governments. Therefore, if minority cultures have any role
to play in the contemporary world, then their rights must be actively fostered
and not only passively and reluctantly protected. Insofar as this is a question of
human rights, only the minority ethnies themselves should be empowered to
decide if or to what extent they wish their cultures, societies, values, and identities to survive in a rapidly changing world.

If we may call the collective rights of ethnic groups ethnic rights, then the
question arises whether such ethnic rights are compatible with, or complementary of, individual human rights. The issue is by no means resolved. It is
of course true, to a certain extent, that the notion of individual human rights is a
liberal, Western concept, and while the notion has spread in modern times to
other cultures, it has not been equally accepted or incorporated by all non-
Western cultures.[45] The issue, then, is if not all contemporary cultures are
equally keen on individual human rights, may not an insistence on collective
ethnic rights become inimical to the enjoyment of individual human rights?
Consider land, the major claim of indigenous peoples around the world. For the
indigenous, the right to land is essential, and land is considered a public, communal good. But for many in the West, the access to, and ownership of, land is
an individual human right. And what of the demand for respect of cultural
identity, when this may imply gross violations of universal individual human
rights, as, for example, the practice of sexual mutilation of young girls in a
number of African countries? To what extent can the traditional authorities of a
rural community demand customary unpaid labour services for public works
from the young men of the village without standing accused of wanting to impose illegal "forced" labour on unwilling youth? (The example comes from
southern Mexico). Yet another case: a linguistic minority is granted the right to
education in its own language; what rights have individual members of the
minority to refuse this education and opt for the majority language and what
right has the community to impose the teaching of this language on its mem-

bers? Or conversely, if a member of the country's majority lives in a "minority" community, will he or she in turn be treated as a "minority"? Such cases are common in Canada, the United States, Yugoslavia, and elsewhere.

When such conflicts arise, as they frequently do, should individual or collective human rights prevail? Are there general principles to be applied, or must each case be solved on an *ad-hoc* basis in terms of the political realities at hand?

While contemporary wisdom holds that all human rights are equally fundamental and none ranks higher than any other, in reality, certain rights do hold priority over others. When conflicts between rights occur, the solution is more often than not neither technical nor moral, but political. In other words, conflicts seldom occur between rights in the abstract, but between holders or claimants of rights. The question is not so much which rights are in conflict, but who holds the rights and how much political (or military) power does he have to impose his claim. If such conflicts occur between individuals in a democratic polity, then usually the State has the means to impose a more or less satisfactory or fair solution. If, however, the conflict occurs between individual rights and collective rights other than those of the State itself, or between holders of competing collective rights, then solutions are not always easy and may lead to political show-downs.

The collective or group rights that ethnic minorities and indigenous peoples claim for themselves are not universally recognized, least of all by the States that are called upon to guarantee them. Still it would seem that there is a tendency in the international human rights field to move beyond universal individual rights towards a structuring of collective rights. And ethnic minorities and indigenous peoples are in the forefront of the struggle to define, establish, and implement these rights. Only time will tell how successful they will be, but at any rate the issues that have been raised represent a major challenge for human rights thinking in our time.

The struggle for the preservation of the collective rights of culturally distinct peoples has further implications as well. The cultural diversity of the world's peoples is a universal resource for all humankind. The diversity of the world's cultural pool is like the diversity of the world's biological gene pool. A culture that disappears due to ethnocide or cultural genocide represents a loss for all humankind. At a time when the classic development models of the post-war era have failed to solve the major problems of mankind (poverty, unemployment, the environment, etc.), people are again looking at so-called traditional cultures for at least some of the answers. This is very clear, for example, as regards agricultural and food production, traditional medicine, environmental management in rural areas, construction techniques, social solidarity in times of crisis, etc. The world's diverse cultures have much to offer our imperiled planet. Thus the defence of the collective rights of ethnic groups and indigenous peoples cannot be separated from the collective human rights of all human beings.

6

Ethnic Conflicts

In the previous chapters, reference has been made to what we may call the two major paradigms of development thinking, the modernization approach and the Marxist theory of class conflict and revolutionary struggle. Significantly, in both approaches little attention has been paid to the dynamics of ethnic conflict and to the so-called "ethnic factor" in development. This is a subject that has been somewhat neglected in the vast literature on development problems over the last few decades, but in recent years it has once again become the centre of attention, basically because ethnic conflicts have become more visible and ethnic demands have become political issues of some importance in a number of countries. Social scientists have put forward competing theories regarding this "ethnic revival," and at the same time some well-established and widely accepted paradigms relating to "development" and "nation-building" have had to be critically reassessed in the light of such phenomena.

But social science theory, as is so frequently the case, has been astoundingly slow in conceptualizing the issues, and much of the recent scholarly debate on ethnicity and related subjects seems to have fallen into ideological squabbles of secondary importance or into endless terminological hair-splitting. There is little consensus among social scientists regarding the true nature of ethnic conflicts or even regarding the acknowledgement of their existence. To the extent that such conflicts do represent life and death questions for millions of people and are now recognized as being the focus of major and massive human rights violations, the search for understanding leads necessarily beyond the admittedly limited propositions provided by mainstream social science.

Perhaps an example may help explain this statement. If we accept that a certain country is a "developing society" (and making such a proposition already entails a series of previously accepted value judgements), then we generally presume that something called "modernization" is taking place, which is a form of social and cultural change.[1] When ethnic conflict occurs in a

74

"developing society," we tend to relate it to our conception of this "moderniza-tion" and will attempt to explain it in the light of what we think "moderniza-tion" is or is not. We may find, for example, that modernization in this country has been incomplete or unequal and that ethnic conflict occurs when an ethnic group considers that it has been "left out." Or it may occur because an ethnic group "resists" modernization; or, on the contrary, a modernizing ethnic group enters into conflict with others who do not wish to modernize. The possibilities are numerous, but what is significant is that if such explanations arise within the "modernization paradigm," then other possibly relevant explanatory fac-tors will tend to be neglected or relegated to second place.

Or we may believe that the only "real" form of social conflict in any given society is "class struggle," and whilst we may give lip-service to cultural, lin-guistic, and religious factors, we will tend to subsume these under the general umbrella of "class struggle"; in these circumstances, it will be difficult to find in ethnic conflicts anything but different expressions of class struggle. For exam-ple, an indigenous community may simply be considered as part of a "landless peasantry" at odds with the local (non-indigenous) landlord class. Or a cultur-ally distinct "middleman ethnie" is only treated as a "merchant class" or a "petite bourgeoisie," regardless of its ethnic characteristics. Moreover, the scholars who adhere uncritically to this approach will neglect to look for any other significant elements except those pertaining to class analysis.[2]

If social scientists, who are, after all, expected to engage in objective analysis of social dynamics, find themselves in such strait-jackets, the task is even more difficult for policy makers and political actors in ethnic conflicts. Whatever the specific issues may be around which ethnic conflicts turn, the fact is that usually both sides to such conflict wield arguments that appear to be morally valid and grounded in a sense of history and apparently supported by rational political analysis. In most cases of ethnic conflict around the world, the parties in conflict hold perceptions that are internally consistent but that are, to a great extent, or at least appear at first glance to be to a great extent, incompatible with the perceptions of the situation held by the opposing party. This is not to say that in each and every conflict in which ethnically defined social groups engage in struggle over rights, resources, or power both sides are always right. Whilst it is not the task of the social scientist to render judgement on whether the claims and demands of ethnic groups in conflict are right or wrong, neither is he or she insensitive or neutral with regard to fundamental moral issues relating to free-dom, liberty, justice, and human rights.

Therefore, the instruments of social science, even when we recognize the limitations pointed out above, may provide useful points of reference when opposing points of view about ethnic conflicts are aired and debated. Not only because a social science approach may take the form of a "third position," thus contributing to break deadlocks or helping to find ways and means of under-standing and dialogue, but also because certain approaches developed by the social sciences may aid the parties in conflict to improve their own understanding of the dynamics of the situation (hopefully, at least; or is this social scientific presumption?).[3]

Ethnic conflict appears to be a permanent form of social and political struggle in the modern world. No major region is free from it. In its more acute manifestations, it may turn into murderous, destructive violence. One recent study demonstrates that between 1945 and 1980, State-sponsored massacres of members of ethnic and political groups were responsible for greater loss of life than all other forms of deadly conflict combined, including international wars and colonial and civil wars. Since World War II, some 40 ethnic or communal groups have been victimized in this fashion, in some cases including genocide.[4]

In certain circumstances, ethnic conflicts have been predictable; in others, however, they seem to come as a surprise to many observers, politicians and academics alike, and sometimes even to the actors in the conflict itself. Not infrequently, ethnic conflict simmers for long periods just under the surface of apparently stable and balanced societies that seem unaware of the potentially explosive nature of the underlying contradictions, until the conflict suddenly bursts out of its shell, upon an unprepared and disbelieving public opinion. Yet once an ethnic conflict has already begun to involve several of the institutions of a society and a polity, then it becomes most difficult to control, unless its root causes can be removed. The term "ethnic conflict" covers a wide range of situations. In fact, it might be argued that ethnic conflict as such does not exist. What does exist is social, political, and economic conflict between groups of people who identify each other in ethnic terms: colour, race, religion, language, national origin. Very often such ethnic characteristics may mask other distinguishing features, such as class interests and political power, that on analysis may turn out to be the more important elements in the conflict. Still, when ethnic differences are used consciously or unconsciously to distinguish the opposing actors in a conflict situation – particularly when they become powerful mobilizing symbols, as is so often the case – then ethnicity does become a determining factor in the nature and dynamic of the conflict.

Ethnic conflict occasionally takes the form of so-called communal or tribal violence. Here, the conflict occurs between two relatively self-contained communities within the wider society, communities that identify themselves and each other in ethnic terms – that is, according to racial, religious, or so-called tribal criteria. Such confrontations may or may not involve the State directly, except as a keeper of the peace. When disorders between communities occur, the State may step in to re-establish order, to arbitrate between the parties in conflict, or to right torts that may have been inflicted on one of the communities by the other.[5]

However, in most cases of open ethnic conflict in the world today, the State is not an impartial onlooker or arbiter, but rather a party to the conflict itself. Indeed, in multi-ethnic societies, the State is frequently either controlled by, or identifies strongly with, a dominant or majority ethnie. If, under such circumstances, ethnic conflict involves an ethnic minority or an oppressed ethnic majority, then the ensuing confrontation may take place between this group and the State itself.[6]

Ethnic conflicts generally involve a clash of interests or a struggle over rights: rights to land, education, the use of language, political representation, freedom of religion, the preservation of ethnic identity, autonomy, or self-determination, etc. At times, an economically or culturally privileged minority may find its traditional interests suddenly called into question by an ethnically distinct, politically powerful majority. When this occurs, the minority may organize to maintain its privileges and interests, while the majority will speak in terms of rights, the collective good, and the national interest. Here we encounter a not uncommon situation: the minority group will defend what it considers legitimate rights that are being denied, whereas the dominant majority will argue against undue privileges by the minority that must be subordinated to the common good and the national interest. Of course, these are usually defined by the majority or dominant ethnie in terms of its own interests; and that is why ethnic conflict in these cases appears irreducible, though frequently there are processes of negotiation, bargaining, and coalition-building that may stave off or prevent open conflict from occurring for some periods of time.[7]

Observers tend to differentiate between stratified, hierarchical, or ranked systems and unranked systems of interethnic relations in which conflicts may arise. Ethnies do not usually face or compete with each other on perfectly equal terms. They generally enjoy differential access to a society's wealth, privilege, power, and other goods and benefits as a result of complex historical processes that will vary from one case to another. Ethnic minorities are frequently – but not always – the victims of discrimination, the underprivileged, subordinate segments within asymmetrical stratified systems; or at least they perceive this to be the case, even if the majority maintains a contrary posture.[8] In unranked systems, ethnic power groups face each other on a more equal footing, and here competition and rivalries between groups may involve complex intra-ethnic arrangements between élites and masses, between leaders and followers.[9]

Conflicts between ethnies arise from a number of causes. A subordinate minority (or majority) may react to years, decades, or centuries of discrimination and oppression, and stand up to say "enough!" Or it may demand rights that it has been denied by others who enjoy them. Or a dominant ethnie (whether majority or minority) may attempt to impose its own norms and standards or its own model of society on a weaker, underprivileged minority (or majority) and encounter resistance when it does so. Or the dominant majority may feel that the minority has been granted or is demanding "too much" and must be kept in its place. No matter what the apparent expressions of ethnic conflict may be, and the underlying causes are usually much more complex, the issues of group interests and group rights are always at the centre of the debate.

Though ethnies or ethnic groups are usually termed the actors in a situation of ethnic conflict, it would be unrealistic to ignore or underestimate the internal divisions within ethnic groups. In situations of ethnic conflict, it is often particular subgroups, special interests, specific organizations, or certain élites within the ethnie who formulate and express the demands and objectives attributed to the whole group.[10] For example, among the Sikh in India, it is mainly the Akali Dal in the Punjab and within this group a particularly militant sect who maintain the high level of conflict of the Sikh movement.[11] Among the Basques, the militant organization ETA and its sympathizers, not all of the Basque people, have been directly involved in the struggle against the Spanish State, just as it is the IRA and not all Irish Catholics in Ulster that engages in protracted conflict.[12]

What are the bases for ethnic mobilization in our time? Can we clearly recognize ethnic demands as against other kinds of demands on the political system? In what way is ethnicity related to the process of development (see chap. 7)? Many authors consider that the individual's identification with his ethnic group is some form of primordial (even non-rational) group attachment of a universal nature.[13] An important school of social scientists linked to theories of modernization and political development affirms that such primary group links constitute an obstacle to nation-building and development, which require the breaking down of these links and the transfer of loyalties from the primary ethnic group to the larger civil society.[14] Others would consider that such primordial attachments are not inimical to the building of a larger society but can perfectly well coexist with the requirements of a modern nation. Perhaps we could go one step further and suggest that ethnic identification and loyalties are again becoming relevant in a modern society where the individual is increasingly alienated, whether in the work-place or in the political bureaucracy. This would, of course, hold more for the industrial societies than for the third world. It may help explain the resurgence of ethnicity in, say, the United States and Western Europe, and more recently in the USSR and Yugoslavia. In many instances, the ethnic community becomes a functional intermediate organization (structured or non-structured) between the individual and the polity, such as is the case, at other levels, with trade unions and similar institutions.[15]

For some authors, the activation of ethnicity represents more of a rational choice for political action rather than a return to primordial sentiments.[16] Ethnic demands are said to be used by certain social groups to achieve satisfaction of economic or political interests that would otherwise be more difficult to obtain. This would presumably be the case in clear-cut ethnic majority-minority situations in liberal democracies, in which cultural minorities will never be able to break majority rule. Here ethnic politics, or ethnopolitics as it has also been called, becomes pressure politics and may be used by the political élites of minority groups in their attempt to redress grievances or obtain a "larger part of the pie" or, on the contrary, conserve their share of the pie against the demands of others.[17]

It is generally accepted that at the root of many contemporary ethnic demands, we find economic grievances, but it would be too simplistic to reduce the whole problem to a form of economic struggle. Wherever we find territorial minorities, such as Indians in Latin America or perhaps scheduled tribes in India, the demands are often for greater control over resources or for greater local autonomy (including, of course, at times political self-government or independence). Wherever ethnic groups do not have a territorial base but are scattered among the larger society, ethnic demands may be couched in more cultural or economic rather than in political or territorial terms. Here we often find the struggle of the ethnic group for recognition of its cultural identity as a group. This might be the case of ethnic groups in the United States or of culturally distinct foreign immigrants in Western Europe.[18]

Some authors consider that ethnic conflicts are not conflicts between interest groups at all, but between identity groups; they are conflicts about basic human needs and values that cannot be bargained over or negotiated, in contrast to the bargaining and compromise reached between groups that happen to have opposing, but negotiable, interests. Therefore, such conflicts are considered as deep-rooted, protracted conflicts, and their resolution involves a far more complex process than mere conflict management.[19] Frequently, this is of course the case. But besides values and identities, specific group interests also play their role in the dynamics of ethnic conflicts.

The activation of ethnic demands as rational choice for political action may serve the interests of a wide segment of the political spectrum. It would be a mistake to identify ethnic movements with any one political ideology. First it must be determined under what concrete historical circumstances such movements arise and how they relate to the major social and economic conflicts of their time and place. Between the two world wars, in Europe ethnic movements had a distinct right-wing coloration, particularly because many of them were inspired by Fascism and the Nazi racist ideology. Today, similar movements tend to be considered rather leftist, because they question the authority of the central State and couch their demands in terms of humanistic values and human rights, though a number of such movements in Western Europe have links to the extreme right. In the third world, ethnic movements are usually of a progressive nature, if only because they arise out of a reaction against oppression and exploitation. In Latin America, as well as in the United States and Canada, the Indian ethnic movements reject the capitalist State, but some of them are equally critical of Marxist ideology, which they consider to be another Western invention.[20] However, this does not prevent them from being used or manipulated at times for purposes other than those they apparently serve. Such might be the case of the Sikh movement in India or of the Miskito rebellion against the Nicaraguan government in the eighties (see below).

When in the course of political development certain ethnically defined élites become displaced or lose previous positions of power and privilege, they frequently react in ethnic terms. This may lead to strife and community conflict, as

is often found in India and other Asian countries. For example, between the two
world wars, the land reforms carried out in several central European countries
affected the interests of the ethnic German landed élites. The landowners
reacted by complaining that they were the victims of national persecution and
mobilized the German government in their defence.[21] The underlying "primordial attachments" are frequently mobilizable in certain situations.[22]

If at the root of so many ethnic demands we find basic economic grievances,
why are these not always expressed in class terms? If tribals or native American
Indians or blacks in the United States or Catholics in Ulster are economically
underprivileged or exploited, should not the class struggle and organization
along class lines be a better vehicle for political action than ethnic mobilization?
This is indeed what some analysts maintain when they suggest that ethnic demands are either a clear-cut instance of "false consciousness" or are simply the
object of manipulation by self-interested élites, used to divert the attention of
oppressed groups from their real (even if unperceived) class interests. There is
certainly a great deal of truth in this approach, but here again, it would be too
simple to reduce ethnicity to class, just as it is equally simplistic to deny the
class factor in so many forms of ethnic struggle. Sometimes, indeed, class interests are better served through ethnic politics than through social class organization. Many blacks in the United States, for example, believe that they may
improve their situation more efficiently through political struggle along ethnic
lines than by subordinating their ethnic demands to general class interests.[23]
This of course does not deny the basic unity of class-based demands, but it
would be a mistake to ignore ethnic and racial cleavages within social classes, in
the United States as elsewhere. And then, of course, it must be recalled that
ruling classes throughout history have tried to justify their rule and privilege by
invoking supposed ethnic superiority.

Let us look briefly at two current cases of ethnic conflict in two vastly different
areas of the world that testify to the complexities involved.

Sri Lanka used to be called a tropical island paradise and it was often cited as
a model of a third world plural parliamentary democracy. For several years
now, ethnic relations have deteriorated badly between Sri Lanka's two principal ethnic groups, and current prospects for a peaceful solution to the conflict are
poor. The Buddhist Sinhala make up the country's majority (70 per cent of the
population), and the Hindu Tamils represent 20 per cent. Both groups settled
on the island from India over 2,000 years ago, but the Sinhala claim original
occupancy. Over the centuries, there have been Tamil and Sinhala kingdoms,
warfare as well as peaceful relations between them. The British ruled Ceylon as
a single colony and it became a unified State after independence in 1947.

For a number of historical reasons, basically British educational policy,
which allowed Tamils to attend British or Christian schools, whereas the
Sinhalese attended traditional Buddhist institutions, the Tamils, who mainly
occupy the northern part of the island, were more than proportionately represented in higher education and in public administration. Attempts were made

by Sinhala-dominated governments to redress this imbalance that were taken by Tamils as discriminatory measures. The situation was aggravated when Tamil plantation workers, who had been brought in by the British from India since the nineteenth century and had made their home in Sri Lanka, were disenfranchised. They are the poorest strata of the Sri Lankan rural population. Also, in 1956 Sinhala was declared to be the only official language, though Tamil continued to be recognized as a national language, and in 1972 Buddhism was constitutionally declared the official religion. Economic development projects have brought Sinhala settlers into formerly predominantly Tamil rural areas, raising fears among the latter that they will become dominated by the Sinhala in what Tamils consider to be their traditional homelands. The Sinhala, in turn, are fearful that they might become "swamped" by 40 million Tamils from southern India, in whom the Sri Lanka Tamils recognize their kin.

The conflict has led to riots and violence that have already produced hundreds of victims and thousands of internal and external refugees among the Tamils. Militant Tamil political organizations seek an independent Tamil State in the north (Tamil Eelam), and initiated a guerrilla war of liberation in the middle eighties. The government countered with military repression. Unable to achieve either a political or a military solution, the Sri Lankan government in 1987 agreed to a military intervention by India, through a bilateral "accord," which allowed Indian troops to occupy the northern Tamil areas, ostensibly to pacify and disarm the Tamil guerrillas. In fact, however, some of the guerrilla organizations continued the armed struggle, even against Indian troops. The number of victims continued to increase after the signing of the accord. On the other hand, radical nationalist Sinhalese organizations, displeased with the accord, increased their own violence against the government and against moderate elements on both sides that were seeking a peaceful solution to the conflict. The Tamils speak of systematic persecution and of "pogroms" organized by the Sinhalese Buddhists. The Sinhala, in turn, speak of subversion, separatism, and endangered national unity. International geopolitical interests of India and the United States in the Indian Ocean place the Sri Lanka conflict within the framework of global strategic concerns. Early in 1989, the Indian troops withdrew from the island, but prospects for peace and justice were still bleak.[24]

Nicaragua. Half-way around the world, in Nicaragua, a popular democratic revolution overthrew the bloody 30-year-long Somoza reign in 1979. Soon, a counter-revolutionary movement, armed and financed by the CIA, began putting enormous pressure on the new regime, creating a permanent situation of armed conflict. The Sandinista revolutionaries had based their movement in the cities and the peasant villages of Nicaragua's western part, where most of the population is concentrated. The isolated Atlantic coast territory, covering almost half of the country, had been spared the civil war. Here a mixed population of Miskito, Sumo and Rama Indians, as well as non-Indian poor peasants, had led a rather unperturbed existence far from Somoza's repressive rule.

The Atlantic coast, however, had its own singular history. Here the British had set up a puppet "Mosquito" kingdom in the eighteenth century in order to control the lucrative lumber trade and harass the Spaniards. An international arbitration in the nineteenth century had formally declared this territory to be an integral part of independent Nicaragua. Still, the Indian population of the Atlantic coast was more closely linked to British and American lumber, mining, and fishing interests than to the central power structures of the country. This enclave economy was strengthened over the years by the missionary and educational activities of the Moravian church, and many Indians bore English names and spoke English rather than Spanish besides their native tongue.

When the Sandinistas came to power, they declared their intent to "rescue" the Atlantic coast from the imperialist interests and integrate this territory and its wealth into the national development process. The Indians, in the mean time, had formed their own militant organization and they resisted the attempt at incorporation, demanding the right to self-determination. The Sandinista government understood this to mean secession and acted accordingly; they disbanded the Indian organizations and jailed the leadership. Armed conflict resulted, the Sandinistas accusing the Indian organizations of playing the counter-revolutionary game. The Indians in turn denied having anything to do with the counter-revolution or wanting to overthrow the Sandinista regime; they simply insisted on their Indian rights within the wider society.

Some Indian organizations did most certainly throw in their lot with the counter-revolution, others waged their own struggle (including armed resistance) against the central government, and still others, who by 1988 had apparently become a majority, agreed to co-operate with the Sandinistas. The government, in turn, recognized the mistakes it had made during 1980–1983 in dealing with the Indian ethnic question and proposed a scheme for regional autonomy that would be respectful of the Indians' cultural rights. Nicaragua's new 1987 constitution provides for regional autonomy in the Atlantic coast and guarantees certain cultural rights to the "communities" in the area, but at the same time, it reaffirms the essential unity of the Nicaraguan nation. Many of the indigenous refugees who fled to neighbouring Honduras during the conflictive years in the early eighties returned home.

As the case of Nicaragua shows, it is clear that contemporary ethnic conflicts can be used as an issue in international power politics, just as it was so used in colonial times. Miskito Indians were virtually unknown outside of their own region a few years ago, and in the eighties they became headline-making news items. The Nicaragua case also shows that an unsophisticated class analysis of a country's situation, as is frequently provided by Latin America's leftists, may run into serious trouble if it ignores or underestimates the ethnic issues involved.[25]

Both the ethnic conflict in Sri Lanka and the one in Nicaragua have been the cause of major human rights violations. Indeed, when ethnic conflicts occur, it is likely that human rights violations take place. Unlike most forms of labour conflict, for example, which is legally and institutionally regulated in most countries (and through international legislation by the International Labour Organization as well), and unlike most forms of non-violent political activity, which is generally regulated by law in democratic countries, ethnic conflict is not legally regulated. In fact, it is not legally recognized. By modern standards of the nation-state, it is not even supposed to exist. Thus, when ethnic tensions or contradictions that may lie latent for many years burst into open conflict, not only are most societies and polities ill-equipped to deal with it, as was stated at the outset, but governments usually tend to deny its very existence. Consequently, when governments act to deal with such conflict, they sometimes adopt repressive measures against one or the other of the opposing ethnies. And when this occurs, human rights violations tend to take place.

Human rights abuses committed within the framework of ethnic conflicts are qualitatively different from human rights abuses against persons in general because they tend to be directed not only at individuals but also at collectivities singled out in terms of ethnic identification. These violations have run across the whole spectrum, from mass killings (genocide) to razzias, illegal and arbitrary detention, torture, mass population removals, deportations and segregation, to lack of due process of law, discrimination in public and private institutions, and other forms of open or subtle antagonism. When such violations of human rights are committed by private individuals or groups, then generally the existing legal system is able to provide a remedy, if the government in power is willing and able to do so. This is of course not always the case. One example might be when human rights abuses are committed by economically or politically powerful groups against a weak, marginalized ethnie, as happens to hill tribes or aboriginals in a number of countries.

When, however, it is the State apparatus itself that engages in human rights abuses (as is frequently the case in situations of serious ethnic conflict), then the ethnic victims of such abuses may find that recourse to existing legal safeguards is less than satisfactory. This is precisely one of the burning human rights issues in many ethnic conflicts in the world today, an issue that has become the subject of increasing international concern. On the other hand, when ethnic conflict has turned into organized violence, and when certain radical organizations of one of the ethnies have adopted terrorism as a tactic, they become just as guilty of human rights violations as any repressive State – no matter how just and legitimate their cause may be. Not only that, but the "diabolical circle of violence" that escalates on both sides generates increasing human rights abuses by both opposing parties.

Most systems of interethnic relations do not necessarily lead to ethnic conflict. This is just one form of interethnic contact that may be latent and protracted, or it may flare up under certain circumstances, triggered by specific events. Ethnic conflict is not necessarily violent, but it may become so. When ethnic conflict occurs, ethnic identities become particularly salient and they, in turn, feed back into the conflict.

Some observers hold that ethnic conflict is fundamentally a psychological problem. Group identity, intergroup hostility and rivalry, in-group and out-group feelings, stereotypes about the "other," group fears and anxieties, etc., are basically psychological issues, the solution to which could be found in "conflict-management" techniques.[26] Others see in ethnic conflict more "structural" forces at work, such as unequal access to resources, economic benefits, or political power between different ethnic groups. The nature of the State and relations between ethnies and the State cannot be ignored in situations of ethnic conflict, particularly in countries with a colonial past. In fact, many current instances of ethnic conflict can be traced to the legacy of colonialism. These alternative approaches to ethnic conflict are not mutually exclusive. There may be structural causes to ethnic conflicts, but the dynamic of the conflicts themselves involves group psychology.

Ethnic conflicts may have an underlying "class" explanation, and some scholars would hold that when such conflicts occur, "ethnicity" represents some sort of "false consciousness," the true conflict occurring between socio-economic classes. This is undoubtedly correct in numerous cases, but in many others ethnic conflicts do cut across class cleavages. Ethnic interests may turn out to be much stronger, in terms of mobilization capabilities and command over group loyalties, than class interests.

Sometimes ethnic mobilization may be profitable politics, and while it does not necessarily lead to conflict, it can turn into ethnic conflict when it affects other group interests. Here the relation between ethnic élites and masses is important. The former have been shown to be able to lead ethnic groups into conflict situations, but frequently also ethnic conflict is a grass-roots phenomenon not controlled by ethnic élites.

Finally, when ethnic conflict becomes violent, it has a tendency to be particularly destructive, leaving deep scars in the body politic and the collective psyche. Massive human rights violations have been associated with ethnic conflicts, ranging all the way from genocide to apartheid to terrorism. The international community is therefore particularly concerned with the wider implications of ethnic conflicts around the world.

7

Ethnocide and Ethnodevelopment

"Development" is a Western construct that has been imposed by the West on the third world. Development theory generally posits a process of "modernization" from so-called traditional or archaic societies to the modern industrial nation-state. Various theories of social and political development specifically stress the evolution from groupings and loyalties based on consanguinity, affinity, religion, and so forth to more functionally oriented and instrumental groups; from ascription- to achievement-orientation, to use common sociological terminology. Within this viewpoint of development, there is little place for the role of ethnic groups. They are dismissed as remnants of the past, as obstacles to modernization. Ethnic attachments would be considered as non-rational, traditional, even conservative.

A major and as yet unresolved task in the development process is to achieve that people really do become the beneficiaries of capital investments, technological innovations, and modernization in general. It has been known for several decades now that development projects, the introduction of a monetary economy in subsistence agricultural systems and other elements of modernization, may have harmful and negative effects on large masses of the population, particularly traditional communities and indigenous and tribal peoples, who are often the "ethnic minorities" within a given country. At the beginning of the famous development decades, such harmful consequences of development policies used to be dismissed by planners and practitioners as the "inevitable social costs" of development, and it was expected that their effects would be transitory and that the affected populations would soon become incorporated into the benefits of the modernization process and would enjoy higher and more desirable standards of living.

Alas, reality has been unkind to the modernizers. The harm that has been wrought upon countless millions of people around the world by "modernization" and "development" has yet to be fully documented and digested. From

85

desertification and deforestation, through pollution and intoxication, to pauper-
ization, marginalization, social polarization, and dependency, the effects of so-
called maldevelopment or perverse development probably add up to one of the
major human tragedies of our time. To be sure, this is not what modernizers
have intended, and there is no denying that numerous benefits to sundry
populations have indeed occurred. But then, as so many recent evaluations and
post-hoc studies have shown, such benefits have much too often accrued to only a
small segment of the target population, to specific social classes or even subgroups within these classes. A frequently cited case in point is the "green revolution" and similar rural development schemes that have only rarely made
prosperous farmers out of poor peasants and have most often than not condemned the already poor to further and often harsher poverty.[1]

A particularly heavy burden has befallen numerous ethnic minorities as well
as tribal and indigenous peoples in a large part of the world. As a result of
conquest and colonization, they have generally come to occupy a position of
clear-cut subordination within the countries in which they live, a situation that
may be defined as *internal colonialism*. In recent decades, after centuries of exploitation and marginalization, not only have many of them become the economic victims of all sorts of development schemes, but in many cases they have
been physically destroyed as viable groups. Quite frequently their collective
disappearance as identifiable communities is not simply a regrettable by-
product of development but actually the stated or implicit policy objective of the
development planners. In contrast to the weaker social classes (peasants, arti-
sans, workers in traditional manufactures, small traders, specialists in obsolete
services, or simply members of communities in depressed areas) that suffer the
backlash or the unintended consequences of development, in many cases ethnic
groups are the victims of a deliberate strategy of destruction by the State or a
country's dominant élites. This process has been called cultural genocide or
ethnocide, and it is a widespread phenomenon in the contemporary world.

Ethnocide entails two principal aspects; one is economic and the other is
cultural. Economic ethnocide is imbedded in the theory and practice of development. It means that all pre-modern forms of economic organization must necessarily disappear to make way for either private or multinational capitalism or
State-planned socialism or mixes thereof. Cultural ethnocide means that all
subnational ethnic units must disappear to make way for the overarching
nation-state, the behemoth of our times. Development and nation-building have
become the major economic and political ideologies of the last quarter century
or more. Both of them, as traditionally expounded by statesmen and academics
alike, have been ethnocidal in that they imply the destruction and/or disappearance of non-integrated, separate ethnic units. This is frequently carried out in
the name of national unity and integration, progress, and of course development.

Governments generally tend to deny that they commit ethnocide or the like.
The concept, after all, has a rather distasteful implication. They usually affirm
that their policies are intended to improve the situation of this or that distinct

ethnic group, that their aim is simply to grant backward or traditional or marginal or primitive groups (the terms used may vary from region to region) the same rights and opportunities as everyone else. Sometimes, however, State policies are clear: minority ethnic groups must assimilate or integrate for the good of the country, and of course for their own good. Examples abound in the North and the South, in the East and the West.

Ethnocide may be defined, briefly, as the process whereby a culturally distinct people (usually termed an ethnie or an ethnic group) loses its identity due to policies designed to erode its land and resource base, the use of its language, its own social and political institutions, as well as its traditions, art forms, religious practices, and cultural values. When such policies are carried out systematically by governments (whatever the pretext: social progress, national unity, economic development, military security), then such governments are guilty of ethnocide. When the process occurs due to the more impersonal forces of economic development, cultural change, and modernization, yet not guided by any specific government policy, it is still ethnocidal as to its effects but may be labelled, in sociological or anthropological terms, simply social change or acculturation.

This distinction between two forms of ethnocide does not lack importance even though the end result may be the same: the disappearance or significant diminution of the group. Governments, as was stated before, do not generally like to be accused of ethnocide; and when social change occurs "spontaneously," so to speak, in which an ethnie tends to disappear as such, it is of course better for everybody concerned to attribute this cultural fact to the "invisible hand" of history. Thus, nobody is to blame. But when governments are responsible for ethnocidal policies, and when such policies are carried out without the consent and the participation of the ethnies involved, then it is likely that the State engages in specific violations of internationally recognized human rights, as shall be discussed later.

Social, economic, and cultural change are of course universal phenomena: no people ever remain static and unchangeable over any length of time. Intercultural influences and diffusion are also universal processes that take place even when States attempt to eliminate them or maintain them at a strict minimum, as occurred in Japan before the Meiji Restoration, in China between Liberation and the Four Modernizations, in Iran under Khomeini. These processes are fairly natural and should not be considered as ethnocide. The latter occurs only when, due to such changes (whether consciously imposed or spontaneous), an ethnie loses the capacity to reproduce itself socially and biologically as an ethnic group and becomes unable to maintain its culture as a creative tool for the solution of collective problems and the satisfaction of its own primary material and spiritual needs. Thus there is a clear difference between social, cultural, and economic change, in which every human group in the modern world is caught up willy-nilly, and ethnocide.

As mentioned before, many economic development projects may be labelled as ethnocidal, even when ethnocide is not clearly their objective. If economic development is to serve the people, then ethnocidal development should be considered a contradiction in terms. Yet it occurs frequently for two principal reasons. Firstly, many development projects and programmes are designed for reasons that have little to do with the well-being of the people, but rather with political, financial, external interests, etc., and their execution will mainly benefit technocrats, bureaucrats, ambitious politicians, or multinational corporations. Secondly, those responsible for development projects and programmes are usually fairly ignorant about the situation of ethnic minorities, do not particularly care about the problem, and usually hold such groups in contempt. This is particularly the case when the dominant State ideology is based on the concept of a single nation that rejects and lacks respect for those other, heteronomous ethnies.

Whereas most countries in the world are multi-ethnic, few States acknowledge this fact and even fewer have developed specific legal safeguards and policies for the protection of the ethnic minorities within their borders. Governments generally argue that by providing equal rights and opportunities to all of their citizens they are respectful of the cultural specificities of particular ethnies. This is of course not entirely correct and it usually doesn't work out that way. Most States have an explicit or implicit assimilationist bias, and despite the formal recognition of fundamental liberties and individual human rights, ethnic minorities are usually at a disadvantage *vis-à-vis* the State. This is particularly the case as regards indigenous and tribal peoples, who are not, strictly speaking, ethnic minorities at all (see chap. 8).

A common feature of many indigenous and tribal peoples is that their traditional habitat has only recently become the object of "national development planning." Areas that used to be remote and isolated from national decision-making centres have now become "poles of growth," reserves of vast amounts of sometimes strategic mineral and other natural resources, the sites of costly dams and mining enterprises, the targets of land development and settlement schemes. For technocrats and planners, multinational corporations, or poor, landless squatters, such areas have become a "new frontier." The best known of such regions is of course the vast Amazon basin in South America. But there are similar, albeit smaller, areas in the jungles, mountains, and savannahs of many third world countries, and recently in the Arctic region as well.

In the scramble for land and riches, it is usually forgotten that many of these areas have their traditional inhabitants and owners, namely, the indigenous and tribal populations. When the expanding frontier and the merry development planners reach the territory of these peoples, conflicts usually occur, which sometimes may become violent. Many indigenous and tribal communities have been physically exterminated by the expanding frontier. The best-known case, sung by poets and idealized by Hollywood, is the American Wild West. But this seems to be no longer of major concern (except to the American

Indian peoples themselves), because it was over and done with by the end of the nineteenth century. But similar events have occurred and are occurring in the Amazon, in southern Chile and Argentina, in central and southern Africa, in India and Bangladesh, in the mountain regions of Thailand and the jungle areas of Malaysia, Indonesia, and the Philippines, in the deserts of north-western Australia.

The first and principal attack on the way of life of indigenous and tribals is the attack upon their land and their ecological resource base. The loss of land and territory has contributed to wipe out many peoples around the world. It is probably the principal factor in the ongoing process of ethnocide of which they are the continuing victims. For indigenous and tribal peoples, land is not only a productive resource, an economic factor. Land is habitat, territory, the basis for social organization, cultural identification, and political viability; frequently associated with myth, symbols, and religion. Land is the essential element in the cultural reproduction of the group.

Development planners and indigenous and tribal peoples continue to clash over the issue of land; what for the former is simply a factor in economic calculus, for the latter constitutes a vital necessity for survival. Land development stands in stark contradiction to the significance of land to indigenous and tribal peoples. As long as this contradiction is not solved, ethnocide will continue in the name of development.

Besides the issue of land, ethnocide proceeds by other ways and means: the monetary economy, which creates new consumer needs, brings in new products and displaces old ones, brings about the disappearance of traditional occupations and the penetration of wage labour into the economy; the national school system, which not only introduces the official or dominant language but also different values and attitudes that replace traditional ones. In short, the process of modernization and secularization (so dear to the development sociologists of the fifties and sixties) has contributed to irreversible ethnocide in many parts of the world. Some governments also adopt clear-cut policies of forced assimilation of ethnic minorities, such as prohibiting the use of the vernacular language in schools and public places; imposing the national or official language as the only one taught in the schools; forcing people to change their traditional names, which identified them as belonging to a given ethnie or nationality; destroying sacred places or burial grounds belonging to the minorities; imposing forced religious conversions, etc. Some of these measures come close to the crime of genocide, prohibited by the United Nations Convention against Genocide (see chap. 5), but many of them are "merely" ethnocide, thus not sanctioned by international law but clearly in contravention of national and international human rights standards. Recent victims of some of such ethnocidal policies, according to public denunciations, have been the people of Turkish origin in Bulgaria, the Kurds in Turkey, the Latin American Indians, the East Timorese, the Chittagong Hill Tribes in Bangladesh, the Vedda in Sri Lanka, the Ainu in

Japan, the inhabitants of southern Sudan, the Berbers in Algeria, and numerous other peoples around the world.[2]

Only during the last few years, perhaps since the middle seventies, have governments and official agencies become aware of the human implications of savage, impersonal, technocratic development. Statements are now in order that the human and social factors of development plans must be carefully studied and taken into consideration before any major policy decisions are taken. The World Bank has now decided to make credit for major development projects in the third world contingent upon safeguards for the well-being of tribal peoples. Governments have been pressured into passing legislation for the protection of indigenous and tribal cultures and communities. Unfortunately, very frequently such safeguards and legislation exist on paper only.

No one has understood the dangers of ethnocide better than the ethnic minorities and indigenous and tribal peoples themselves. While their resistance to ethnocide and genocide is as old as these destructive practices, the political organizations of many of these peoples, at least on the international scene, is a fairly recent phenomenon. In placing their problems before international public opinion, they have been aided by a number of intergovernmental, nongovernmental, academic, professional, and human rights organizations. The gist of their various activities has been the recognition of the need for a new approach to the problématique of economic and social development of ethnically distinct peoples within the context of the modern so-called nation-state. As against policies that lead to ethnocide or preserve internal colonialism, there has arisen a call for self-determination, autonomy, and *ethnodevelopment*. This means basically that indigenous and other ethnies demand the right to decide about their own affairs, to participate in the decision-making bodies and processes where their future is discussed and decided; to political representation and participation; to respect for their traditions and cultures; to the freedom to choose what kind of development, if any, they want. Ethnodevelopment means that an ethnie, whether indigenous, tribal, or any other, maintains control over its own land, resources, social organization, and culture and is free to negotiate with the State the kind of relationship it wishes to have.

Ethnodevelopment, like the concept of self-reliant development that was developed in the seventies, means looking inward; it means finding in the group's own culture the resources and creative force necessary to confront the challenges of the modern, changing world. It does not mean autarchy or self-imposed isolation, and much less retreat into a museum of "tradition," though ethnies that may wish to remain isolated (as some tropical forest tribes in the Amazon basin) should by all means be free to enjoy the basic human right of isolation. Ethnodevelopment does not mean breaking up existing nations and subverting the process of nation-building (a major task of our time, particularly in the third world), but rather redefining the nature of nation-building and enriching the complex, multicultural fabric of many modern States, by recognizing the legitimate aspirations of the culturally distinct ethnies that make up the national whole. Ethnodevelopment does not mean blurring the very real social and economic class divisions that characterize the modern world capitalist system by stirring up some artificial "tribalism," but rather it assumes that not only class but also ethnic identity and community are socially integrating principles. Thus class-based social movements in the modern world can only benefit and improve their performance if they recognize the validity and legitimacy of ethnic demands (such as has occurred in the revolutionary movement in Guatemala or the struggle in Northern Ireland). Ethnodevelopment, finally, means rethinking the nature and objectives of local-level development projects, from hydroelectric dams to the introduction of plantation crops, by keeping in mind, first and foremost, the needs, desires, cultural specificities, and grassroots participation of the ethnic groups themselves.

A United Nations report recommends:

In multi-ethnic societies, action must always be based on criteria which, at least in principle, assert the equality of the cultural rights of the various ethnic groups. The State has the obvious obligation to formulate and implement a cultural policy which will, among other things, create the necessary conditions for the co-existence and harmonious development of the various ethnic groups living in its territory, either under pluralist provisions which guarantee that one group will not interfere with another, or under other programmes which guarantee equal and genuine opportunities for all.[3]

Thus the question arises whether there exists a human right to cultural identity. It seems that the international community is moving in this direction, though the concept itself is open to discussion.[4] Certainly the indigenous peoples demand that such a right be recognized internationally and domestically.

In this respect, two basic issues arise that have not yet been solved. The first relates to the process of cultural change, adaptation, and reinterpretation. Indigenous and tribal cultures are not static, and no protective cultural policy should be designed to keep them, as it were, as living museums, an accusation that is often levelled at those who demand protection for indigenous cultures. The solution to this issue is that indigenous and tribal peoples simply be allowed to manage their own cultural affairs and develop their own cultural potential, with the support of, but not the interference by, the State. Why the support of the State? Because if left entirely on their own, these cultures would indeed tend to disappear as a result of ethnocidal processes that take place in society with or without State intervention.

The other basic issue regarding a possible human right to cultural identity is that certain traditions and customs in indigenous cultures are considered by outside (mainly Western) observers to be in violation of universal individual human rights (for example, sexual mutilation of children and adolescents, the formal and social inferiority of women). Which holds priority, the collective right to cultural identity or the universal individual human right to liberty and equality? The question has not yet been answered satisfactorily.

In international human rights circles, there is currently going on a lively discussion concerning the so-called third generation human rights or the rights of solidarity. Some authors would deny that these are human rights at all, others insist that they should be so considered.[5] A particular point of controversy is the right to development, adopted by the UN General Assembly in 1986, which is of special interest to indigenous and tribal peoples, as well as ethnic minorities. As has been shown repeatedly, the liberal, transnational, or State bureaucratic model of development can be deadly to indigenous areas. The process of ethnocide has been widely documented.[6] If indigenous peoples are not only to survive but also to be able to improve their standards of living on their own terms and increase their status relative to the rest of society, then development ought to take the form of *ethnodevelopment*.

8

Indigenous and Tribal Peoples: A Special Case

In 1970, the UN Sub-Commission on Prevention of Discrimination and Protection of Minorities recommended that a complete and comprehensive study of the problem of discrimination against indigenous populations be undertaken. The study took over 10 years to complete and is generally known as the Martínez Cobo report, after the name of the special rapporteur appointed by the Sub-Commission. At various sessions over the years, the Sub-Commission received progress reports, and the full report, entitled "The Study of the Problem of Discrimination against Indigenous Populations," contained 22 chapters. In 1987, the United Nations published the concluding two chapters of the monumental study, which is the only publication available to a wider public. In a statement to the Sub-Commission, the special rapporteur observed that

the social conditions in which the majority of indigenous populations lived were favourable to the specific types of discrimination, oppression and exploitation in various fields described in the study. In many countries they were at the bottom of the socio-economic scale. They did not have the same opportunities for employment and the same access as other groups to public services and/or protection in the fields of health, living conditions, culture, religion and the administration of justice. They could not participate meaningfully in political life.[1]

Over 30 years earlier, a major study undertaken by the International Labour Office stated that indigenous peoples all over the world had in common "considerable economic backwardness by comparison with the remainder of the population" as well as "inequality of opportunity and the survival of anachronistic economic and land tenure systems that prevent indigenous peoples from fully developing their production and consumption and contribute to perpetuating their inferior social status."[2] Furthermore, the report observed that "as a rule, the living standard of the aboriginal populations in independent countries is extremely low, and in the great majority of cases is considerably lower than that of the most needy layers of the non-indigenous population. The aboriginal groups in many regions stagnate in conditions of economic destitution."[3]

More recently, a report prepared for the Independent Commission on International Humanitarian Issues declared:

The present situation of indigenous peoples is rooted in their colonial past. If they are largely landless, underprivileged and discriminated against, it is because of the relationship of conqueror and conquered which was established during the early years of colonial contact. A higher proportion of indigenous peoples in all countries today remain unemployed than in society as a whole. . . . Indigenous people also suffer comparatively poor health. . . . The perpetuation of the underprivileged position of most indigenous peoples has been ensured by the low priority accorded to their education by governments. . . . The result is that almost everywhere the indigenous are the worst educated group in society.[4]

The situation of many indigenous peoples around the world has been amply documented in recent years. Observers seem to agree that the low standards of living, the poor health conditions, and other expressions of poverty among the indigenous are not the result of inherent backwardness and isolation, but rather the direct consequence of the impact of "modern civilization" upon the indigenous peoples. Bodley, for example, underlines the dire consequences for the indigenous of the resource appropriation and land settlement undertaken on indigenous territories by the national society.[5] Burger undertakes a wide survey of the situation of indigenous peoples in the various regions of the world and concludes that in almost all countries indigenous minorities face discrimination and suffer disadvantage.

They are more likely to be unemployed than the majority population, they will probably receive less remuneration than comparable workers and will almost certainly be concentrated, when they do find work, in the more menial and poorly paid occupations. Indigenous peoples, as they are integrated into the national life of the society, will usually take their place on the lowest rung of the ladder. . . . They will receive less opportunity for schooling and non-academic training; they will have less access to medical care and other social welfare services; where they have moved to urban areas they will invariably occupy those suburbs or ghettos with the most rudimentary facilities and housing.[6]

For decades, indigenous peoples have been powerless and helpless regarding their situation. To be sure, indigenous rebellions have occurred throughout history and all over the world; and of course indigenous peoples have been able to petition national governments, and sporadically even international organizations. Usually, however, indigenous peoples have had to trust in paternalistic government action for redress of ancient torts or for projects conducive to development or improvement of their standards of living. Government responsibility for indigenous peoples has frequently taken the line of assimilation or incorporation. This ideology has found expression in international instruments. Thus, an Inter-American Indianist Congress met for the first time in 1940, and while it declared its respect for indigenous culture and personality, as well as complete equality before the law for all peoples, it also fostered the idea of national integration and indigenous assimilation to "national culture." The ILO's first efforts went in the same direction. Its Convention 107 on Indigenous and Tribal Populations, adopted in 1957, was basically assimilationist and integrationist. Article 2 of the Convention stated unabashedly:

1. Governments shall have the primary responsibility for developing co-ordinated and systematic action for the protection of the populations concerned and their progressive integration into the life of their respective countries.

As a result of increasing criticism of this Convention by indigenous organizations, the ILO initiated a lengthy process of revision, and the Organization's General Conference adopted a new convention in 1989, now numbered 169. The new convention retains some of the suggestions made by the indigenous organizations, who were able to participate in part of the process of revision. Generally, indigenous organizations complained that they were not formally represented in the procedures, and only a smattering of them were invited as non-governmental organizations to present their points of view at the sessions of the General Conference. The new convention includes the concept "peoples" instead of "populations," as insisted upon by the indigenous organizations. Article 2 of Convention 169, as well as other articles, is now much less "integrationist." While it states the responsibility of States, it also underlines the full participation of the peoples concerned in the development of co-ordinated and systematic action intended to guarantee the respect of the integrity of these peoples and their rights.[7]

However, in the last 15 years, important changes have taken place, if not in the social and economic situation of indigenous peoples as such, at least in the political awareness and the political participation of their organizations, both at the national and international levels. Indigenous movements and organizations have become politically vocal; international meetings have taken place at the United Nations and elsewhere. The UN Sub-Commission created a Working Group on Indigenous Populations in 1983 that has been meeting yearly since then (except in 1985, due to budgetary constraints). At its sessions in 1988 and 1989, the Working Group was attended by over 300 participants from dozens of countries and numerous indigenous organizations. At these sessions, the Working Group advanced towards the drafting of a Declaration of Indigenous Rights that is expected to be adopted eventually by the UN General Assembly.

Even though this Declaration is still in draft form, and there is no guarantee that it will be adopted by the various UN bodies without modification, it is noteworthy that for the first time such a UN document reflects the proposals and suggestions provided by numerous indigenous organizations throughout five years of sessions of the Working Group. Part I of the Draft Universal Declaration on Indigenous Rights is devoted to general universal human rights; Part II, to collective cultural and ethnic rights, including protection against ethnocide; Part III, rights to land and resources; Part IV, economic and social rights, including the maintenance of traditional economic structures and ways of life; Part V, civil and political rights, including respect for indigenous laws and customs, participation in decision-making in all matters affecting their life and destiny, as well as the collective right to autonomy; and Part VI regards recommendations for fair procedures for resolving conflicts or disputes between States and indigenous peoples.[8]

With the adoption of the new ILO convention and the UN Declaration on Indigenous Rights, a new international environment, however limited, will have been created for the rights of indigenous peoples that perhaps will help them improve their relative situation within their own countries. It remains to be seen, however, to what extent such documents will be ratified and implemented. To the extent that they are instruments drafted by governments for governments, in organizations that serve the interests of the member States, indigenous peoples remain understandably suspicious of them. Still, they do reflect up to a certain point the claims that indigenous, aboriginal, and tribal peoples have been pushing for decades and that represent the principal issues that so often are at the root of conflicts between States and indigenous peoples.

What are these issues? For the purposes of this chapter, it may be useful to group them under the following headings:
1. Definition, membership, and legal status
2. Land, territory, and resources
3. Economic development
4. Language, education, and culture
5. Indigenous law and social organization
6. Self-government, autonomy, and self-determination

We shall take up each of these issues in turn, though there is obviously some overlap between them.

DEFINITION, MEMBERSHIP, AND LEGAL STATUS

It may seem surprising that the question of definition of, and membership in, indigenous groups is an issue of some concern both to the indigenous themselves and to the States in whose territories they live. Yet the question arises because the definition of indigenous peoples often is directly linked to the nature of the relationship between the group and the State, as well as with other groups. And the issue of membership is frequently linked to the enjoyment of certain rights and privileges, or conversely, to the imposition of disabilities and the limitation of political and civil rights. Therefore, in recent years, the question of definition and membership has become a claim put forward by indigenous organizations and is being dealt with by international organizations.

Thus, as early as 1953, the ILO reviewed the various definitions and criteria used by national governments and social scientists, and concluded that there was no single, universally valid definition of indigenous peoples. It therefore proceeded to offer a provisional description as a "purely empirical guide to the identification of indigenous groups in independent countries," as follows:

Indigenous persons are descendants of the aboriginal population living in a given country at the time of settlement or conquest (or of successive waves of conquest) by some of the ancestors of the non-indigenous groups in whose hands political and economic power at present lies. In general these descendants tend to live more in conformity with the social, economic and cultural institutions which existed before colonisation or conquest . . . than with the culture of the nation to which they belong.[9]

This description served as a basis for the definition that was later included in Article 1 of ILO's Convention 107, now superseded by Convention 169.[10]

The UN "Study of the Discrimination against Indigenous Populations" also goes into an in-depth analysis of the various definitions used by governments and others to define indigenous peoples, and likewise recognizes that such definitions vary greatly. The special rapporteur concludes that "the question of a definition is one that must be left to the indigenous communities themselves." He proposes that "the right of indigenous peoples themselves to define what and who is indigenous must be recognized" and that "the correlative of this faculty is, obviously, the faculty of defining or determining what or who is not indigenous." Moreover, for the purposes of international action, the special rapporteur proposes the following definition:

Indigenous communities, peoples and nations are those which, having a historical continuity with pre-invasion and pre-colonial societies that developed on their territories, consider themselves distinct from other sectors of the societies now prevailing in those territories, or parts of them. They form at present non-dominant sectors of society and are determined to preserve, develop and transmit to future generations their ancestral territories, and their ethnic identity, as the basis of their continued existence as peoples, in accordance with their own cultural patterns, social institutions and legal system.[11]

The reader will notice certain differences between the ILO and the UN definition, basically that the former refers to "persons" and the latter to "communities, peoples and nations," a distinction that reflects the changing concerns of the international community and the indigenous peoples themselves. They have in common, however, the idea that indigenous peoples are somehow the descendants of the original inhabitants of a territory, that they were overwhelmed or subordinated to other peoples through invasion and/or conquest, that they occupy a non-dominant position in a society, and that they are culturally distinct from the non-indigenous populations.

The World Council of Indigenous Peoples, a non-governmental organization, has insisted that the UN recognize the indigenous as separate nations within a political State and claims that the right to define who is and who is not an indigenous person should be left to the indigenous peoples themselves. It rejects artificial definitions such as those that appear in some national legislations and that impose on the indigenous definitions that the latter do not accept.[12]

Governments do indeed vary as to how they define indigenous peoples and/or persons, and as to what significance such definitions have. In Canada, for example, the Constitution Act of 1867 enabled the Government of Canada to legislate in relation to "Indians, and Lands reserved for Indians." According to one author,

this power has been exercised in the passage of special legislation called the Indian Act. This statute sets forth a complex system for registering Indians, administering their lands and regulating their lives. The idea of such a definitional system has existed since the early legislation concerning Indians was enacted in 1850 and has been maintained in all subsequent statutes. . . . The net result is that the present Indian Act contains a hybrid status definition system that precludes any Indian control over the decision-making process.[13]

This situation has led to a number of court cases regarding Indian rights, at least one of which has been considered by the UN Human Rights Committee.[14]

In the Latin American countries, the legal status of Indians varies considerably, depending upon the definitions employed. Thus, even though Mexico has a government policy designed to improve the situation of Indian communities (called *indigenismo* in the Latin American countries), there exists no legal or administrative definition of Indians. This has led some observers to speak of "statistical ethnocide" of Indians; that is, the systematic under-enumeration of Indians in the national censuses.[15] In Colombia, a law of 1890 that is still in force distinguishes between civilized and uncivilized Indians and attaches different legal rights to them. Similarly, the Indian Statute of 1973 in Brazil defines "isolated" and "integrated" Indians as well as those in the process of "being integrated," and each category is the possessor of certain (limited) rights. The new Brazilian constitution of 1988 includes a chapter on Indian rights for the first time in Brazilian constitutional history, as a result of the long and strenuous efforts of indigenous organizations and their supporters in the Brazilian body politic.[16]

In most south and south-east Asian countries, the concept of indigenous peoples is not generally used. Rather, the term tribal peoples or ethnic minorities is employed. India maintains a list of "scheduled tribes" that enjoy constitutional protection, a fact that has not saved them from discrimination and the catastrophic effects of certain development policies (see below). In insular South-East Asia, indigenous tribal peoples are systematically underestimated by government sources, a situation that, according to some observers, facilitates policies detrimental to these peoples' interests.[17] Government definitions of indigenous or tribal groups often seem to depend on the countries' self-definition as nations.

At the present time all of the countries of mainland Southeast Asia deny tribal peoples legitimate ways to maintain and promote their own cultural identities. Given the definitions of the nation that each of the modern states have adopted, tribal peoples have been relegated to marginal positions or even excluded from participation in national life.[18]

National governments may define indigenous groups for administrative purposes or to provide legal status; such definitions may serve to grant or withhold rights and privileges. Indigenous organizations complain that definitions in which they have not been directly involved are generally used, not in their best interests, but rather in the interests of the States. When no definitions exist, and the fiction of a homogeneous mass of equal citizens is maintained, then frequently indigenous populations are also short-changed, as exemplified by the Chilean government's answer to the ILO's questionnaire regarding the revision of Convention 107, in which it denied the existence of a specific indigenous population subject to specific rights, whereas it is well documented that the Mapuche Indians, among others, were particularly hard hit by the repressive policies of the military government then in power.[19]

The right of indigenous peoples to self-definition and self-identification, as well as to determine membership, has thus become a major issue in recent debates and negotiations between the indigenous and the State, at both the national and international level. The question has to do with the relative importance accorded to collective and individual human rights. When an indigenous or tribal people possess a clearly identified territory and constitute a recognizable administrative and/or social unit, then the question of definition and membership should not pose a particularly difficult problem, except if governments refuse to recognize a group as such, which is often the case. A more complex situation arises in the case of indigenous peoples who emigrate from their original communities to become part of the modern, urban industrial and service economy. For example, in the United States many members of Indian reservations work in the urban construction economy; in Latin America, members of highland Indian communities move to the cities and join the ranks of the services and so-called informal sector. Similar phenomena occur in other countries. Indigenous identification and membership may be important for some people in the urban environment, even when they are distant from their original communities, but it poses special problems, for example, as regards the uses of law and language, or in relation to educational facilities.

As may be apparent from the above discussion, it is not an easy task to arrive at a valid estimate of the number of indigenous and tribal groups and their populations that exist in the world today. If we include the tribal populations of India (*adivasis*) and other Asian countries, the Amerindians of the American continent, the Inuit in the Arctic, the aboriginals in Australia and other Pacific States, as well as so-called "primitive" isolated ethnic groups in Africa, the number of people in the world who may be classified as indigenous may run well over 200 million, and the groups thus defined would number several thousands. Still, these are only estimates and the final figures, as the above discussion has shown, will depend on who does the defining and the counting and for what purpose.[20]

LAND, TERRITORY, AND RESOURCES

The land issue has become the principal claim of indigenous peoples at the present time. Article 12 of the Draft Universal Declaration on Indigenous Rights proposes "the right of ownership and possession of the lands which they have traditionally occupied," and Article 13 stresses "the right to recognition of their own land-tenure systems for the protection and promotion of the use, enjoyment and occupancy of the land."[21] The same right appears as Article 13 in the ILO's new Convention 169.[22]

Ever since European expansion in the fifteenth and sixteenth century, the land issue has been in the forefront of the conflicts between States and indigenous peoples. The Europeans considered that the "newly discovered" territories lacked inhabitants and/or owners and appropriated for themselves vast expanses of land all over the world, on the flimsy theories of "right of discovery," the concept of *terra nullius*, or the idea of waste or idle lands. Indigenous prior occupancy and property rights were largely ignored and hardly ever recognized or respected. On the American continent, indigenous peoples who formerly roamed freely on their lands were pushed into reservations or onto barren lands, and frequently had to find refuge in mountain fastnesses and impenetrable jungles. But capitalist expansion kept pursuing them, and particularly in recent decades the onslaught on indigenous lands has again taken on dramatic proportions all over the world.

Indigenous peoples have always had a special relationship with land. Land has been, and to a great extent still is, the source of their basic sustenance. Indigenous peoples are to a large extent agriculturalists, hunters, or gatherers. Their culture and way of life is linked to the land. But the land is not only an economic factor of production; it is the basis of cultural and social identity; the

home of the ancestors, the site of religious and mythical links to the past and to
the supernatural. This is something special that government planners and economic developers have consistently refused to understand when they simply
push indigenous peoples off their land or when they glibly offer "monetary compensation" or relocation in exchange of land expropriations. The World Council of Indigenous Peoples has stated this special relationship eloquently:

The Earth is the foundation of Indigenous Peoples. It is the seat of spirituality, the
foundation from which our cultures and languages flourish. The Earth is our historian,
the keeper of events and the bones of our forefathers. Earth provides us food, medicine,
shelter and clothing. It is the source of our independence; it is our Mother. We do not
dominate Her: we must harmonize with Her. Next to shooting Indigenous Peoples, the
surest way to kill us is to separate us from our part of the Earth.[23]

For most indigenous peoples in the world, land thus has a double role. On the
one hand it is frequently the basis for the economic sustenance of the group,
tribe, or community. On the other, for many indigenous peoples a given territory is considered their homeland, it is the physical, historical, and often
mythical space with which the group identifies and without which the group's
very survival is at stake.

From early colonial times onward, indigenous land has been coveted by con-
querors, colonists, and settlers. The purposes and mechanisms of this giant
historical land-grab have varied from place to place and from time to time.
Certainly the need and desire for arable land by new agriculturists has been a
major factor, as, for example, in the "conquest of the American West," which
was accompanied by massive genocide of the pre-existing indigenous populations. Similarly, in Argentina, the settlement of the Pampas by cattle ranchers
in the nineteenth century led to the practical disappearance of the earlier indigenous occupants. In neighbouring little Uruguay, the Indians were completely wiped out, as had happened a few centuries earlier in the Caribbean
islands.

But the appropriation of indigenous lands by colonists for direct agricultural
production has been only one aspect of the problem. In colonial and independent Latin America, the colonizers and later the local landholding élites also
exerted pressures upon Indian territories in order to obtain cheap or servile
indigenous labour for their estates. By taking away the land, the colonial system
obtained a double benefit: the land itself and the labour required to make it
productive. In the colonization of America, the Spanish Crown attributed to
itself the legal ownership of practically the whole continent, vast expanses of
land that it later granted or donated to the Church, to private individuals, and,
most generously, but only in the last instance, to the indigenous peoples themselves from whom it had been taken. Thus, the appropriation of indigenous
lands also served the purpose of establishing political and administrative control by the Crown and the Church over the population. Not to mention the fiscal

income that the colonial State derived from taxing the lands over which it had unilaterally declared its eminent domain. Similar processes occurred in colonial Africa (the Congo, for example), where vast tracts of forest, occupied by semi-nomadic agriculturists, hunters and gatherers, were turned by the colonial State into cash crop plantations.

Economic development and the integration of a world system of production and consumption have renewed pressures on the remaining lands of indigenous peoples in our time. "Since the Second World War" – states the Independent Commission on International Humanitarian Issues – "the number of incursions into indigenous peoples' lands has escalated worldwide. Once thought of as barren wastelands of little economic and political value, indigenous territories have now been identified as areas of vital national and even international importance. . . . With no untroubled or uncoveted regions to retreat to, the native inhabitants have been forced to accept these invasions reluctantly, or else fight back." [24]

The rights to land that the colonial State established for itself by conquest and military power have now been taken over by national governments. The Brazilian government, for example, deems itself the legal owner of the vast Amazonian territories that have since time immemorial been inhabited unhindered by hundreds of Indian tribes. This government, over the last few decades, has ceded large tracts of this territory to multinational corporations, with disastrous effects on the lives and fortunes of the indigenous populations. For example, the situation of the Yanomami in northern Brazil has aroused concern all over the world. As a result of international pressure, a Yanomami park has been decreed; but still land invasions by non-indigenous squatters and miners continue, and legal instruments designed to legalize these invasions and further intrusions have been submitted to the Brazilian parliament and have been resisted by the supporters of the Yanomami. In the mean time, the socio-economic and cultural integrity of this group is threatened. [25]

Land claims are basic to the conception of aboriginal rights in Canada, and they have been negotiated between the aboriginal peoples and the federal and provincial governments for decades. Despite some progress, one specialist concludes that in the last decade "the social and economic difficulties faced by the Aboriginal People have increased, while their longstanding political, moral and legal grievances have continued unresolved." [26]

In the Amazon as well as in the tropical jungles of southern and south-eastern Asia, indigenous and tribal peoples have retreated into a "last frontier," from which they are currently being dislodged. They occupy forests rich in tropical timber, an increasingly scarce resource for which there is great demand in the international markets. Logging companies, which have received permits from compliant governments, have opened roads into indigenous territories and are cutting down precious tropical forests at an alarming rate, destroying the last existing ecological niche in which indigenous and tribal peoples have found refuge. In the process, they force the indigenous into the market economy, prostitution, alcoholism, and other socially and culturally destructive situations. Victims of these processes are the hill tribes of Thailand and Burma, the forest dwellers of India, Malaysia, Indonesia, and the Philippines, the jungle tribes of central Africa, the lowland Indian communities of the Amazon basin in South America. Usually after the loggers have cut down and cleared the forest, they pull out their operations, leaving the indigenous territory in shambles and the indigenous and tribal peoples in disarray.

In some countries, sympathetic but weak governments have attempted to provide some protection to the indigenous peoples; in others, the government has been openly favourable to the intrusion of the timber companies onto indigenous lands. In recent years, the indigenous peoples have begun to resist and fight back, through their own political organizations, recourse to the laws and the courts, political action at the national and international levels. On occasion, violent encounters between the indigenous and the new invaders have taken place, in which the victims of course tend mostly to be the indigenous.[27]

Another cause of ongoing conflicts over land rights relates to mining. In many parts of the world, the indigenous peoples sit on rich reserves of minerals that are coveted by multinational corporations and governments alike. Even when indigenous land rights are granted or recognized, possession of subsoil resources is reserved by the government for itself. Thus, when governments grant prospection and mining rights to private companies, the latter come in and tear up the land with little regard for the local indigenous occupants. In some countries, such as the United States and Canada, legislation allows the indigenous tribes to obtain a profit from such activities, but in many other countries, such safeguards do not exist, and the effect of prospecting and mining by private or State-run companies can be catastrophic for the indigenous, similar to what happens in the jungles as a result of logging. A recent report puts it succinctly:

Mines, perhaps more than other economic development, contribute to the breakdown of the close association of indigenous peoples with their land. Mining transforms familiar landscapes. Mountains and valleys which have been immutable for centuries are turned into featureless wildernesses. Surface "strip" mining is even more destructive, leaving land unreclaimable. For indigenous peoples, such physical assault on the land itself is seen as desecration. . . . Sacred sites have been mined throughout Australia and in one instance an entire sacred mountain in Western Australia was dug up and shipped out in the form of iron ore, without any consultation with its Aboriginal owners. Adding insult to injury is the fact that the mining projects on indigenous peoples' land, despite the enormous wealth generated, bring little in return to those who are dispossessed and displaced.[28]

Little wonder that indigenous peoples everywhere have organized to resist such invasions of their lands and are struggling with governments over control of mining operations, the distribution of benefits, and the limitation of damages. Governments, however, refuse to relinquish what they consider to be "national" assets, which are frequently described as such in laws and even constitutions. Indigenous organizations would like to have their right over subsoil resources recognized internationally, just as is their right over land and surface resources. It is highly unlikely, however, that governments will agree to this. The Draft Universal Declaration on Indigenous Rights rather timidly suggests that it is "the duty of States to seek and obtain their (i.e. the indigenous peoples') consent, through appropriate mechanisms, before undertaking or permitting any programmes for the exploration or exploitation of mineral and other subsoil resources pertaining to their traditional territories. Just and fair compensation should be provided for any such activities undertaken."[29] Article 14 of the ILO's Convention 169 is drafted in almost identical language.[30] In neither document are indigenous rights over subsoil resources actually recognized; governments are simply advised to seek the consent of the interested peoples when mining activities on indigenous land is decided upon. Nothing is proposed if the indigenous withold their consent, and experience shows that in the end, governments and multinational corporations do what they please.

Yet another motive for the invasion of indigenous territories by States is military and political, though it often has to do with "strategic resources." Many indigenous peoples live in border areas, some straddle international boundary lines; others occupy areas that have never been carefully mapped and that two or even three neighbouring States claim as their own. Governments frequently invoke reasons of "national security" and proceed to militarize border areas where indigenous peoples have long been living peacefully. As a result, in some countries "indigenous affairs" become the administrative responsibility of the defence ministries; in others, members of indigenous tribes are recruited for military activity, and often the indigenous peoples are considered security risks and potential enemies. In countries where civil conflicts occur, indigenous and tribal peoples are often drawn unwittingly into either insurgency or counter-insurgency activities; in others that may be at war, they are frequently conscripted forcefully into military service. Again, the long-term consequences of these processes on the indigenous societies can be catastrophic. Perhaps the most dramatic examples in recent years come from the hill tribes in South-East Asian countries. The Brazilian military has long considered the existence of a large number of Amazonian indigenous peoples and their traditional territories as a prime question of national security. The Miskito Indians in Nicaragua and Honduras have felt the impact of militarization around their traditional Río Coco habitat; many Miskito refugees who left Nicaragua in the early eighties to cross the border into Honduras have since returned to their villages. The return of Mayan refugees in Mexico to Guatemala is a slower and more complicated process at the present time. Native Hawaiians have long complained about US Army practice ranges on traditionally sacred islands. India has established military controls over a number of tribal areas along its borders. In both Indonesia and the Philippines, military activity and control have engulfed numerous tribal regions.[31]

One report states that

massive displacement and other violations of the fundamental human right to effective recognition of indigenous rights have been underway in insular Southeast Asia since the onset of colonial rule. More recent official development programs and rapidly expanding populations have accelerated the processes. Transmigration in Indonesia, and "public" land policies in the Philippines, for example, were designed with little or no thought given to the presence of long-term occupants in areas designated for resettlement or capital-intensive, export-oriented development. While corporations and elite entrepreneurs profit from this political economy of ignorance, indigenous occupants throughout insular Southeast Asia are being forced to flee their ancestral homes, often at gunpoint. Property rights to large tracts of ancestral land are transferred to urban-based national elites, whose lack of local knowledge regarding the sustainable use of an ecologically fragile natural resource base is wreaking havoc on the environment. Concerned responses and concrete action are evident, particularly in the Philippines. But for the most part, the overall situation of indigenous occupants in insular Southeast Asia remains tragically precarious.[32]

Indigenous peoples are aware of the fact that unless they are able to retain control over their land and territories, their survival as identifiable, distinct societies and cultures is seriously endangered. Traditionally, the greatest threat to their ancestral habitats came from the national government; nowadays, the multinational corporations also play an increasingly important role. More and more governments have been impelled to recognize the legitimacy of indigenous land claims, and protective legislations have been adopted in many States. Still, as resources become scarcer, as the world economy becomes more transnationalized, as the last "frontier areas" become incorporated into so-called "development," the indigenous and tribal peoples continue to be the most vulnerable victims of Statist and capitalist logic.

ECONOMIC DEVELOPMENT

Much damage has been done to indigenous peoples through economic development projects, particularly hydroelectric dams and other regional development schemes (see chap. 7).The isolated, marginal areas often occupied by indigenous peoples constitute the last great and until recently unexploited reserves of natural resources. Neither State planners nor multinational corporations nor international development agencies have hesitated to implement strategies to "incorporate" these areas into the national and international economy. In the process, indigenous and tribal peoples have suffered genocide and ethnocide. Usually the grandiose development schemes that third world governments are so fond of are not designed to benefit the local population but rather the urban and rural élites. Indeed, when local, frequently indigenous or tribal, populations exist, the idea is that they must be removed to make way for "progress." Examples abound. In Brazil, the mammoth Greater Carajás Programme, occupying an area the size of Britain and France, has already, in the words of one observer, "brought irremediable ecological damage and social upheaval to the region. . . . In the name of development, this vast area, 50% of it tropical rainforest, will be turned into a massive agro-industrial park, and its people transformed into a destitute, landless labour pool."[33] Billions of dollars have been invested in this project by the World Bank and by the European Economic Community; hundreds of thousands of hectares of forest have been destroyed and tens of thousands of indigenous peoples have lost their land and livelihood. Also in Brazil, the widely publicized Polonoroeste development project has produced similar results. Other Indian areas are likewise threatened by hydroelectric projects.[34]

Elsewhere in the world, similar development schemes have similar effects. In central India, two giant hydroelectric power projects are expected to have disastrous effects on the local tribal populations. One observer writes: "Damage to environment from deforestation and inundation are not the only deleterious consequences expected from the projects. . . . There is reason to fear that wholly inadequate measures will be taken to resettle and compensate the deprived tribals."[35] One observer estimates that over the last decades, approximately half a million tribal people have been displaced in India as a result of regional "development" projects under the worst kind of circumstances.[36] Likewise in the Philippines, where the government plans to build 40 major dams in the next 20 years to generate electric power. Most of these dams will flood areas now occupied by national minorities, that is, indigenous peoples, and the projects threaten their very survival.[37]

Not only do power projects threaten indigenous peoples in tropical countries. In Norway, the Saami reindeer pastoralists are threatened in their traditional way of life by the Alta/Kautokeino Hydro project. Despite Saami protests, the Supreme Court of Norway upheld the position of the State, in favour of the project, in 1982.[38]

The Independent Commission on International Humanitarian Issues concludes that

large dams are disastrous for indigenous peoples. They destroy their economies and habitats, disrupt their social systems, and submerge and otherwise desecrate sites of religious or cultural importance. Indigenous communities are dispersed, losing their original cohesion and unity; they are left impoverished, often landless and dispirited.[39]

Many of these development projects are designed and financed by the World Bank and other international development agencies. After having been accused

repeatedly of neglecting environmental and human damage to tribal and indigenous peoples in the projects it supports, the World Bank finally decided on
the adoption of guide-lines for the protection of the environment and the local
populations and declared it would withold aid to governments that did not
respect them.[40] Many observers consider, however, that the guide-lines are not
being implemented adequately, and lately World Bank officials have stated that
protection of indigenous peoples or environments is not among their priority
concerns.[41]

In the Chittagong Hill Tracts of Bangladesh, for years, thousands of poor
Bengali colonists from the lowlands, with government support, have been coming into tribal areas to settle. The result has been the massive destruction of the
society of the hill people. One report states:

The Bengali poor will seize any survival chance they are presented with. Illiterates have
limited horizons and they are not fully aware that the government's scheme to settle
them in the Chittagong Hill Tracts is not essentially an attempt to improve their lot. It is
a political act to nullify the question of tribal rights to self-determination by increasing
the number of Bengalis in the hill tracts to a majority.[42]

A Chakma tribal relates: "The Bangladesh Government has been carrying out a
programme of systematic extermination of the indigenous nationalities of the
Chittagong Hill Tracts because they are ethnically, religiously and culturally
different from the Muslim Bengalis."[43] According to reports, massive violations
of human rights of the tribal populations, verging on genocide, have taken place
in the hill tracts due to the government's settlement policies. At the UN Working
Group on Indigenous Populations, the Bangladeshi delegates routinely deny
these accusations.

Similar massive violations of human rights have occurred in Indonesia's out-
lying islands, Kalimantan, West Papua, and East Timor, as a result of Indonesia's "transmigration programme," whereby hundreds of thousands of Javanese
and inhabitants of other overpopulated islands are resettled, with World Bank
support, in the less-densely populated, ethnically distinct, islands. Many people
have pointed out that this programme is motivated more by political than economic considerations, in order to ensure the Indonesian government's control
over the vast archipelago. The impact of this programme on the tribal populations has been disastrous.[44]

LANGUAGE, EDUCATION, AND CULTURE

In many countries, for example those in Latin America, in the absence of other
valid criteria, the only test for the existence and quantification of indigenous
peoples is their language. In fact, indigenous peoples the world over are recog-

nized by the thousands of different languages they speak, most of them unwritten. Hundreds of indigenous or tribal languages are used, for example, in countries such as Brazil, India, and Indonesia. In Mexico, where the indigenous population represents approximately 15 per cent of the total population, 56 different Indian languages and many more dialects have been identified.

A language is basically a means of communication, but it is much more than that. Languages are an integral part of cultures; through its language, a given group expresses its own culture, its own societal identity; languages are related to thought processes and to the way the members of a certain linguistic group perceive nature, the universe, and society. It has often been related, for example, that the Inuit language has a number of different words for the different shades of the colour white, a fact that is important for life in the Arctic environment. And in the tropical jungles, the languages of local tribes are capable of designating and naming the myriad objects and forms of the jungle environment, which no other language is capable of doing. In other contexts also, languages express cultural patterns and social relations and in turn help shape these patterns and relations. Western observers have always been astonished by the way Japanese, or Arab languages, for example, reflect and express behavioural patterns in their respective linguistic communities. Moreover, languages are the vehicles for literary and poetic expression; they are the instruments whereby oral history, myths, and beliefs are shared by a community and transmitted from generation to generation. Just as an Indian without land is a dead Indian, as the World Council of Indigenous Peoples states, so also an ethnic community without a language is a dying community. This was well understood by the romantic nationalists of the nineteenth and twentieth century who strove for a revival of "national" languages as part of the politics of nationalism in many parts of the world (see chap. 2).[45]

On the other hand, language has always been an instrument of conquest and empire. Nebrija, a Castilian grammarian and adviser to Queen Isabella I the Catholic in the fifteenth century, published his Spanish grammar the same year Columbus reached America, and advised his queen to use the language as an instrument for the good government of the empire. Both the Spanish Crown and the Church took the advice to heart, for Spanish did become one of the universal languages of the modern world. So did English, of course, for the British Empire knew well the power of the word as an instrument of world-wide power and control.

In the process of colonization, the languages of the colonized peoples – especially if unwritten – were usually downgraded to mere "dialects," a term that connotes something less than a full-fledged, structured language and therefore casts doubt on the status of the culture that uses it. Thus indigenous and tribal peoples are still considered at the present time by a non-informed public opinion to speak only dialects and not languages, a position frequently shared by government bureaucrats. This is of course linguistic nonsense, but it carries a political intention. As some anonymous wit has expressed it: a language is a dialect with an army. Or to put it another way: a dominant group is able to impose its language on subordinate groups. Linguistic dominance is more often than not an expression of political and economic domination.[46] To be sure, there are exceptions: in Africa and Asia there are a number of *linguae francae*, vehicular languages used for trade and commerce that do not necessarily denote political domination. In Indonesia, a foreign language, Malay, that, however, has been spoken in the area for centuries, is now the official national language, and is considered to be a factor in national unification. In the insular Caribbean, Papiamento, a new language made up of a mixture of original European, African, and Indian languages, is widely spoken. In Paraguay, to cite another example, most of the population speaks the indigenous Guarani language, but the indigenous peoples in that country are victims of ethnocide and genocide.[47]

In the predominant statist view of national unity, assimilation, and development, the languages of indigenous and tribal peoples, particularly when only spoken by small minorities, have usually been destined to disappear. Government policies have generally been designed to help this process along. In most countries, indigenous languages are not given legal recognition, are not used in official administrative and judicial dealings, are not taught in schools, and the people who do use them are discriminated against and treated by the non-indigenous as outsiders, foreigners, barbarians, primitives, and so on. Very often, the men of the tribe or indigenous community, who move around in the outside world for economic reasons, learn the official or national language of a country and become bilingual. Women tend to be more monolingual, which increases their isolation and the discrimination that they suffer. Small children, before school age, speak the maternal language, but often as soon as they reach school they are not allowed to speak their own language in class. Observers have noticed that this creates serious psychological and learning problems among school-age children of many indigenous and tribal peoples. Or, because of language and other forms of discrimination to which they are exposed, families avoid sending their children to official or missionary schools at all.

The UN special rapporteur, who bases his assessment on replies sent by many governments to his questionnnaire, reports that "the policies followed in a great many States were based on the assumption that indigenous populations, cultures and languages would disappear naturally or by absorption into other segments of the population and the 'national culture.'"[48] But, he continues, in the typical low-key language of UN documents, "it is believed today that these policies, which in some cases have prevailed for centuries, do not seem to have been well-grounded, to judge by their effects." And further, "public schooling oriented towards doing away with indigenous characteristics and the policies of marginalization, relegation and elimination of indigenous languages followed by most States, many of which inherited them from the colonial period, have been questioned and utterly rejected."[49]

As a result of policies of persecution and general attitudes of discrimination against them, many indigenous and tribal peoples have internalized the negative attitudes of the dominant society against their languages and cultures. Particularly when they leave their communities, they tend to deny their identity and feel ashamed of being "aboriginal" or "native" or "Indian" or "primitive." Hiding an identity is not always possible, given that in many countries ethnic and cultural differences are accompanied by biological distinctions, and cultural discrimination is often indistinguishable from racial discrimination. This has been particularly the case in European settler societies where the biological differences between the upper classes and the indigenous populations are particularly visible; it is less so in societies that have undergone a process of racial intermarriage and mixing, such as many Asian and Latin American countries.

In recent years, indigenous and tribal peoples have begun to resist the "natural" or forced disappearance of their languages and cultures, and slowly a growing awareness has arisen among social scientists, humanists, educators, and even politicians that the maintenance of indigenous languages within the concept of cultural pluralism is not necessarily undesirable for a given country. The UN special rapporteur states:

The vigorous presence of indigenous peoples and languages in many parts of the world is an established fact. Defence by these groups of their languages is determined and tenacious. . . . There is increasing acceptance of the need to recognize, once and for all, the plurilingual and pluricultural nature of the countries where indigenous populations live and to adopt unequivocally policies which permit and promote the conservation, development and dissemination of the specific ethnic nature of those populations and its transmission to future generations.[50]

The Draft Universal Declaration on Indigenous Rights prepared by the UN Sub-Commission now establishes

9. The right to maintain and use their own languages, including for administrative, judicial and other relevant purposes.
10. The right to all forms of education, including in particular the right of children to have access to education in their own languages, and to establish, structure, conduct and control their own educational systems and institutions.[51]

Are language rights human rights? This is one of the questions being debated currently among specialists. Article 27 of the International Covenant on Civil and Political Rights establishes that persons belonging to ethnic, religious, or linguistic minorities shall not be denied the right to use their own language. But aside from the fact that this article is a very weak statement of cultural rights as applying to ethnic minorities, in fact the organizations of indigenous peoples around the world refuse to be categorized among "ethnic minorities" in general, which is one of the reasons why a specific declaration of indigenous rights is being prepared in the specialized UN bodies.

Language rights certainly seem to be a major issue among indigenous organizations at the present time. At the regional level, the periodic inter-American indigenist congresses, meetings of governments belonging to the Organization of American States, have reaffirmed for several years the linguistic rights of the indigenous populations of the American continent, even though a number of member States do not appear to pay much attention to these resolutions domestically. Unesco has also affirmed the importance of the use of vernacular languages as an integral part of the cultural policies of States, and particularly as regards education for minority groups. A number of countries have recently changed their traditional postures of discrimination against and neglect of indigenous and tribal minority languages, and have designed policies to protect and promote these languages. In Latin America, in some recent national constitutions and general laws, indigenous languages have finally been recognized as part of the "national culture." [52]

The survival of indigenous and tribal languages is of course closely related to the educational and cultural policies of governments. Whereas Article 27 of the International Covenant on Civil and Political Rights establishes the right of ethnic minorities to enjoy their own culture, Article 13 of the International Covenant on Economic, Social and Cultural Rights directs that "education shall be directed to the full development of the human personality and the sense of its dignity," and the States that are parties to the Unesco Convention against Discrimination in Education agree not to allow restrictions or preference in education based solely on the ground that pupils belong to a particular group, it is a fact that most governments have systematically neglected the education of indigenous and tribal peoples. The UN special rapporteur writes that the right of indigenous populations to education has not been duly guaranteed and is not really observed, and that States frequently do not recognize traditional indigenous education based on autochthonous educational processes and often deliberately aim at doing away with it and replacing it by formal, alien, and alienating educational processes. [53]

In fact, in many countries, ever since colonial times, the schooling of these peoples has frequently been left in the hands of Christian missionaries, first by the colonial and then by the national governments. Numerous members of indigenous and tribal peoples have passed through missionary and sometimes government schools over the decades, and many often have become integrated into the "national" society and economy, its professional and occupational structure, and have adopted the values of the dominant society. In that sense, they have become assimilated, they have left their traditional society behind, because this has been precisely the objective of the formal school system. However, it must be recognized that many of those who have passed through such schools and have acquired the ways of the dominant "national" society have now become the leaders of authentic indigenous movements who claim the linguistic and cultural rights that are their due, and who reject the kind of education to which they themselves were exposed and that is considered to be fundamentally destructive of indigenous and tribal societies and cultures.

As a result, in numerous countries indigenous organizations and sometimes sympathetic governments are experimenting with new linguistic and educational policies that take indigenous claims into account. A basic premise of these new schools is teaching the vernacular language, the mother tongue. In order to achieve this, many unwritten indigenous languages have had to be turned into written tongues; alphabets have had to be prepared; educational materials in the vernacular tongues must be provided; teachers – often from the indigenous communities themselves – must be trained. This is a lengthy and complicated process, and amongst educators and government officials, debates continue to rage as to the relative merits of one or another kind of educational system. In countries where there exist myriad small indigenous linguistic groups, governments argue that such educational innovations are costly and basically inefficient, and furthermore, they consider that fragmenting the educational system along linguistic lines is a threat to national unity. In these countries, if there exists a majority national language, government policy tends to favour the teaching of the national or official language. In other countries, where the indigenous communities are numerous, particularly if they have a certain amount of political clout, the education in indigenous languages tends to become accepted.

In fact, in most countries where indigenous language schooling takes root, what is taking place is bilingual education. The indigenous language is taught together with the official or national language (or sometimes, as in India, the official State language). Just what the pedagogical mix between the two (or sometimes three) languages is depends on local conditions. Some authors consider the formal schooling (learning how to read and write) in an indigenous language as merely a step towards the appropriation of the official or national language. Others consider it as an end in itself, which is what the indigenous peoples themselves claim. In most countries, the teaching of indigenous languages is carried out only at the lower levels of elementary schooling and is not taken any further. In others it covers elementary and secondary levels, and higher technical schools also. A UN-sponsored seminar on discrimination held in 1981 in Nicaragua suggested the creation of an "Indian university" in Latin America, but so far nothing has come of the resolution.

A more complicated educational problem is making bilingual schooling truly bicultural or intercultural. Just as school children in the urban industrial environment formally learn about their own "national" culture, so also children in indigenous schools must learn about their own culture, aside from what they learn about the "total society." This poses a formidable task for educational planners regarding curriculum development, preparation of textbooks, reading and audio-visual materials, and so forth. Indigenous peoples have been claiming the right to establish and control their own educational institutions, which means exercising control over their own curriculum and educational contents. In some countries this is being achieved, and interesting educational experiments are taking place in many areas. In other countries, particularly in the poorer third world, this must be the government's responsibility, and governments, as has been pointed out above, are not always eager to undertake such innovations, particularly because they have been identified for so long with the assimilationist approaches.

Even if indigenous education is achieved in the terms set out above, another problem remains, that of indigenous cultures as a whole, as living totalities. Cultures are complex patterns of social relationships, material objects, and spiritual values that give meaning and identity to community life and that are a resource for solving the problems of everyday life. Indigenous and tribal cultures have been particularly vulnerable to attack by the dominant society and government. Too many States since colonial times have adopted the stance that indigenous cultures must disappear and its members become acculturated into the dominant, so-called national culture. Discrimination and persecution of indigenous cultures span a wide variety of aspects, including

- Religion (prohibition to practise indigenous religion, forced conversion, taking of children from families and putting them into Christian schools. In this respect, international missionary institutions such as the Summer Institute of Linguistics, which works among hundreds of indigenous and tribal peoples in the world, have been particularly destructive of native cultures)[54]
- The use of traditional dress or names (in October 1988 a Brazilian judge refused to deal with Indian litigants who wore their ethnic attire; the Indians in turn refused to deal with the judge unless so dressed)
- The violation of sacred and burial sites (indigenous peoples claim that numerous objects and artifacts in museums and private collections around the world have been vandalized, stolen from sites and monuments that still have cultural and symbolic meaning for contemporary peoples. Litigation undertaken occasionally on behalf of the indigenous has sometimes led to the satisfaction of indigenous claims. Sacred sites are constantly being destroyed by land developers, government projects, military activity, grave-diggers, or treasure hunters)
- The exploitation of the artistic expressions of indigenous peoples (handicrafts, dances, ceremonies, music, etc.) for tourism, with complete disregard for authenticity and preservation, thus contributing to what many observers have termed the prostitution and degeneration of indigenous and tribal cultures[55]

The UN Draft Universal Declaration on Indigenous Rights includes an article on "the right to manifest, teach, practise and observe their own religious traditions and ceremonies, and to maintain, protect and have access to sacred sites and burial grounds for these purposes," but it does not, at least in its present form, establish the duty of States and other actors to guarantee this right and to protect such sites for the indigenous.[56] In Latin America and elsewhere, governments have admittedly protected and enhanced the remains of glorious ancient civilizations (such as the Aztec, Maya, and Inca), but have done precious little to conserve the contemporary cultures of the direct descendants of these civilizations.

Cultural policies designed to protect and strengthen today's indigenous cultures are being developed slowly by some States and international bodies. A beginning in this direction is the recognition that States in which indigenous and tribal peoples live are multi-ethnic and multicultural societies, a concept that many States still do not wish to admit. The UN special rapporteur says, in this respect:

In multi-ethnic societies, action must always be based on criteria which, at least in principle, assert the equality of the cultural rights of the various ethnic groups. The State has the obvious obligation to formulate and implement a cultural policy which will, among other things, create the necessary conditions for the coexistence and harmonious development of the various ethnic groups living in its territory, either under pluralist provisions which guarantee that one group will not interfere with another, or under other programmes which guarantee equal and genuine opportunities for all.[57]

INDIGENOUS LAW AND SOCIAL ORGANIZATION

A principal factor that has enabled indigenous and tribal peoples to survive in the face of the persistent assaults against them by the dominant society is their internal coherence, their social organization, as well as the maintenance of their own traditions, laws, and customs, including local political authority. The distinct personality of indigenous peoples is not only a question of language or other cultural expressions but the result of the permanent social reproduction of the group through the functioning of its own social, political, and frequently religious institutions. Of course there are exceptions, and in general terms indigenous and tribal peoples who lose their social institutions will also, in the long run, tend to lose their ethnic identity. There may also be cases in which, despite internal divisions and strife or the breakdown of traditional institutions, a given group is able to conserve its identity. Generally, however, the preservation over time of ethnic and cultural identity is closely linked to the functioning of local social and political institutions.

Many governments consider that the existence of such institutions distinct from the constitutional or legal mechanisms developed by the State constitute a form of separatism, a threat to national unity. Most national legal systems do not recognize indigenous law and political institutions. On the contrary, they may argue that if equality before the law, as established in all international human rights instruments, is to be a reality, then no particular ethnic group should have a right to its own legal and political institutions. Many observers, however, have pointed out that equality before the law is a pious fiction when indigenous and tribal peoples are concerned, and that one of the best instruments that these people have to defend their human rights is precisely the validity of their own institutions. The UN rapporteur considers on this point: "Where traditional law continues to be observed by indigenous populations, the question of legal systems arises. While some countries do not recognize the validity of indigenous laws and customs, in the face of the undeniable fact that such legal norms continue to exist, other countries have recognized their existence for some purposes." [58]

Indigenous peoples have demanded that their own customary legal and political institutions be recognized by the State. The UN Draft Universal Declaration of Indigenous Rights is clear on this point:

21. The right to participate fully in the political, economic and social life of their State and to have their specific character duly reflected in the legal system and in political institutions, including proper regard to and recognition of indigenous laws and customs.

The non-recognition of customary indigenous law by established national legal systems may lead to serious violations of individual human rights. This has been documented, for example, in various Latin American countries.[59] The Inter-American Indianist Congress held in 1985 recommended, among other issues, that the customary laws of the Indian peoples be recognized by the States.[60]

SELF-GOVERNMENT, AUTONOMY, AND SELF-DETERMINATION

The question of legal systems and customary law is directly related to tribal and community government, and to the political status of the indigenous peoples within the contemporary so-called nation-state. From time immemorial, indigenous and tribal peoples have been jealous of their sovereignty and independence. Most of them were incorporated against their will, through military and political pressures, into administrative systems not of their own choosing. They were reduced to "minority" status, their lives and fortunes determined and controlled by special ministries or departments, or by religious institutions. They lacked political rights and were excluded from political participation and representation. Many of them never knew what States they actually "belonged" to till recent times. In some countries, during European colonial expansion, treaties were signed between sovereign indigenous nations and an independent national government (Canada, United States, New Zealand). Soon, however, these treaties were violated and/or abrogated unilaterally by the State, with no regard to indigenous sovereignty and rights. In the United States, a series of "Indian wars" in the nineteenth century reduced to almost nothing what little sovereignty and rights the indigenous had left. In 1871, Congress ceased to make treaties with the Indians and thereafter dealt with Indian tribes by legislation, executive order, or agreement. During the Roosevelt administration, in the thirties, Congress passed the Indian Reorganization Act, which recognized Indian tribal governments on reservations. In 1953, however, Congress passed a resolution that established what has become known as termination policy, which the Indian tribes resisted fiercely. In the late sixties and early seventies, government policy changed once again, in favour of strengthening tribal governments and lessening federal control over tribal governmental affairs. The concept of Indian self-determination was used for the first time.[61] In Alaska, a different approach has been used by the federal government. Here, the Alaska Native Claims Settlement Act (ANCSA) of 1971 severely limited the Alaskan natives' (Indians, Inuit) former titles and treated them as so many commercial corporations. Alaskans have resisted the act and are struggling for the recognition of their right to self-determination.[62]

In Canada also there has been a long history of unequal and broken treaties between the government and the Indian tribes. As one author puts it: "The commissioners saw the treaties in one way; the Indians in quite another. A reading...shows that the two groups came together with radically different expectations. The Indians sought to be protected from land-grabbing settlers and from the evils they sensed. . . . The commissioners saw Indian reserves as places where Indians could learn to be settlers and farmers."[63] In 1982, Canada adopted a new constitution, in which aboriginal and treaty rights of the aboriginal peoples of Canada are recognized and affirmed. These would include, according to one scholar, the right to live under traditional forms of government, which are tribal, and to be governed by customary laws; in short, a constitutional right to cultural survival. The constitution was amended in 1983 as regards aboriginal rights.[64]

Aboriginal peoples in countries where treaties had been made in colonial and independent times (Australia, Canada, New Zealand, and the United States) have long claimed that because of such treaties they must be recognized as sovereign nations. The governments involved have denied this claim, but have nevertheless attempted to provide satisfactory solutions to the indigenous demands. The International Indian Treaty Council has lobbied the United Nations for redress for several years. At its session in 1988, the UN Economic and Social Council, on the recommendation of the Commission on Human Rights, appointed a Special Rapporteur of the Sub-Commission on Prevention of Discrimination and Protection of Minorities, with the mandate to prepare an outline on the possible purposes, scope, and sources of a study on the potential utility of treaties, agreements, and other constructive arrangements between indigenous populations and governments for the purpose of ensuring the promotion and protection of the human rights and fundamental freedoms of indigenous populations.[65]

While *de facto* tribal and indigenous community governments exist in many countries, the formal and legal recognition of such institutions by governments has been achieved only partially and unevenly. Some governments recognize indigenous law and institutions when these do not conflict with national laws or only when members of the indigenous or tribal community are involved. As soon as relations between indigenous and non-indigenous peoples occur, then the national law tends to predominate.

Indigenous organizations the world over are claiming the right to self-government and autonomy. Some countries have granted this. Panama's constitution of 1972 recognizes the tribal territory of some indigenous groups, and others in that country are demanding similar treatment. In Nicaragua, the new constitution of 1986 establishes a measure of autonomy for the communities of the Atlantic coast and recognizes their right to establish their own forms of social organization and to administer their local affairs according to their own traditions. A further Statute of Autonomy of the Regions of the Atlantic Coast spells out the social, economic, political, and cultural rights of the local communities.[66]

Quite another situation prevails in some Scandinavian countries. In Norway, the Saami have been considered an ethnic minority, discriminated against by some, but have received the benefits of the Norwegian welfare state. Still, the Saami organizations have been aspiring to more; specifically, they have demanded that the fundamental aboriginal rights of the Saami be written into the Norwegian constitution, as well as the right to establish a Saami elected committee or parliament that can administer these rights and express the common will of the Saami people. The Saami have identified themselves ideologically with other indigenous peoples and are founding members of the World Council of Indigenous Peoples. They also regularly send representatives to the UN Working Group on Indigenous Populations.[67] A different situation prevails in Greenland, long a Danish colony. Here the majority Inuit population achieved political power through traditional party politics and established home rule, that is, virtual independence and self-government.[68]

Self-determination has recently become a major political claim of indigenous peoples, especially in international bodies. They base their demands on the human right of self-determination of peoples as spelled out in Article 1 of the two international covenants.[69] They claim that being the original "first nations" of the territories that they inhabit, and having been submitted generally against their choosing to the suzerainty of other States and governments, usually in the form of invasion, conquest, and colonialism, they have the right to self-determination just as so many other peoples who have shaken off colonialism. Moreover, they demand the right to be considered "peoples" and not mere "populations," as has been the custom in international organizations. Likewise, they reject being considered as "ethnic minorities" and thus refuse to be dealt with according to Article 27 of the ICCPR. These demands have been taken up by the specialized bodies of the UN that are currently dealing with the rights of indigenous peoples. Thus, both the new draft ILO Convention 107 and the Draft Universal Declaration on Indigenous Rights use the term people instead of the former word populations.

CONCLUSIONS

The subordination of indigenous peoples to the nation-state, their discrimination and marginalization, has historically, in most cases, been the result of colonization and colonialism. Within the framework of politically independent countries, the situation of indigenous and tribal peoples may be described in terms of internal colonialism. The processes whereby indigenous and tribal peoples have been subjugated by today's dominant societies has occasionally been accompanied by genocide, not only in the nineteenth century during the heyday of colonial expansion, but also in some parts of the world during the present century and in contemporary times. Denunciations about the genocide of ethnic minorities in general and of indigenous and tribal peoples in particular have been brought to the attention of the international community regularly, but the latter has usually been unable or unwilling to do anything about it. This has been one of the major failures of the UN system in recent years, despite the existence of the Convention on the Prevention and Punishment of the Crime of Genocide.

More commonly, indigenous and tribal peoples have been the victims of cultural genocide or ethnocide, which, as was expressed in the previous chapter, entails two principal aspects, one economic and the other cultural.

Governments have carried out different kinds of policies at different times *vis-à-vis* the indigenous and tribal peoples within their territories. Aside from extermination and genocide, which fortunately constitute exceptions at the present time, policies of segregation, assimilation, integration, and amalgamation have been carried out more or less successfully. Such policies have provoked the increasing resistance of indigenous organizations in recent years, and some States have experimented with new kinds of policies, including pluralism, self-reliance, self-management, autonomy, and ethnodevelopment. Ethnodevelopment, as was pointed out in the previous chapter, means finding in the group's own culture the resources and creative force necessary to confront the challenges of the modern, changing world.

In 1977, the first international conference of non-governmental organizations on Indigenous Peoples of the Americas was held under UN auspices in Geneva. This was followed by another NGO Conference on Indigenous Peoples and the

Land in 1981. Since then, an increasing number of indigenous and tribal organizations have attended the sessions of the UN Working Group on Indigenous Populations and have submitted statements and documents that have been publicly discussed and many of which are being taken into account in the UN Draft Universal Declaration on Indigenous Rights. The first NGO Conference of 1977 produced a Declaration of Principles for the Defence of the Indigenous Nations and Peoples of the Western Hemisphere, which states, *inter alia*, that indigenous people shall be accorded recognition as nations, and proper subjects of international law, provided the people concerned desire to be recognized as a nation and meet the fundamental requirements of nationhood.[70] Other declarations of indigenous rights have been proposed by other conferences and other non-governmental organizations. A general tendency to be observed is the claim of the right of self-determination of indigenous peoples. This claim will surely remain a key issue in the national and international debates on indigenous rights in the coming years.

9

Immigration and Racism in Western Europe

IMMIGRANTS IN EUROPE

Migrations have long been a fact of life for millions of people. The nineteenth century saw massive migrations out of Europe into the "New World" and the British and French colonies. After the Second World War, the flow of international migrations seems to have changed direction. Two new major poles of attraction of migrants have arisen in recent decades, one is Europe and the other is the Gulf States. In the latter, temporary worker migrations from various Asian countries have had far-reaching economic consequences, for both the sender and the receiver countries. Problems of cultural adjustment of migrants to the local societies have been mentioned but have not been analysed in detail.[1] In Europe, the situation is different. While temporary migrant workers from third world countries arrive in droves, many of them, in contrast to what happens in the Arab world, come with their families and the intention to settle permanently. Over the last few decades, many Western European countries have become multiracial and multicultural countries as a result of massive immigration. A host of new problems for both the countries and the migrant groups have arisen that relate to new patterns of interethnic relations in the European countries. A study published in 1978 reported that 15 million people had migrated to Western Europe in the previous 20 years, and these migrations are closely related to Europe's post-war economic prosperity.[2] In 1985, the European Economic Commission estimated that 15 million migrant workers and their families were currently living in the countries of the European Community, without counting the illegal immigrants.[3] At an earlier stage, most migrants to Western Europe's prosperous industrialized countries came from other, mainly southern, European countries. Nowadays they come increasingly from the third world. They have become the new ethnic minorities in Western

120

Europe, not only because they come mainly from Asia and Africa, but also because many of them are Muslims in Christian countries.

Economic factors are of course the prime movers behind these migratory movements. Migrant workers have become a structural feature of Western European countries. They are present in the automobile industry, in construction, services, and other sectors. They also occupy the lowest rungs of the economic scale, moving into jobs that Europeans no longer want for themselves. They are more mobile, more malleable, more adaptable, more passive (less unionized), less skilled, but more efficient (they have come to make money), less demanding in terms of working conditions, promotions, work hours, wage increases, etc., than local workers. They are found among the lowest and most disadvantaged sectors of society.

Several European countries that regularly receive foreign migrant workers have signed treaties with sending countries, but these treaties have not significantly improved the situation of the workers. Migrants tend to send a part of their incomes to their families in the home countries (as occurs with Asian migrants to the Gulf States), and many of them expect to return home after a stint in Western Europe. However, increasingly, migrant workers do not wish to return and try to stay in the host country.

The cultural implications of these economic migrations are important. Immigrants, in fact, live in two cultures. On the one hand, immigrants wish to acquire the instruments that will allow them to adapt more easily to the host society, particularly the language, but on the other, they do not wish to cut their links with their home country, especially when they are looking forward to returning. But trying to maintain their own culture in the foreign environment of the receiving country creates serious psychological problems. Only a few receiving countries (such as Sweden) have developed policies that favour the difficult cultural choices that immigrant workers have to make. When immigrants manage to stay with their families, second- and third-generation members in turn face other problems. Here we find the rise of a new minority culture that stems from the traditional culture of the migrants but is in many respects different from it.[4] Particular difficulties are faced by Muslims in the predominant Catholic or Protestant societies of Western Europe. Belonging to Islam is not only an intimate, private choice of religious preference; it means public, collective, community religious activity, educational facilities for religious schooling, expression of religious practices on holidays and feasts. In France, for example, Islam has become the second religion; in Germany, Islam is the religion of the large Turkish community. One French writer insists that the French secular nation-state now has to rethink itself in terms of the importance that Islam has acquired in France as a result of immigration from Africa and the Arab countries.[5] Particular cultural problems attach to the situation of women, either female immigrant workers or the wives and daughters of such workers. They are usually doubly handicapped, as foreigners and as women. A report states:

For the woman from the Maghreb countries, who has been raised in a tradition of submission, things are more difficult. If she looks for work, this poses serious problems for the married couple, insofar as the Maghreb male will not easily accept the erosion of his power. More generally, if the woman, who is after all the guarantor of cultural traditions, "modernizes", then the whole cultural system of origin is being questioned. Even the smallest evolution of the role of the Muslim woman has considerable influence on the relations between the couple, in the family and in the immigrant community.

Certain immigrant women cannot bear their inferior position in relation to the male any longer, an inferiority which has been institutionalized and dogmatized by the Koran. The status of the emancipated European woman is not without influence on these women, and a number of them have begun refusing their condition of subordination.

This evolution will be more marked among the young women of the new generation. Therefore it is not suprising to learn about an increase in the number of elopements and attempted suicides by young Maghreb girls who do not accept that their future husband be chosen according to tradition by their father. For a number of them, the Islamic religion is seen as an obstacle to their development.[6]

Still, the new generation tries to adapt to the host environment, and perhaps is able to do so better than the first generation of immigrants. New cultural forms emerge among the youth of immigrant families, such as the "Beurs," the children of Arab immigrants in France, or the Rastas or Rastafarians in Britain.[7]

There are also political aspects to foreign immigration of workers in European countries. Migrants are now frequently demanding political rights and political participation, particularly as the economic and cultural policies of the host countries directly affect their well-being. Migrants are increasingly participating in union activities, voluntary associations, cultural organizations, but direct political participation still eludes them. OECD countries are now discussing the possibility of granting double citizenship or nationality to immigrants or their descendants. But in general, the political rights of foreign immigrants in Europe are still very limited.

THE NEW RACISM IN EUROPE

One of the more dramatic consequences of the massive migrations from third world countries to Western Europe has been an alarming rise of racism and attendant expressions of extreme right-wing ideologies in Europe, which prompted an inquiry by the European Parliament.[8]

In fact, racism in Europe is not a new phenomenon at all, but there is a "new" racism that it might be convenient to distinguish from the older kind, and place it within its historical and structural context. We should not, however, take the contrast too far, because there is no doubt an underlying continuity in the underpinnings of racism between the "old" and the "new." Still, for analytical and practical purposes, it might be possible to make a useful distinction.

There are two fundamental historical roots of racism in Europe, namely, the formation of the modern so-called nation-state, beginning in the eighteenth century, and the colonial expansion of Europe around the same time. The two phenomena are related and reached their climax in the nineteenth century. The formation of the modern nation-state was based on the idea of a shared ethnic identity, a national language, a common culture. This implied two processes: the elimination or absorption of non-national groups by the dominant ethnic majority, and the creation of "national myths" based on a common (usually heroic) history and the eulogizing of that abstract entity: the people, *le peuple, das Volk*. The Germans put it succinctly: *ein Land, ein Volk*, one land, one people.[9] Elsewhere it was claimed that every nation had to have its own State and every State was to be composed of one nation. A people, a nation, thus became ethnically distinct from other peoples, other nations. And some nations developed an acute awareness regarding not only their allegedly common culture and history, but also their supposedly shared biological characteristics. Thus arose those "imagined communities," the modern nations. This problématique later became known as "the national question" and it still bedevils the world today.[10]

Nations became nation-states and States begot nations at a time when the consolidation of modern capitalism required the structuring of territorial units for the mobilization of resources, labour, and markets. Intense economic and geopolitical rivalry between the European States, oftentimes turning into military conflict, strengthened the "national ideal" and helped further the perception of the ethnic distinctiveness that set one nation against another during so much of modern European history.[11] Consequently, national consciousness, soon followed by nationalism as a political ideology, became a vehicle for ethnocentric attitudes that in turn were able to generate chauvinism and xenophobia, two collective phenomena that have time and again been whipped up in periods of conflict to strengthen the power of the State and of sundry ruling groups.

On the other hand, the colonial expansion of the industrializing European countries during the nineteenth century (particularly England, France, and Germany) presented the European societies with a situation in which it became necessary to find ideological justification for the economic exploitation and the political oppression of distant peoples who were moreover biologically and culturally distinct from the average European.[12] Racial ideologies such as those developed by Gobineau and Chamberlain and their followers quickly filled the gap. Pseudo-scientific theories attempted to establish the alleged superiority of one race and the supposed inferiority of others. Race was said to be a crucial factor in the cultural and economic achievement of whole peoples as well as in the abilities and psychology of individuals. The "white" race, that of the European colonizers, was deemed to be superior to all the others.

The emergence of racism was thus linked to the formation of the ethnically distinct nation-state and the establishment of overseas colonies by the European powers. Thereafter racism as an ideology became embedded in the political and popular cultures of the time, developing rapidly among different social classes, but mainly serving the interests of the ruling bourgeoisie, till it reached its perverse and genocidal climax under German Nazism.

After the Second World War and the founding of the United Nations, with the approval by the General Assembly of the Universal Declaration of Human Rights in 1948, which proclaims the principle of non-discrimination, the Genocide Convention of 1950, and the International Convention on the Elimination of All Forms of Racial Discrimination, which entered into force in 1969, and with the establishment of the European human rights machinery (convention, commission, and court), it was felt that institutional racism (as distinct from individual racist or discriminatory attitudes) would disappear forever. Once Nazism had been defeated in Europe, observers and politicians alike felt that racism on this continent was no longer possible. Anti-racist laws had been enacted in some countries, the non-discriminatory clauses of the Universal Declaration had been taken over by a number of national legislations, the European Court of Human Rights was hailed as a major forum to deal with human rights violations, including racism, and the rest was to be left to the educational system. Perhaps, after a generation or two, racism would be remembered only as a bad dream.

This process was bolstered by the fact that even in the United States, where racial discrimination was legal and accepted by the majority of the population, the 1950s witnessed a progressive breaking down of the legal supports of racism. On the other hand, the sixties became the decade of decolonization, as numerous erstwhile European colonies in Africa obtained their political independence and joined the UN as equals with their former metropolis. The economic and political bases for the existence of institutional racism were thought to have disappeared once and for all, and only South Africa remained with the aberrant and abhorrent apartheid system, an outcast among the world's nations.

Yet this noble dream was not to be. Changes in the world economy occurring since the sixties have transformed the structure of European society and have produced major demographic and sociological realignments. On the one hand, increasing labour migrations brought first thousands, then millions of workers from overseas into the industrial heartland of Europe. At first, these migrations came from southern Europe: Italy, Spain, Portugal, Yugoslavia. Later the source of migrants was the Middle East, North Africa, Africa south of the Sahara, and southern Asia. At a later stage, labour migrations were supplemented by the arrival of political and economic refugees from a number of third world countries.

Such mass migrations are not new in world history, but their particular characteristics were indeed new to post-war Western Europe, particularly since the sixties. The nature of these migration flows has been widely documented in the specialized literature of our time. Among the questions that have been addressed more or less systematically, we may point to the following: Who are the migrants; why do they come; what do they come for; how long do they stay; how do they relate to the economic and social structure of the host country; what kind of relations do they establish with the national population; what are the respective reciprocal attitudes of the different population groups that come into contact with each other due to such migrations; what policies do governments follow with regard to the migrants; what are the migrants' needs, aspirations, problems, demands, claims, and complaints; how do they relate to their country of origin; and how do such migrations affect relations between countries? What might the long-term effects of migration be, what should be done to "integrate" migrants in the nation-state? etc.[13]

Two major characteristics of these migrations stand out. Overall, the migrants, particularly the economic migrants, flow into unskilled working class and low status occupations that have traditionally been the object of social class discrimination in Europe as elsewhere. Secondly, the immigrants tend to be biologically distinguishable from the natives (mainly by skin colour), a fact that enables people to construct so-called racial distinctions between the two groups (the natives and the newcomers), which in turn provides a rationale for the emergence of the practice of racial discrimination. Thirdly, the immigrants are the bearers of a "foreign" culture: language, religion, social practices, values, etc., that clashes with native culture and institutions. Such foreign cultures are exotic but respectable in their own countries, where they may be appreciated by the tourists, but when they happen to appear next door, then they threaten "our" identity, "our" way of doing things, and they question the model of the monoethnic nation-state that provides security and identification for its members. In contrast, the immigrant is the stranger, the unknown, who is perceived as a potential threat, even though his contribution to the labour force is needed and appreciated.

As part of the working class in the industrialized capitalist economies, the third world immigrants bring home to the once arrogant world empires the full significance of the contradictions of colonial exploitation. *Le colonialisme chez nous*, the French complain. Indeed, there is not only similarity but also continuity between the traditional exploitation of labour under colonialism and the insertion of immigrant labour into the work force of the industrialized countries. As the post-war boom and the welfare state enabled the local working class to aspire to, and at times achieve, middle class status, the economic situation in the former colonies as well as in other so-called third world countries became progressively more difficult for millions of poor peasants and urban dwellers. At the same time, in Europe the less well paid and less-desirable positions, the back-breaking or lowly service jobs, became available, not only because more such jobs opened in an expanding economy, but also because their traditional occupants, the local working classes, moved into other, more highly skilled and better-paid occupations.

Immigrant labour thus came to occupy a special status in many European countries. Not only did it, generally speaking, come to fill specific slots in the occupational structure (there are exceptions, of course: white-collar workers, traders, small businessmen, liberal professions; but I am here referring to a general tendency); it also complemented and frequently competed with the traditional local working class. This process gave rise to what some observers have called a "dual" or "split labour market," one for the local working class and one for the immigrants.[14] Job requirements, skills, working conditions, pay and benefits differed between the two markets, reserving the lower scales for the immigrants, who found it increasingly difficult to rise up and out. At the same time, the working class itself became fragmented and divided, a situation that did not favour unified class actions for better pay and improved conditions of work and life and that enabled the market to press down on wages.

No wonder, then, that these conditions became fertile ground for the emergence of what we may now call the "new" racism in Western Europe (and other industrialized countries). This was so because the split labour market distinguished between white and black or coloured, and the working class came to be divided along racial lines. Whereas "race" was not originally a factor that necessarily compressed immigrant labour into specific occupations or activities, it increasingly became a factor in conditioning social and economic relations among different segments of the population.[15] In other words, there took place what one author defines as the "racial categorization" of class relations.[16] And this racial categorization of class relations led to institutional racism as a sociological fact, spilling into all spheres of social life. Whereas "race" as such is not an observable reality and lacks any kind of scientific meaning, racism is a reality in the sense that it finds expression as such in political, economic, social, and cultural life. It is not the existence of "races" that nurtures racism, but rather the racist ideology that creates the "races" upon which it feeds.[17]

To the extent that for the reasons mentioned before the racist ideology exists latently in European cultural history, it re-emerged in the sixties under a new guise, focusing on the masses of immigrants from overseas. Whilst the majority of these immigrants were at the beginning only temporary labourers, over the years their demographic composition has changed. Many are now permanent settlers with their families; children of immigrants have been born in Europe and are citizens; in recent years, political refugees, with their own particular problems, have increased their numbers. The racist ideology has caught them all in its net. And according to recent studies, including the report of the European Parliament, racism is on the rise, strongly linked to the re-emergence of extreme right-wing political activity in several European countries.[18]

The new racism is not only directed against individuals who are perceived to be biologically different. Biological differences, whatever their nature, only become socially significant when linked to other factors, such as behaviour, economic activity, cultural values, social relations, and so forth. Racism is a virulent ideology not only because it posits the supposed superiority of one "race" over another, but because it correlates racial characteristics of individuals with social and cultural variables of groups and entire peoples. Thus, racism leads from subjective ranking of individuals according to biological traits to generalizations and value judgements about whole cultures and societies.[19]

The new immigrants in Europe come from culturally diverse backgrounds; they bring with them their languages, religions, social structures, and value systems. The racist ideology rejects these "foreign" elements in the name of nationalism and patriotism. The victims of the new racism are no longer just the biologically distinct individuals (blacks, Arabs, Indians, Orientals), but the culturally and socially different ethnic groups. Racial discrimination becomes ethnic discrimination. Whether this should also be called racism or not is an open question about which there is still much debate. Some scholars would limit the term racism to discrimination based on physical or biological traits. Others include ethnic discrimination in general under this term. The fact is, however, that regardless of skin colour and other biological traits, immigrant ethnic groups (just as other national and regional minorities before them) have become the object of discriminatory treatment because of their social and cultural patterns, their way of life. And usually it will be difficult, if not impossible, to separate racial from ethnic discrimination in practice.[20]

For many specialists and practitioners, the solution to racism must be twofold. On the one hand, the racist ideology and racial as well as ethnic discrimination must disappear. This can be achieved through legal action and the educational process. Full equality of all social groups (whether they be defined and identified in racial or ethnic terms) must be achieved, in accordance with the principles of the international instruments of human rights. If and when racism has disappeared and formal equality has been attained, then the human rights of minority groups will be protected.

But on the other hand, in most countries one hears calls for the rapid integration and incorporation of immigrant groups into the social and cultural mainstream. This ideal is presented as a solution to racism, and conversely, racism is seen as a major obstacle to the achievement of this objective. Underlying this perspective is the idea that it is precisely the ethnic and cultural differences of minority groups that determine or at least condition racism. Were these differences to disappear, then again formal equality would be attained and the human rights of minority groups (who by then would no longer be considered as such) would be protected.

The objective of "full integration" is a virtuous one. It is hoped that through integration many of the obstacles to the well-being and improved standards of living of the immigrant minorities will disappear. At the same time, the majority population will feel less threatened and insecure and the old ideal of a homogeneous ethnic nation will be preserved.

But the integrationist approach has two drawbacks. For one, by virtually blaming the victim for the existence of racism (let us recall the old slur about the Jews being the cause of anti-Semitism), it neglects and underestimates the power of "racial categorization," mentioned above, in creating socially significant differences where there were none, or scarcely any, before. Secondly, it does not recognize a most important phenomenon of our time: the claim by numerous ethnic groups around the world to their own identity, to their survival and reproduction as culturally specific social groups or peoples, within the wider society. The right to be different from the dominant ethnic majority, *le droit à la différence*, has become a major issue in the contemporary world and no doubt a fundamental human right that is recognized as such in international law. Integrationist policies, then, may, with the best of intentions, actually violate some basic human rights of minority peoples, including immigrants. Thus, we also find social and cultural policies designed to protect the cultural heritage and the social identity of such groups. If successful, and if immigrants and their descendants wish to preserve their culture and identity, then undoubtedly the traditional nature of the monoethnic nation-state will be modified. And the struggle against racial and ethnic discrimination will also have to include policies for the recognition and respect of ethnic differences within the nation-state.

Such policies may, however, not be popular among certain sectors of the native population that may perceive their own national ethnic identity to be threatened by the ethnic and cultural dynamics of the immigrants. Here, the collective human rights of different population groups may indeed enter into contradiction. And sometimes, these contradictions do lead to political conflict.

In conclusion, the "new" racism in Europe is actually not so new, because the racist and ethnocentric ideology is in fact rooted in European national and colonial history. It is new only insofar as it is now exercised on immigrant populations and their descendants rather than on the more traditional territorial and religious minorities (though these also still suffer different forms of discrimination; for example, the Roma, or Gypsies). As a widespread social and economic phenomenon, today's racism can only be understood in the framework of the structural changes that have taken place in the economies of the industrialized European countries. This is not to imply that racism is merely an epiphenomenon of material forces, but neither is it simply a set of unsupported subjective attitudes that will disappear with a little bit of goodwill and humanitarian education. In every case of racism, at least two factors are at issue: the structure and dynamics of the economy (particularly the composition of the labour force and its relation to capital), and the prevailing cultural value systems and ideological trends.

A deeper understanding of the conditions that have produced and continue to provide a justification of the different expressions of racism is necessary if the struggle against racism is to be successful.[21]

10

Ethnic Rights and National Policies

States deal with minorities under their jurisdiction in various forms. As mentioned in earlier chapters, some States ignore the existence of minorities altogether and provide no legal framework whatsoever to deal with minority issues. They may do so at a political level, but they find no guidance for their policies in existing legislation. The fiction of the homogeneous, monoethnic nation is widespread. It is usually accompanied by different kinds of assimilationist policies that may range from the "melting-pot" hypothesis to deliberate actions of ethnocide, and in extreme cases, genocide. The ideal behind these assimilationist policies is that culturally distinct ethnies will simply disappear and melt into the wider society, the unified nation.

Some States have laws and policies whereby the relations between a dominant ethnie and one or several subordinate minorities are regulated. These are so-called "domination devices" used by the ethnocratic State to preserve its power and to keep minorities in their place. South Africa's apartheid comes to mind here, but there are many other examples where constitutions, for example, determine an official religion or language and place restrictions on the free exercise of the ethnic rights of minorities.

A number of States have developed variations of pluralist arrangements by which ethnic minorities may have some form of legally recognized representation or participation in the political system. Such pluralist techniques may include group autonomy on territorial principles, which in turn might range from full federalism through regionalism or devolution, administrative centralization to local self-government and the relative autonomy of community development authorities. A more complex set of issues arises when ethnic minorities are protected through electoral laws and the composition of the legislature. A number of different mechanisms have been set up to provide for adequate minority representation; for example, separate electoral rolls and separate blocs of seats for the different ethnic groups or communal seats in fixed proportions, but with common voting. A common mechanism is proportional representation. Ethnic minorities may also participate in various manners in executive government through formal or informal power sharing.

Finally, there also exist numerous forms of administrative protection of minority groups.[1]

The United Nations University study of State laws related to minorities covered some 40 different countries, which allows for some generalizations. The first point to note is that an undifferentiated human rights/non-discrimination formula is the preferred style in much of the Americas and Africa; group differentiation is more common in Europe and Asia.[2]

LATIN AMERICA

The "no-minorities" homogeneity principle is carried through fairly consistently into general Latin American legal arrangements. The American Declaration of the Rights and Duties of Man 1948 makes no reference whatever to minorities, though it forbids discrimination on grounds of "race . . . language, creed or any other factor" (Article 2). The omission recurs in the American Convention on Human Rights 1969. Assimilation is the general policy followed in Latin America, and discrimination is universally prohibited in the constitutions and equality proclaimed. Latin American delegates at the United Nations have repeatedly stressed that there are no minorities in Latin America, referring particularly to foreign immigrants. These immigrants, treated as individuals and not groups, are supposed to integrate and assimilate. Equality and non-discrimination often mean that the State proclaims only one official language and that newcomers are required to learn it and their children will be educated through the medium of this language. This also applies traditionally to indigenous groups, which have not been recognized as "minorities" by national governments in Latin America. However, in this respect there have been significant changes in recent years. The 1972 constitution of Panama respects the regional autonomy of some Indian groups and provides for bilingual education. The new constitutions of Guatemala (1986), Nicaragua (1987), and Brazil (1988) guarantee Indian rights for the first time in the constitutional history of these countries.[3] At the subconstitutional levels, Argentina and Peru have adopted laws that recognize certain Indian rights to territory, language, and culture. As far as Indians are concerned, the traditional idea of complete assimilation into the dominant "national" (that is, non-Indian) mould is slowly changing in Latin America.

NORTH AMERICA

Exhibiting another style of diversity, Canada is an outstanding exception to the general American pattern described above. In Canada, neither of the two original contending European powers – Britain and France – was able to establish complete cultural and political supremacy. The British North America Act of 1867, now styled the Constitution Act of 1867, and *a fortiori*, the Constitution Act of 1982, reflect the sharing of power and influence in Canadian society. The new constitution reflects the triple heritage of Canada – Part One is the Canadian Charter of Rights and Freedoms, which establishes the relationship between the French and English heritages of Canada, including linguistic equality between English and French; Part Two is headed Rights of the Aboriginal Peoples of Canada, and consists of one brief section:

35:(1) the existing Aboriginal and Treaty Rights of the Aboriginal Peoples of Canada are hereby recognized and affirmed. (2) In this Act, Aboriginal Peoples of Canada includes the Indian, Inuit and Metis Peoples of Canada.

The reference to the existing rights of aboriginal peoples introduces a feature of the colonization process in North America, the full implications of which are yet to be worked out for the benefit of the Indian groups. Unlike the equivalent process in Latin America, colonization was achieved in the main through treaties with Indian tribes and nations, many of which were, regrettably, broken by the colonists but that can still form the basis for land claims. The Canadian view is that the treaties, while binding, are not treaties in the international law sense.

Whatever genuine international law character the treaties once possessed in the United States, there too the prevailing view is still that articulated by Chief Justice Marshall in 1831. The Indian tribes are to be regarded as "domestic dependent nations . . . living in a state of pupillage. Their relationship to the United States resembles that of wards to guardian. . . ." International law seems to have endorsed the view that, as lawyers would have it, Indian groups are not subjects of international law: i.e., they are within the legal system of States and are not independent entities of international law (see chaps. 8 and 11). Nonetheless, within the municipal laws of States, Indian tribes may still have autonomous status. They have been described as semi-independent and a separate people – they are "nations," even if "dependent." Recent US case law has demonstrated that respect for the rights of individuals must be balanced against the right of the tribes to maintain distinct identity.

AFRICA

African States display a philosophy of minorities similar to that prevailing in Latin America. Discrimination on grounds of race, tribe, colour, or creed is typically prohibited in constitutional law. Like Latin American States, many African States have reported to international bodies that they have no minorities or no "minority problems." Like Latin American States, African States

purport to regard "minority" as a foreign concept. On any deductive application of the definitions of minorities provided by the Capotorti report (see chap.
8) to Africa, the presence of "objectively" identifiable minorities displaying
"subjective" willingness to retain their cultural capacity is amply demon-
strable. Many African States would figure highly on any register of ethnic and
religious complexity. There are more than 250 distinct ethnic groups in Nigeria's 90 million population. On Uganda, a source states that "the present day
national borders of Uganda cut across ethnic and language boundaries, and
place together over 40 ethnic groups which formerly had little in common, and
which even today may not understand each other's languages."[4] Such patterns
of complexity are normal in Africa. So why not minorities? Why not constitutional recognition of diversity? The reasons are not far to seek.

A cursory glance at African boundaries with the lines of longitude and lati-
tude provides the clue that divisions between African States may not be coterminous with population distributions; it suggests that the States are artificial,
not organic. To take only a few examples, the Ewe people are divided among
Ghana, Togo, Burkina Faso, and Nigeria. Somalis live in the Somali Republic,
Ethiopia, Kenya, and Djibouti. Some State boundaries do not respect the ethnic
principle in any form. An All-African Peoples' Conference in 1958 passed a
special resolution on frontiers, boundaries, and federations:

The Conference (a) denounces artificial frontiers drawn by imperialist powers to divide
the peoples of Africa, particularly those which cut across ethnic groups and divide peoples of the same stock; (b) calls for the abolition or adjustment of such frontiers at an
early date.[5]

The revisionist approach to boundaries proved quite unrealistic. Realign-
ment would be as disastrous in human terms as the original, colonial conquests,
or more so. The new States chose instead to develop nationality within their
colonial inheritance. Nationality has therefore to be forged; it has not come
ready-made to the rulers of the new States. Arbitrary borders have been
accepted as a basis for statehood – there is often no equivalent pre-colonial polity
to return to – and have been defended tenaciously. The Charter of the Organization of African Unity (OAU) 1963 describes the purposes and aims of the OAU,
which are, *inter alia*, "to defend the States' sovereignty, their territorial integrity
and independence." The member States proclaim their adherence to principles
including "respect for the sovereignty and territorial integrity of each State and
for its inalienable right to independent existence." In the African context, the
principle of intangibility of colonial frontiers has been accepted as a first principle by the International Court of Justice (as in the 1986 border litigation between Mali and Burkina Faso). Challenges to this principle have generally been
unsuccessful. Somalia is unusual among African States in maintaining
irredentist claims and seeks unification in a State of all ethnic Somalis.[6] But its

ambitions, which have brought Somalia into conflict with neighbouring States – principally Ethiopia – have not been supported.

The OAU took its stand against irredentism by Somalia during the Ethiopia/ Somalia conflict in 1977. It has taken a similar stand against separatism or secession. If the boundaries of the African States are legitimate, then they must be defended against internal as well as external subversion. The attempted secession of Biafra from Nigeria was condemned by the OAU, though five States departed from the "territorial integrity" line. Other attempted secessions or ethnic realignments of States have been similarly unsuccessful. The separatist ambitions of the Ashanti and Ewe, of the Southern Sudanese, of Katanga, of Eritrea and Tigrey, of the Buganda, of the Bakongo, have not prospered.

All of this has discouraged any pro-minority sentiments in Africa. The African experience has fed into general international law in disallowing self-determination for minorities. African nationalism is not predicated on European patterns of ethnicity but on inherited reality within given borders, however artificial. The African concept of self-determination is essentially majority rule in African States, freedom from external interference, and termination of white racist rule in South Africa and Namibia (the latter having obtained its political independence in 1990). This self-determination is deemed to be the basis of all human rights, a valuation that has sometimes meant that self-determination as national consolidation displaces human rights.[7] Minorities have inevitably been victims in the process of nation-building. Unhappily, genocide has its place in recent as well as colonial African history.[8]

Much African experience with human rights is summarized in that most recent of international human rights instruments, the African Charter of Human and Peoples' Rights, adopted by the 18th (Banjul) Assembly of Heads of State and Governments of the Organization of African Unity in Nairobi in June 1981. The charter is now in force. It is a unique statement of collective peoples' rights and individual human rights. While there is not an explicit ranking of the two classes of rights, the preamble cites the States' parties' recognition that "the reality and respect of peoples' rights should necessarily guarantee human rights," which may imply some practical priority for the former class of rights. Individual rights have only lexical priority: the first 187 articles of the charter are devoted to them, including civil and political rights and economic and social rights. Individuals also have duties, including the duty to "preserve and strengthen social and national solidarity," and even more instructively, "to preserve and strengthen the national independence and the territorial integrity of their country." Peoples have rights but no duties in the charter; the rights are essentially variations on the theme of self-determination including the right to "economic, social and cultural development."

Consistent with African attitudes, there is no reference to minorities in the charter: The "African" character of the charter is asserted in the preamble, which refers to "the values of African civilization" that should "inspire and characterize" the States' parties' "reflections on the concept of human and peoples' rights." The charter rights are guaranteed without distinction of any kind, including distinction based upon "ethnic group" as well as those based on "race . . . colour, sex, language, religion, political or any other opinion, national and social origin, fortune, birth or other status." The preamble to the charter selects discrimination on such grounds as especially deserving of elimination from Africa.

In sum, the charter amplifies and strengthens the legal concept of self-determination and adapts individual rights to the African context through, *inter alia*, a novel emphasis of the charter that the "people" is the whole State in each case and not minority tribes, ethnic groups, races, or religions. The adaptations of human rights in the charter do not go very far in the recognition of any middle terms between the State and the individual – references to duties to the family, society, and "other legally recognized communities" (Article 27) may count for little in this context.

The legal systems of many African States accordingly devote themselves to nation-building, modernization, and the combatting of tribalism: the tribe may be taken as a rough equivalent of minority or ethnic group in the European context in that it represents a level of association intermediate between State and individual (or family). The nation-building process is particularly fierce in some States.

Much of the constitution of the Republic of Somalia is devoted to the development of a progressive culture for the Somalis – the State promises as much to the people (Article 51). Article 52 promises that the State will preserve good customs and will "liberate society from outdated customs and those inherited from colonialism, especially tribalism, nepotism and regionalism." The programme of the Somali Revolutionary Socialist Party, as well as sub-constitutional legislation, continues the attack – the Party struggles, *inter alia*, "to transform the old and reactionary traditional structures based upon tribalism and to form a democratic government belonging to all the peoples." Tribalism is declared to be "the number one enemy of the Somali society and the revolution."

Ghana's Provisional National Defence Council Law 42 includes in its "directive principles of state policy": "a spirit of loyalty to Ghana overriding sectional, ethnic or other loyalties, is to be cultivated among the people of Ghana"; and "traditional cultural values are to be adapted and developed as an integral part of the growth and development of the society."

The constitution of the Republic of Benin (formerly Dahomey), recognizes the polyethnic nature of the country but emphasizes national unity. Article 3:

The Popular Republic of Benin is a multinational unified State. All nationalities are equal in rights and obligations. To consolidate and develop their union is a sacred duty for the State, which guarantees to each of them full development in unity, through a just nationalities policy and interregional equilibrium. Any act of regionalism is rigorously prohibited. All nationalities enjoy the liberty to use their spoken and written language and develop their own culture. The State actively helps the nationalities that live in less-developed localities to attain the economic and cultural level of the country in general.[9]

ASIA

The most complex of all constitutions, the Constitution of India, notably recognizes the claims of communities as well as individuals on the State. The constitution combines provisions on equality with principles designed to protect and consolidate the identity and integrity of groups. Elements of positive discrimination for certain groups are present – "for the advancement of. . . socially and educationally backward classes of citizens or for the scheduled castes and scheduled tribes." Equality for these groups means actual and not mere formal equality. For group indentity, Article 29(1) of the constitution provides that "any section of the citizens residing in the territory of India . . . having a distinct language, script, or culture of its own shall have the right to conserve the same." Whereas Article 29 refers to citizens, Article 30(1) describes minorities: "All minorities, whether based on religion or language, shall have the right to establish and administer educational institutions of their choice." This tolerance provision is fortified by the second paragraph of the article, which establishes in effect the minorities' rights to State support in the granting of aid to educational institutions. Article 350A provides that it is the goal of every State and local authority "to provide adequate facilities for instruction in the mother tongue at the primary stage of education to children belonging to minority groups." Linguistic group rights in the constitution are balanced against the general direction of State policy, which decrees that the official language of the union shall be Hindi in the Devanagari script; also "it shall be the duty of the Union to promote the spread of the Hindi language, to develop it so that it may serve as a medium of expression for all elements of the composite culture of India. . . ." Broad guarantees are also provided in relation to religion, as well as extensive sections devoted to scheduled castes and scheduled tribes.

Whereas, despite the preponderance of Hindus in India, the State is officially secular, the constitution of India's neighbour, Pakistan, proclaims the State religion as Islam – Article 2. The preamble to the constitution describes Pakistan as a "democratic state based on Islamic principles of social justice." Article 222 does not commence in a very promising way for non-Muslims: "All existing law should be brought into conformity with the injunctions of Islam. . . ." However, the rest of the article recites that "nothing in this part shall affect the personal laws of non-Moslem citizens or their status as citizens." Pakistan, like many Middle Eastern and Asian States – including those within the realm of Islam – is not governed entirely by principles of legal territoriality, but also by the principle of personality: members of religious groups may be legally subject to the demands and benefits of their religion as well as to State law in general.[10] Other articles of the Constitution deal positively with minorities and their rights, which include in this case due representation in the federal and provincial services and provincial and national assemblies. Rights are for individuals as well as religious communities, which have the right to organize and establish educational institutions. Linguistic as well as religious minorities are catered for. Thus Article 28 recites the right of "any section of the citizens speaking in a distinct language, script or culture. . . to preserve and promote the same and, subject to law, establish institutions for that purpose." Despite a much more Draconian approach to non-Muslim religious minorities in Bangladesh, the validity of religious laws and customs of religious minorities has been recognized by the government in such matters as personal and family laws.

A perhaps surprising example of this kind of relationship is to be found in Israel, which retains the former Turkish millet system, whereby the leadership of religious communities is responsible to the government for these communities. Religious laws of members of a recognized community govern in matters of personal status, defined in Article 51 of the Palestine Order in Council as suits regarding "marriage or divorce, alimony, maintenance, guardianship, legitimation of minors, inhibition from dealing with property of persons where legally incompetent, succession, wills and legacies, and the administration of the property of absent persons." Israeli law reflects a certain tension between territorial law and personal law, and Israel has extended the application of territorial law to some matters of personal status.

WESTERN EUROPE

A large variety of arrangements specific to minorities are found in Europe. Forms of autonomy (enhanced self-rule falling short of independence) or home rule, separate representation, federalism, and distinct cultural, religious, and linguistic rights exist in different countries. Forms of minority representation in the State include separate electoral rolls and communal voting, proportional representation systems, power sharing in the executive government, regional devolution, and other devices.[11] Most of these forms reflect an impulse to recognize or support diverse traditions within the State. Some are backed by international treaties to benefit specific groups; some are not. The effect is to dilute the concept of the homogeneous nation-state. It is somewhat ironic that so many exceptions to this concept are found in Europe, crucible of nation-state doctrines.

A range of differential human rights is displayed in such constitutions. Belgium represents an extraordinary example of such differentiation in the constitution, recognizing linguistic communities and regions.[12] The whole intention of the division into Flemish-, French-, and German-language communities in the Belgian scheme is to maintain cultural distinctiveness even at the expense of individual choice. In Belgium, the territorial principle is dominant – the principle that an individual's rights depend not altogether on preferences but upon geographic location. The equilibrium between the linguistic groups is maintained from the level of the Belgian cabinet down to the local and communal level, and affects commerce as much as education. The effect of this complicated bifurcation of rights and responsibilities is that each linguistic community is treated as a corporate entity with its own or collective rights. The interests of individuals are mediated through the community to which they belong, and group rights exist to complement individual rights or to compete with them. This is some distance from the model of the Universal Declaration.

The Cyprus arrangements represented an attempt to cope with majority/minority arrangements through the recognition of a group dimension.[13] In this case, the constitutional arrangements were backed up by international treaties and did not endure. The constitution was engineered on a pragmatic basis. The community principle was applied in a thorough-going way. Article 1 of the basic structure of the Republic of Cyprus initiated the community motif: "The State of Cyprus shall be a republic with a presidential regime, the president being Greek and the vice-president Turkish, elected by universal suffrage by the Greek and the Turkish communities of the island respectively." The House of Representatives exercised "authority in all matters other than those expressly reserved for the communal chambers." The communal chambers exercised authority "in all religious, educational, cultural and teaching questions and questions of personal status." In the judicial system, civil disputes relating to questions of personal status and religious matters that were reserved for the competence of the communal chambers were dealt with by tribunals "composed solely of judges belonging to the community concerned." Voters were registered in separate Greek and Turkish electoral rolls. In the House of Representatives, separate majorities were required for measures imposing duties and taxes. Divisions extended to the level of the local commune. Rights and duties were also in this case assigned to communities as such.

Less far-reaching arrangements in other States may nonetheless involve some sacrifice on the part of individuals, in that rights may vary on territorial or personal criteria. Spain is a nation that shows a recent development from centralism to wide-ranging recognition of minority groups. Unity and autonomy are both expressed as desiderata in the Spanish Constitution of 1978: "The Constitution is based on the indissoluble unity of the Spanish nation, the common and indivisible country of all Spaniards, and recognizes and guarantees the right to self-government of nationalities and regions of which it is composed and solidarity amongst them all" (Article 2). Article 3(1) provides that Castilian is the official language of the State, but "the other languages of Spain shall also be official in the respective self-governing communities in accordances with their statutes." Article 3(3) expresses a theorem that many have tried to argue in relation to minorities; that they consolidate rather than threaten the nation: "The wealth of the different language variations of Spain is a cultural heritage which shall be the object of special respect and protection." Article 143 states the general framework and motivation of the Spanish system: "In the exercise of the right to self-government recognized in Article 2 of the Constitution, bordering provinces with common historic, cultural and economic characteristics, island territories and provinces with historic regional status may accede to self-government and form self-governing communities. . ." in accordance with constitutional provisions. Article 148 provides that the self-governing communities may exercise a broad range of functions within their territorial bases, including cultural and linguistic matters. The State as a whole permits cultural collaboration between the communities. The elaboration of these provisions rests on specific autonomy statutes, including those for the Basque country (Euskadi) and Catalonia.

Italy is another country with a centralist tradition that, since World War II, has sought to effectuate constitutional requirements towards the recognition of particular groups. Article 5 of the constitution describes a "Republic. . .one and indivisible. . . ." It is nonetheless a republic that "shall recognize and promote local autonomy" and "shall bring about the widest administrative decentralization in the services of the State, and adapt the principles and procedures of the legislation to the requirements of autonomy and decentralization." It is thus in concept a unitary republic with substantial devolution. Article 6 provides that "the Republic safeguards linguistic minorities by means of special provisions." Article 116 recognizes regional autonomy in accordance with special statutes for Sardinia, Trentino-Alto Adige, Friuli-Venezia Giulia, Valle d'Aosta, and Sicily: all regions with some claim to ethnic particularism. The general background is, once more, a broad Rights of Man constitution. Ethnic identity in some of the regions becomes at least as important as membership of the wider Italian community. In the case of the South Tyrol, following some further autonomy revisions, identity governs which school a child attends, access to employment in public administration, housing, and qualifications for those standing for elections. An official declaration of ethnic group membership determines the relevance of much legislation to individuals. The homogeneous nation is individuated into regional particularisms with reference to underlying ethnic factors.

The Swedish/Finnish agreement of 1921 relating to the Aaland Islands was a stage in elaborating a system of protection for the Swedish-speaking inhabitants of the Aaland Islands that some have considered to be – along with the general treatment of Swedes in Finland – "the best treatment of a minority group by a host nation anywhere in the world."[14] Under the Aaland Autonomy Act, the Swedish character of the islands is maintained through regulations on language, education, regional citizenship, and the acquisition of property on the island.

The provisions in education result in the situation that a Finnish-speaking child (and Aaland *is* Finland) requires the consent of the local commune before he/she may be taught Finnish. On land acquisition, five years' unbroken residence in the province of Aaland gives general regional citizenship, which is a prerequisite for land acquisition and voting. Special repurchasing rights are also given to those with regional citizenship against those who have not. There is something more than individualism in these arrangements: in a non-European context, such provisions as are contained in the Aaland statute might well be caricatured as a form of apartheid. With respect to the general theory of human rights, we may say that "the individual and collective rights of the islanders are balanced against the rights of other Finnish citizens to equal treatment." [15] Another way of stating the factors is that the equality/non-discrimination aspects of human rights give way to a pragmatic resolution that involves virtual self-determination for a minority group.

European examples of forms of separate representation of ethnic and linguistic groups can be multiplied. Little of this freedom is reflected in the provisions of the European Convention on Human Rights, in which the only reference to minorities is that contained in Article 14, which prohibits discrimination on grounds of, *inter alia*, "association with a national minority. . . ." There is nothing in this convention that inscribes any kind of positive recognition to minorities; efforts to insert more positive provisions that would be fully in keeping with European experience have come to nothing. In a case brought before the European Court of Human Rights in 1968 relating to certain aspects of the laws on the use of languages in education in Belgium, the Belgian linguistic territorial distinctions were found mostly not to violate the article since they were based on the public interest and strike a fair balance between the protection of the interests of the community and respect for the rights and freedoms of individuals.

SOCIALIST COUNTRIES

Socialist constitutions also have a marked tendency to recognize the constituent elements of the nation. Article 36 of the 1977 constitution of the USSR provides that "citizens of the USSR of different races and nationalities have equal rights." The article describes a policy for the nationalities: the exercise of their rights "is ensured by a policy of all round development and drawing together of all the nations and nationalities of the USSR." Article 2 provides the right of each union republic "freely to secede from the USSR." Soviet legal theory regards the republics as subjects of international law – they have sovereign rights (Article 81). Of course, as both Lenin and Stalin warned, the existence of a right is one thing, its exercise is another, and the exercise of self-determination may be counter-revolutionary (see chap. 2). The Soviet legal system was put to a severe test early in 1990 when the Republic of Lithuania declared its independence, a unilateral decision not recognized by the Soviet government. So in practice, the constituent elements of the USSR remain in place.[16]

The 1982 constitution of the Peoples Republic of China displays some similar features. Again, the people of all the nationalities of China are invoked as creators of a glorious revolutionary tradition (preamble). The State is not federal, like the USSR, but a "unitary multinational" State. Big-nation chauvinism and little-nation chauvinism are equally condemned. The instigation of secession in this case is prohibited (Article 41) – citizens have a duty to safeguard national unity (Article 52). There are extensive and generous provisions on official use of minority languages – though the State council is empowered to promote the official common language. Minority nationalities are entitled to appropriate representation (Article 59) in the Peoples' Congress. The general State structure also affords minority representation, and general laws may, within limits, be tailored to meet local requirements (Article 99). National regional autonomy is the structural key in the Chinese case. The constitutional provisions are given detailed implementation in the Law on Regional Autonomy for Minority Nationalities of the PRC, 1984, the preamble of which commences: "The PRC is a unified and multinational country jointly founded by people of various nationalities. . . . Regional autonomy for minority nationalities is a basic policy of the CCP (Chinese Communist Party) for solving the problems of nationalities on the basis of Marxism-Leninism. . . ." But the model is one of diversity, influenced by ideology, and the effort to address minority issues is conscious, not accidental. This appears to be true of other socialist States; Yugoslavia is an outstanding example.

CONCLUSION

Minority rights as a legal and political concept are at the juncture between individual and collective rights. While some authors believe that there is a fundamental contradiction between individual and collective rights, others consider that there is no such fundamental contradiction; that both types of rights can and in fact in many countries, as we have seen, do coexist. Even the most liberal countries, where emphasis is placed squarely on the individual regardless of racial, linguistic, or ethnic factors, allowance has been made in the legal system for minority rights, as Vernon van Dyke has so aptly shown.[17] Another author has usefully summarized what he calls, perhaps a bit ambitiously, a "provisional theory of minoriy rights":

1. Minority rights are group rights. They may be claimed by an individual, but they are asserted as a result of membership in a group that seeks a measure of differential treatment distinct from the majority of the population. Equal treatment is not the basis of the rights.

2. Minority rights may include individual rights, as in the well-recognized principle of nondiscrimination to be found in most of the world's constitutions and in the basic United Nations documents. . . .

3. Multicultural societies must, at least, consider whether they have significant groups that are effectively treated as minorities and should develop some principled basis for the recognition of the legitimacy of minority group status. . . .

4. Minority rights include the idea that individuals should be free to remain in the minority group or, if able, to leave it voluntarily. . . .

5. Minority rights should not be compulsory or a pretext for discrimination. . . .

6. A failure of multicultural societies to recognize the existence of a substantial minority is a denial of minority rights. . . .

7. Under conditions of extreme deprivation, minority rights justify special treatment and advantages for groups victimized by persistent prejudice.

8. Minority rights include rights to political representation and to social and economic justice.

9. Minority rights do not include the right to revolution and secession except upon the same basis as do individual rights. . . .[18]

11

Educational and Cultural Issues

Among the principal problems facing ethnic minorities and indigenous peoples in the world is the question of educational and cultural policies by governments. Traditionally, in most nation-states, such policies intend to promote the assimilation of ethnic minorities into the dominant ethnic model, but some countries have faced the difficulties involved by designing policies to accommodate the needs of different ethnic groups. The first issue, of course, is language. Linguistic minorities (in India, Spain, Belgium, Canada, and countless other countries) demand respect and status for their languages, which are an essential element in the maintenance of ethnic and cultural identity. This requires adequate solutions to questions such as the official or legal status of a minority language, the language or languages used in schools and other educational institutions, as well as in the mass media. These issues have led to countless projects of bilingual and multilingual education in multi-ethnic States, involving numerous complexities regarding educational techniques and human and financial resources. Such projects also face serious social and political problems when, for example, two linguistic groups in a territory do not agree on a common solution (for example the reaction of anglophones in Quebec to the policy of francophone schooling, or the WASP backlash against bilingual education in the United States).

An even more complex issue relates to cultural policies by governments in relation to ethnic minorities. It is claimed that education should not only be bilingual, but also intercultural; that is, that minority cultures should receive their due place not only in the educational system but also in the image or model of the "national culture." This viewpoint is not often accepted by the governing élites, particularly in the younger third world States whose purpose is to promote "national integration and unity" and who may feel that strengthening minority cultures creates obstacles to such an aim, and moreover may further political demands for autonomy or even secession. A similar position is

142

held by governments in certain countries that have been formed by successive historical waves of immigrants from different parts of the world and that insist on the assimilation or "melting-pot" model that requires immigrants to divest themselves of their original cultures and adapt to the dominant language and cultural model. Still, there are numerous examples of government policies that do attempt to deal adequately and equitably with the conflicting needs and demands of majority and minority ethnic groups.

Among the specialized organizations of the United Nations system, it is Unesco that has the responsibility for furthering culture and education. Unesco has developed activities in the field of cultural rights and cultural policies, on the basis of the mandate of its constitution and the Universal Declaration of Human Rights. The latter recognizes the "right to culture" in several places, as when it explicitly states that everyone, as a member of society, is entitled to cultural rights (Art. 22); everyone has the right to freely participate in the cultural life of the community (Art. 27). Furthermore, Article 15 of the International Covenant of Economic, Social, and Cultural Rights recognizes the right of everyone to take part in cultural life.

In 1968, Unesco organized an international meeting of experts that discussed these problems and that produced a Statement on Cultural Rights as Human Rights, one of whose conclusions was

6. One of the characteristics of our contemporary world is the domination of men by strong centralized nation-states which have the power to increase cultural uniformity and homogeneity within their borders and outside. While such cultural uniformity and homogeneity is understandable from the point of view of the political and economic interests of the ruling groups of such societies, means have to be found to mobilize those cultural traditions, the richness of which can provide people with a sense of belonging to coherent groups and which can contribute to the development of a sense of personal identity in the face of forces which often tend to alienate or estrange men from the organized centres of power. While most of us may agree with this article of faith – that elements of traditional culture should not be lost and means should be found to clarify their relevance – it is probably a task for the future to deal with these problems systematically and concretely.[1]

The language used by the Unesco experts expresses their lack of conviction that such an objective was attainable at all. In general, Unesco documents emphasize the need to develop culture, the right of all peoples to their culture, the desirability of furthering cultural identity. But usually these terms refer to "national" cultures, and very little attention has been paid to national subcultures or to the cultures of ethnic minorities within State boundaries. A 1970 intergovernmental conference on cultural policies recognized that in States in which a federal structure prevails, cultural autonomy is accepted as a guiding principle; it also expressed its apprehension at the fate of indigenous cultures around the world and recommended that local cultures be maintained and protected. The European regional conference on cultural policies held in 1972 made scant reference to national and immigrant minorities in European countries. The Asian regional conference of 1973 emphasized the development of national cultures and identities and considered that "subcultures" or "cultural survivals" were a hindrance to the development of national cultures. A similar tendency prevailed at the African regional conference held in 1975, at which national unity and national integration, as well as respect for the African personality, were underlined. But here concern was expressed about popular and traditional cultures, oral traditions, non-written languages, and cultural pluralism.

The Latin American regional conference was held in Bogotá in 1978; here the lack of attention paid to Latin America's indigenous cultures is really astounding. The indigenous cultures were mentioned only once, in relation to the cultural pluralism that intervened in the make-up of Latin American societies. The final declaration of the conference makes no mention at all of indigenous languages or specific cultural policies for Latin America's Indians.

Eighteen years after the original world conference on cultural policies, Unesco organized another such conference (known as MONDIACULT in Unescoese) in 1982. Here there were slightly more references to the cultural rights and needs of cultural minorities. In the final declaration, no specific reference is made to ethnic minorities, except that inequalities resulting from membership in ethnic minorities or in other groups that may hinder full participation in cultural development is frowned upon (point 22). And point 33: national languages must be furthered as vehicles of knowledge. In contrast with the first world conference held 12 years earlier, this Unesco meeting did reflect a changing awareness about cultural diversity, the right to be different, the importance of local, native, and vernacular cultures, the respect of minorities; but in general, as in previous conferences, and as behooves meetings of government delegates, priority was given to the national interests and cultural policies of States.

In Europe, the Council of Europe has sponsored several international meetings at which the cultural problems of minority ethnic groups have been dealt with. The special problems of territorial minorities as well as immigrants have been given attention, most recently at a meeting of experts held in 1986 under the auspices of the European Parliament. A proposed charter of regional languages and cultures and a charter of rights of minorities are still in the form of a project. European ministerial conferences on culture have also taken place regularly, but here again the cultures of minorities are only given lip-service, whereas the principal objective seems to be intercultural communication and the development of a unified European culture.[2]

Governments have developed various kinds of cultural policies, and sometimes these policies deal with ethnic minorities; frequently, however, they ignore them altogether. In the framework of its activities related to world culture, Unesco has published a series of country reports on cultural policies, based principally on government documents. These reports are rather representative of the status of cultural policies around the world. A comparative analysis shows the way different countries deal with their minority cultures. Some countries do not address the question of minorities directly, but allow for a certain amount of regional decentralization in the formulation and execution of cultural policies. This is the case of France and the United Kingdom, for example. In Italy and Spain, regional autonomy has been granted in some cases, whereas in the Federal Republic of Germany and Switzerland, a federal solution has been adopted.

In Belgium, where linguistic conflict exists between Flemish and Walloons, cultural policy is the domain of two distinct ministries for cultural affairs, one each for each linguistic community. A dual administrative structure in cultural affairs also exists in Czechoslovakia (Czechs and Slovaks) and in Canada (anglophone Canada and Quebec).

The United States report, in contrast, makes no mention at all of the Hispanic populations, nor of the native American Indians, and just barely touches upon the cultural contributions of blacks (jazz. . .). Japan does not report on its own minorities either (Ainu, Koreans). Algeria emphasizes the importance of Islam and the process of Arabization within its cultural revolution, without even mentioning the Kabyl ethnic group, and deals with the Berbers as belonging to the pre-Muslim period that has now been overcome. Bulgaria, in turn, does not mention its Greek and Turkish minorities, despite that the ethnic problems that have arisen in relation with these minorities have produced conflicts with Bulgaria's neighbours.

The Latin American reports hardly refer to Latin America's Indian peoples, except as something out of the past (museums, folklore), and only a few countries (Mexico, Ecuador, Peru) report on current *indigenista* educational and cultural policies and the existence of several Indian languages.

As we have seen in chapter 4, this situation is changing in Latin America, and the recognition of the cultural rights of indigenous peoples has slowly entered into the national consciousness, and therefore, into cultural and educational legislation and policies over the last few years.

An interesting example is provided by Mexico, a country in which the majority population speaks Spanish and can be identified culturally as mestizo but where around 15 per cent of the population belongs to 56 different Indian or indigenous ethnic groups that trace their descent from the original inhabitants of pre-Hispanic times and that maintain to greater or lesser degree their languages and cultures distinct from the official or national models.

The Mexican government has dealt with the linguistic diversity of the population in various ways over the years. In colonial times, the Catholic missionaries used the native languages to convert the population to Christianity. But, on the other hand, Spanish was recognized and used as the language of empire. In the nineteenth century, the independent Republic of Mexico abolished all legal distinctions between Indians and non-Indians. All Mexicans were considered equal before the law and Indians were not to be discriminated against nor to receive any special privileges. Schooling was carried out in Spanish only and the Indian languages were considered a nuisance.

The Mexican social revolution of 1910–1917 put the Indians back squarely into the limelight. The new social policies were designed to raise the standard of living of the peasants, a large majority of whom were Indians. This was to be achieved through two principal means: land reform and education. Government policy towards the Indian groups was a policy of assimilation and incorporation. The official ideology considered that the Indian communities represented backward social and economic conditions and that development implied their becoming full-fledged members of the national society. In doing so, they would have to abandon their Indian ethnic cultural characteristics, including their native language, and acquire what is officially called national culture. National culture, of course, is mainly of Spanish origin, though it has incorporated many originally Indian elements over the centuries. And the national culture has a single national language, which is Spanish. Thus, Hispanicization of the Indian groups became the mainstay of the Mexican government's policy *vis-à-vis* the Indian populations.

Educational policy in Mexico is the responsibility of the federal government, and its main instrument is the Ministry of Education. Since the early years after the revolution, the Ministry set up a special Department of Indian Affairs, which has been reorganized on several occasions and is now called Department of Indian Education.

As late as the 1920s, the Indian population in Mexico was almost totally illiterate. The non-Indian population, particularly in the rural areas, was only slightly more literate. None of the Indian languages had a written standard. To be sure, ancient Maya and Nahuatl had scripts, but these did not survive the Spanish conquest. The grammars and dictionaries of Indian languages prepared by the early missionaries were forgotten. A few select scholars "cultivated" Maya or Nahuatl, using Latin script, but the mother tongues of the Indian groups were all non-written languages. Literacy in Spanish was the privilege of only a handful of persons in some of the Indian communities.

In the early 1940s, the government launched a vast adult literacy campaign that managed to reduce illiteracy from over 60 per cent to less than 30 per cent according to official statistics. But it was carried out almost exclusively in Spanish and its impact on the Indian communities was slight. By the 1970s, illiteracy had again become a national problem. It had grown anew over the intervening period because the national school system had not been able to keep up with rapid population growth and because so many rural areas had simply not been covered by the massive educational effort launched by the federal government in the 1920s and 1930s and kept up over the years. Thus, in the mid-1970s, another literacy campaign was carried out that, by latest counts, has been able to reduce illiteracy to around 15 per cent in 1980. It is difficult to assess the impact of this latest campaign on the Indian groups, because available statistics are not broken down by ethnic group, but it would be safe to guess that again the main progress has probably taken place in the urban and non-Indian areas.

Indianist educational policy has not been concerned so much with adult literacy as with schooling at the primary level. It is here that different objectives, policies, and methods have been applied over the years and that lively debates among scholars and officials have taken place. In the 1920s, the federal government initiated a massive effort to enlarge the educational system by establishing schools in hitherto isolated rural areas. For the first time, backward, long-forgotten villages were incorporated into the school network. Hastily trained teachers were sent out into the backwoods, and children in the rural areas were able to learn their three R's. Many monolingual Indian communities received their first contact with the national school system at that time. But the prevailing ideology considered that "being an Indian" was an obstacle to progress and "civilization." School was taught in Spanish, and it was hoped that the Indians would soon learn the "national language," become fully integrated into "national" society, and forget their "backward" customs and manners. The use of the native mother tongue in schools was strictly forbidden. Teachers were sent into the villages from the outside, to transmit the "new" way of life and the "benefits of civilization and culture." Children who spoke their own language in school were considered offenders and punished. They were taught to feel ashamed of their own culture and to despise it. The brighter Indian students were taken out of their communities and sent to boarding schools and special institutions in the cities, where they were expected to become fully "integrated." Many of them, of course, did become so integrated or acculturated to urban ways that they never returned home.

The mediocre results of this policy, and the negligible impact that such schooling had on the community, soon became apparent. By the 1930s, a number of voices were raised, demanding a bilingual education and the respect of local cultures and values. A small number of pilot projects in Indian areas were set up, under the supervision of linguists and anthropologists, to test the new ideas about bilingual education and literacy in the native language. The government invited a United States-based Protestant missionary organization, the Summer Institute of Linguistics, to come to Mexico and help with this effort. The institute had some previous experience in developing scripts for non-written languages and methods for teaching reading and writing to adults in these languages. Though over the years the institute did provide technical assistance in these matters and produced a considerable amount of specialized knowledge about Mexico's Indian languages, it was mainly concerned with missionary activity and encountered increasing resistance among many Indian communities and other groups of Mexican society (including teachers and social scientists who accused the institute of serving foreign political interests). In

1980 the Mexican government officially severed its relationship with the SIL, but did not expel it or prohibit its private activities, as has happened in many other countries.

During the 1940s and 1950s, a small number of devoted linguists and teachers continued working on the unwritten Indian languages, but official interest in these questions waned, and not much progress was achieved.

Indian education, as it were, consisted in the continued expansion of the national rural school system to the Indian areas. Teaching programmes were identical all over the country, regardless of regional or urban-rural cultural differences. All teaching was carried out in Spanish.

Textbooks and programme content were highly biased in favour of middle-class urban outlooks. Those who questioned the wisdom of this approach were answered that it was contrary to a nationalist and democratic viewpoint to establish differential education and that, if some areas or ethnic groups were culturally or economically backward, the national school system would simply have to make an additional effort in order to "raise" the standards of the rural and particularly the Indian population to what was considered to be the national norm.

Among the small groups of specialists who were concerned with Indian education in governmental institutions, serious discussions took place during the 1950s. On the one hand were those who argued that the only way to introduce Spanish as the national vehicular language into the Indian communities was to teach it directly in the same fashion as it was taught in Spanish-speaking environments, and to teach all subjects in Spanish as well. This was the traditional method, and to date many educators still adhere to it. On the other hand were those who felt that this method could not be successful in an environment where the mother tongue was not Spanish, and they argued for other methods whereby Spanish would be taught as a second language in primary school and even to pre-school children. Several such methods for teaching Spanish as a second language were tried in a number of pilot projects around the country. This meant preparing primers and training the right kind of personnel. It was felt that the regular subjects of elementary schools could only be taught in Spanish once literacy in this language had been acquired by the Indian school children.

Still another group of experts maintained the earlier arguments in favour of a bilingual education. They considered that literacy, to be successful and meaningful to the children, should be carried out in the native language. Only after the children had mastered the techniques of reading and writing in their mother tongue should Spanish be introduced as a subject in itself and be used as the language of teaching all other subjects. The end objective, of course, was still the Hispanicization of the Indian school children; literacy in the mother tongue was considered only as a necessary stepping-stone towards this end.

The two basic methods of alphabetization competed with each other for several years. Each method had its supporters among specialists as well as in official institutions. The main handicap to the rapid extension of the second method (literacy first in the native language) was the lack of trained teachers competent in each one of the Indian languages and the lack of teaching materials in these languages. Therefore, this method, while gradually becoming accepted by officials responsible for Indian education, made only little headway in the 1950s and early 1960s.

Still, efforts were finally being made to train as teachers young men and women from the Indian communities who had at least completed primary schooling themselves or who, in a few exceptional cases, had been to secondary school or teachers' college. They had the difficult task, with the help of some linguists, of preparing primers in their own tongues, teaching reading and writing in the mother tongue, teaching Spanish as a second language simultaneously, and, to boot, imparting the basic subjects (natural sciences, arithmetic, history) either in the native language or in Spanish on the basis of the only existing officially provided school textbooks in Spanish.

Obviously, such efforts could not make an impact on the Indian communities unless backed by massive and sustained support by the federal government. This finally became forthcoming in the middle 1960s. The principle of early literacy in the native language plus the teaching of Spanish as a second language became the official policy, and the training of teachers from the Indian communities became the highest priority of the Indian education programme.

By the middle of the decade of the seventies, a highly vocal, well-organized group of what became known as "bilingual teachers" from the various Indian ethnic groups had become integrated into the federal school system and was on the federal payroll. Their number increased from a handful in the 1950s to several thousand at the beginning of the 1980s. Most if not all of the over 50 Indian groups now have trained school teachers who are able to teach up to at least the third year of elementary school in the Indian language; primers exist in all of the Indian languages, and the official primary school textbooks (produced and distributed by the government at no cost to the students) are gradually being translated into all of these languages and adapted to local cultural contexts. For this purpose, a master's programme for the training of ethnolinguists from the Indian groups was begun in the late 1970s.

Gradually, the "bilingual teachers" have become aware of the wider issues involved in the apparently only technical questions of whether to teach Spanish first or later, or whether literacy should be fostered in the native tongue or in Spanish. For some years now, the bilingual teachers associations, supported by knowledgeable social scientists and public officials, have been demanding not only that the Indian languages be used in the teaching of reading and writing but also have insisted that the whole educational programme in the Indian communities should be truly bilingual and bicultural, or as is now stated, "intercultural." This means that, for the first time in the educational history of

Mexico, the Indian languages and cultures are being given due recognition in school programmes. It is hoped that all subjects during the whole of the primary school cycle will be taught in the mother tongue in those areas where this is spoken by a local majority; that Spanish will be introduced from the beginning as a second language and that the Indian students will become fully bilingual; that in all relevant subjects the local culture will be prominently dealt with (for example, local and regional history, geography, customs, traditions, ethnobiology, etc.) At the same time, at the national level, the curriculum should be organized in such a fashion that school children all over the country will become aware of the pluricultural make-up of their nation, and respect for and knowledge of the minority cultures should become a part of the national curriculum. Of course, the full Hispanicization of all minority ethnic groups is still the stated objective, but no longer to the exclusion of the minority cultures as such.

To achieve a truly intercultural educational system, at least in the core areas where the minority ethnic groups are concentrated, will be a long and complicated task, but the first important steps have been taken, and recent governmental decisions lead one to believe that bilingual and bicultural education in the Indian regions are now official policy, in contrast to the earlier policy of assimilation and integration.[3]

In contrast to Latin America, the countries of Sub-Saharan Africa do attribute great importance to the presence of multiple ethnic groups in their territories. Their main objective is to further "intertribal understanding and national unity." Due importance is given to the various national languages, traditional customs, and the oral traditional black African cultures. The great task of the recently decolonized African countries is to build a national culture on the basis of a multitude of different ethnic groups within the borders inherited from colonial times. The document prepared by Senegal for the Unesco series on cultural policies states:

It is very desirable that attention be paid, particularly in the African countries, to provide a national cultural awareness for the various ethnic groups which recently were isolated from each other, each one with its own specific cultural traditions, but who are now placed in the need of living within politically and geographically wider borders.[4]

The terms bilingualism and pluriculturalism come up frequently in the African Unesco documents, but in the background there always looms the fear of tribalism, a potentially destructive force, and the desire of liberation from the consequences of colonialism. The cultural policy carried out by Tanzania illustrates well the trends in African cultural policies:
1. Due recognition given to certain traditions and customs
2. Strengthening and conservation of the country's cultural heritage
3. The use of culture as an instrument of development and unity of the nation
4. The fusion of the various tribal cultures into a single national culture

5. The contribution of the country's culture to the progress of humanity and of other cultures to the country's own progress
6. The need to revise the educational systems inherited from the colonial powers and the need for Tanzanians to liberate themselves from the influence of colonial mentality[5]

Asian countries also pay attention to the various national languages and the building of a unified national culture, but policies vary. In its report to Unesco in 1973, Sri Lanka, for example, never even mentioned the Tamil minority; and in the eighties, Sri Lanka was in the throes of a violent ethnic conflict. Afghanistan never mentioned its minorities in its report on cultural policy in 1975; by 1982, however, perhaps as a result of changing political circumstances, Afghanistan did report to the World Conference in Mexico City that the protection and furthering of the cultures of minority ethnic groups had become a part of its cultural policy.

India has developed the most far-reaching and complicated linguistic and cultural policies of the Asian countries. In 1953, the Indian States were reorganized on a linguistic basis. As one author remarks, the reorganization of linguistic States as political and administrative units was based on the principle of reducing the conflict between the major minority-language speakers of India. But in the process, it gave a new dimension of conflict and tensions to different minority-speech communities that earlier enjoyed peaceful coexistence. The First Report of the Commissioner for Linguistic Minorities stated:

The division of States on a linguistic basis has given rise to the inevitable result that the regional language should gain prominence and should in course of time become the official language of the State. The other languages which are the mother-tongue of the minority communities living in the State, naturally do not get equal prominence or status. The result is that those whose mother-tongue is the minority language have not only a sentimental grievance but certain practical difficulties and inconveniences from which they suffer.

India developed the "Three Language Formula" as part of its linguistic educational policy, which means teaching (1) the regional language and mother tongue when the latter is different from the regional language; (2) Hindi or, in Hindi-speaking areas, another Indian language; and (3) English or any other modern European language. Still, this policy has not been able to solve all the problems of linguistic minorities. For example, in 1956 there were only 16 States in India, whereas now there are 22 States and 9 Union territories. The process of bifurcation of States has some relevance for the minorities. Maharashtra was bifurcated in 1960 into two States because of the two prominent speech communities – Gujarati and Marathi, and in 1966 Punjab was divided into Punjabi Suba and Haryana because of the conflict between two ethnic groups – Hindu and Sikh, the former adhering to Hindi and the latter to the

Punjabi language. Sikhs are primarily concentrated in Punjab, but even there they were in a minority, as is evident from the 1961 census statistics. They were in fact 33 per cent of the total population of the State. After the reorganization, the Sikh population in Punjab rose to 60 per cent, but Hindi became the minority language. In the eighties, ethnic conflict between the Sikhs and the national State had a religious and no longer a linguistic basis. In India, no State has fewer than 12 mother tongues; in fact, the mother tongues range from 123 to 410![6]

Another instructive case of language policy, which stands in direct contrast to India, is Indonesia, where 600 languages and dialects are spoken, the largest of which, such as the Javanese languages, are spoken by 50 million people, while some of the other languages are spoken by only a few hundred thousand people.

During the colonial period, the dominant language was, of course, Dutch. Second place was taken by the Malay language, which was the lingua franca in South-East Asia for more than a thousand years. The leaders of the anti-colonial struggle recognized that they would only be successful if they could be united into a single social and cultural, and especially political, force. That was the decisive meaning of the oath of the youth in Indonesia in 1928 for *one country*, *one nation*, and *one language*, all called Indonesia. It is significant that the Javanese population, consisting of about 50 million people, and the Sundanese of 25 million, gave up their languages in favour of the Indonesian national language, which was for them a foreign language. A number of sociocultural factors intervened in the establishment of another more or less foreign language as the official language of the country. Currently, pupils in Indonesian schools have to learn and utilize the Indonesian language from the first year on. If necessary, the teacher is allowed to use the local language, which helps him in his communication with his pupils. In this process, specialists foresee that the other, smaller Indonesian languages will tend to disappear, and even Javanese and Sundanese, spoken by many millions, are declining in importance, since all laws and official pronouncements, all newspapers, magazines, and books, all education from the primary school until the university are in the Indonesian language. The Javanese and Sundanese languages could well be developed into modern languages, according to scholars, but "in this phase of Indonesian social, cultural, and especially political life, which emphasizes the unity of the country and its people, such a development is out of the question."[7]

In recent years, changes in "unifying" or assimilationist national cultural policies have sometimes come about as a result of the pressures, lobbying, and political activities of the subordinate minorities. The linguistic reorganization of India was the consequence of political pressures by linguistic groups. Australia established bilingual education in its Northern Territory for the Aboriginal population as a result of long struggles by the Aboriginals for their rights. Nicaragua has constitutionally conceded autonomy to the Atlantic Coast region as a consequence of serious conflicts between the Miskito Indians and the revolutionary Sandinista government. Even officially bilingual and bicultural Canada has adopted new cultural and educational policies in the eighties regarding its indigenous and other ethnic, mainly immigrant, minorities.[8] In the United States, educational policy is formulated at the county and State (not federal) level. Some States have gone far in providing bilingual education for linguistic minorities (for example, Hispanics in the South-West), and of course Indian education is provided for in federal law. But an "anglophone" backlash has arisen that has led to "English only" educational legislation being adopted by referendum in several formerly bilingual or multilingual States. A recent court decision has overturned some of this legislation. The possibility of increasing linguistic and ethnic conflict in the United States as a result of these tendencies is not to be underestimated.

In Eastern Europe, at least up to the late eighties, cultural policy was directly related to Marxist-Leninist ideology. A new, socialist culture is the objective of State policy, according to the USSR's report to Unesco. Most socialist countries recognize the existence of national minorities (China, Viet Nam), others of "nationalities" (Ethiopia, Romania, Yugoslavia), or "Autonomous Socialist Republics or Regions" (USSR), and the new culture is considered to be socialist in content and national in form only.[9] Another common concept of the socialist period is that of the cultural revolution and the conviction that cultural progress can only take place within the framework of the revolution. In Ethiopia for example, whose government declared itself officially to be Marxist-Leninist, the different languages spoken in the country are vehicles for the dissemination of scientific socialism. The different cultures are respected to the extent that they are politically useful for the dominant group. Other countries have also developed the concept of cultural revolution, such as Cameroon, Zaire, and Bolivia (and of course China many years earlier). Among the socialist countries, only Yugoslavia seems to have developed a decentralized and "self-managed" cultural policy, without too much emphasis on a national "Yugoslav" culture; still, even here the need for the development of a national culture is politically important.[10]

In some countries, ideological centralism is taken almost to extremes, and its effects on minority cultures can be mortal. Thus, in Ethiopia:

As far as art, literature, music and theater are concerned the cultural revolution must further the creation of progressive anti-feudal and anti-imperialist works, inspired by "socialist realism" and not by the idea of "art for art's sake"; it must serve to educate the masses and raise their cultural level in order to promote the construction of socialism, of nationalism and national unity. . . . Culture is one aspect of our development which we enrich by only keeping the progressive heritage of the past. On the contrary, those elements of our cultural heritage which are not directly related to our development or which are in contradiction to it, must be placed in the museums of history.[11]

In other African countries, respect for minority cultures is officially proclaimed, despite the desire for national unity. Thus, in Cameroon, the cultural and artistic movement is expected to be committed to the ideals proclaimed by the ruling party in order to strengthen national unity, and at the same time the respect for pluriculturalism and bilingualism as a factor enriching national unity is recognized.[12]

In general, a review of Unesco's international conferences and national reports on cultural policy testifies to the fact that ethnic minorities do not appear prominently in cultural policies. They usually appear with reference to other subjects, such as cultural development in general, the equal dignity of all cultures, popular cultures, oral traditions, popular arts and traditions, or minority languages. Not one of the special Unesco conferences on cultural policies has dealt with the problem of minority cultures directly, and only a few final resolutions refer to this issue.

Cultural policies of States have only been defined as such in the last two decades by most countries, and this is partly the result of the efforts of Unesco and the Council of Europe, among other international organizations. This occurs within a context in which the problem of "cultural control" arises, as a result of the development of the mass media and the technological revolution, but also as a consequence of the multiplication of small nation-states in the world, which require a certain hierarchy of cultural priorities in which the cultural needs of ethnic minorities fade before the raison d'état.[13]

The study of cultural policies is eloquent in this respect: the cultural identities of minorities are considered mostly in terms of national identity. For the States, the question of national identity is paramount among these multiple identities. Culture and cultural identity are increasingly seen as necessary factors in the development process and the national image of countries on the international scene. Nowadays, the nation-state is the primary actor in the international system, and consequently the tendency to develop a national cultural identity is often a state-inspired and state-controlled objective. Older States wish to reinforce their cultural identity (for example, the francophone movement headed by France), whereas newer States insist upon the creation of such a national identity, or sometimes on a supra-national identity (négritude, pan-Arabism, Latin American culture, the culture of the English-speaking peoples through the Commonwealth). Thus culture, through cultural policies, becomes an instrument of national ideology. Sometimes such instrumentalization of culture reaches extreme forms, as when governments, through their cultural policies, decide which are the "good" or "bad" or the "positive" and "negative," or the "progressive" and "regressive" cultural elements that ought to be maintained or discarded. Usually, ethnic minorities have to pay the price of this hierarchization of cultural elements.

Cultural policies reflect political forces and realities. The culture of ethnic minorities depends in large measure on the political power of minorities in relation to State power. Cultural policies are cultural politics and refer back to the centralization of the State, which is not frequently questioned as such. Thus, on the one hand, we witness a strengthening of national cultures and on the other, a furthering of supra-national, regional, or world cultural identities. In this process, local and particular (ethnic, tribal, communal) cultural identities are weakened, but when endangered, they often resist and react by producing ethnic or linguistic "revivals" and "reawakenings." States and the interstate system have only recently learned to respond to such demands.

At the same time, in certain countries new cultural identities emerge as a result of international migrations (see chap. 10) that pose new challenges for the nation-state. Thus, in recent years in Europe, for example, the cultural policies are more concerned with the problems of immigrant minorities than with those of the ancient territorial minorities. In contrast to the latter, the immigrants do not pose a threat to the State's control over political and geographic space; their challenge exists at another level. In the nineteenth and early twentieth century, the problem of territorial minorities contributed to a reshaping of Europe. Nowadays, Europe seems to pay less attention to the question of territorial minorities and is more involved in the challenges posed by the new immigrant minorities, including the problems of interethnic relations, racism, and relations between States with regards to immigrants.

No matter what the particular ideology of a State might be, cultural policies appear more concerned with "national" and supra-national identities than with subnational and particular identities. Latin America is a case in point (see chap. 4). At the international level, Latin American culture is proposed as expressing a certain homogeneity that in reality does not exist. A number of Latin American countries are still seeking their own national identity but share in a common Latin American culture. At the national level, a number of States have developed specific cultural policies for their own indigenous populations, but at the international level, when area-wide cultural policies are discussed, the problems of the indigenous peoples are hardly touched upon. This ambiguity reflects the difficulties of Latin American élites to face up to their intrinsic diversity (after all, there are over 400 different indigenous groups with 30 million people in Latin America). Africa, on the other hand, recognizes the multiplicity of its ethnic cultures and languages but subsumes them under the imperative of the construction of "national identities" that result out of the artificial borders left by the colonial heritage and on a pan-African culture to be constructed in the future. Is there a contradiction in this approach?

As Coulmas states, less than 4 per cent of all peoples live within boundaries coinciding with the extension of their ethnic groups. Consequently, the populations of most countries include one or several minorities. Specialists estimate that between four to eight thousand different languages are spoken in the world, the great majority of them by very small populations, minority groups living in States dominated by speakers of more widely spoken languages, such as English, Spanish, French, Russian, Hindi, or Chinese. The linguistic composition of the world is characterized by a great disparity between number of languages and number of speakers of these languages. Nevertheless, there is hardly a state that does not have one or several linguistic minorities. In fact, monolingual States are extremely rare (for example, Iceland, Portugal, Tonga). World-wide, States where more than one language is spoken are the vast majority. There is a significant difference between "linguistic minorities" and "speakers of a minority language." The concept of "linguistic minority" refers to the relative part that the speakers of a language constitute within the total population of a country; "minority languages," in contrast, are minor languages that do not serve as standard or national languages in any country. What is the future of these languages? How do they fit into the pattern of cultural policies developed by States, which have been considered before? These are some of the unresolved issues that are being faced by many countries, particularly in the third world today.[14]

Epilogue

From the Australian Aborigines to the Welsh, from the Armenians to the Tamils, from the Ainu to the Yanomami, ethnies around the world are mobilizing and engaging in political action, sometimes in violent conflict and confrontation, to establish their identities, to defend their rights or privileges, to present their grievances, and to ensure their survival. In all likelihood, the ethnic question will not only continue but also increase in importance in the coming years.

Ethnic mobilization directly defies the fundamental concepts on which the modern nation-state has been built and therefore presents a formidable challenge to policy makers and "nation-builders." Not all States in the world have faced this question directly in their constitutions and legislations, and those that have done so continue to deal with unresolved problems that arise time and again. The world system has not yet found a satisfactory answer to the apparent contradiction that exists between a limited number of sovereign nation-states and a large number of culturally and linguistically diverse ethnies and peoples.

Ethnic mobilization may have multiple causes; in part it is a response to the problems, maladjustments, and tensions engendered by the process of economic development. In fact, unequal development is linked to the structure of internal colonialism, in which subordinate ethnic groups, often regionally localized, bear the social costs of capital accumulation and unequal exchange and are impelled to react or resist in regionalist, nationalist, or ethnic terms. The ethnocratic State provides ideological and legal cover to such processes that, under the guise of nation-building, frequently result in ethnocide. Particularly vulnerable to this situation are tribal and indigenous peoples, who are engaged in the search for alternative development models, one of which is ethnodevelopment.

Ethnic conflicts are frequently the expression of underlying social and political conflicts between classes, population segments, or interest groups within the wider society. The politicization of ethnicity is simply one form of politics, but it

157

is a form that tends to increase cleavages within a society and to harden divisions and barriers through the use of symbols and myths that openly question the ideological bases of the nation-state. In the political struggles of our times, the cross-cutting cleavages of ethnicity and social class frequently complicate the terms of social conflict and make institutional responses more difficult. The ease with which ethnic myths and symbols become powerful political instruments testifies to the strength and resilience of ethnic identities as a fundamental expression of human solidarity and societal integration. The social and economic policies of States can ignore these forces only at their own peril.

One of the myths of the contemporary world holds that in the process of development, modernization, and nation-building, ethnic identities and interests must perforce lose salience; the contrary seems rather to be the case. Assimilationist and "melting-pot" policies, while successful at times, have frequently increased tensions and provoked conflicts. In the process, serious questions of human rights violations have occurred. The universalization of individual human rights, based on the principle of non-discrimination and equality, has undoubtedly been helpful in the protection of the human rights of ethnic minorities whenever these have been violated, but not only individual human rights are involved. The question of collective rights has repeatedly been raised concerning ethnic minorities and tribal and indigenous peoples. The international system has been concerned with the protection of minorities, and the right of self-determination of peoples has also been invoked when the demands of indigenous peoples are discussed.

Governments have adopted different kinds of policies regarding ethnic groups and minorities. Such policies may range from neglect or complete denial of the existence of such minorities, through devices for assimilation and integration, to autonomy and self-government, affirmative action or preferential politics and the recognition of pluralism. Constitutional and other legal arrangements are often complemented by specific policies in the linguistic, educational, and cultural fields. The recognition and acceptance of ethnic pluralism has become a major issue of our times. It is a question of human rights, it relates to problems of peace and security, it is ingrained in the process of economic and social development, and it is directly linked to the challenge of human survival.

Since the major portions of this book were written, in 1988–1989, new ethnic conflicts have arisen and have assumed international proportions in various areas, including the Soviet Union (Baltic, Caucasus), Yugoslavia, and India (Kashmir). Ethnic conflict was the detonator of the democratic revolution in Romania. Lebanon continues to be in the throes of religious-sectarian violence, with no end in sight. So do the ethnic conflicts in the Horn and eastern Africa. Latent ethnic tensions simmer in other African States. In Western Europe, some ethnic regional movements maintain a high degree of visibility (Basques, Ulster), and racism against ethnic immigrants has become an urgent political issue in a number of countries. Québecois nationalism is re-emerging in Canada

after a period of quiescence. Structural racism and socio-ethnic cleavages also trouble the social scene in the United States. In Latin America, the social and political organizations of the indigenous peoples are challenging traditional thinking about the nature of the nation and the State.

The Sub-Commission for the Prevention of Discrimination and the Protection of Minorities of the United Nations appointed a special rapporteur to prepare a study on minority rights and another one for a study of treaties between indigenous peoples and States for possible action on these issues by that international body.

The ethnic question poses a challenge to the social sciences as well as to statesmen and policy makers. The present volume is but a modest attempt at a better understanding of a complex problématique, which is highly relevant to the prospects of the world at the end of the twentieth century.

Notes

CHAPTER 1

1. There are many difficulties involved in identifying and classifying ethnic groups that do not coincide with States. That is why specialists come up with different estimates as to their numbers. For example, are Australian Aborigines to be defined as a single people or as a number of distinct ethnic groups? Is there one Arab nation or several? Are the German-speaking peoples to be classified as one nation or as separate entities in the different countries in which they live? There is no consensus about these questions, and the answers depend more on political and ideological factors than on scientific ones.

2. See Francesco Capotorti's (special rapporteur of the Sub-Commission on Prevention of Discrimination and Protection of Minorities), *Study on the Rights of Persons*. He distinguishes two sorts of criteria in the definition and identification of minorities: the objective and the subjective. The former includes a numerical criterion and the existence of stable ethnic, religious, or linguistic characteristics. The latter has been defined as a will on the part of the members of the groups in question to preserve their own characteristics (paragraphs 566 and 567). For a careful study of the terminological complexities involved in ethnicity research, see Fred W. Riggs, ed., *Ethnicity. Concepts and Terms Used in Ethnicity Research* (Intercocta Glossary) (International Conceptual Encyclopedia for the Social Sciences: Vol. 1) (Honolulu, International Social Science Research Council, 1985).

3. See Unesco, *Delcaration on Race and Racial Prejudice*. For a collection of Unesco's earlier contributions to the question of race and racism, see Kuper, *Race, Science and Society*. For a critique of the "race" concept, see, *inter alia*, Jacquard, "La science face au racisme."

4. Cf. Breton, *Les Ethnies*.

5. This statement is disputed by some authors; see, for example, Blaut, *The National Question*.

6. See Smith, *State and Nation*. Also Asiwaju, *Partitioned Africans*.

7. See, among many others, Smith, *Nationalism in the Twentieth Century*.

8. For an analysis of third world nationalisms, see Seton-Watson, *Nations and States*;

Kedourie, *Nationalism in Africa and Asia*; Shafer, *Faces of Nationalism*; and Emerson, *From Empire to Nation*.

9. Cf. Connor, "Nation Building or Nation Destroying."

10. For a good summary of the controversy surrounding Weber's thesis and its possible application to extra-European contexts, see Eisenstadt, *The Protestant Ethic and Modernization*.

11. Cf. Weber, *The Religion of India*.

12. Bellah, *Tokugawa Religion*.

13. Sombart, *The Jews and Modern Capitalism*.

14. Léon, *La conception matérialiste*. For a more general theory on ethnic groups as "middlemen," see Bonacich, "A Theory of Middleman Minorities."

15. This has been recognized by some contemporary economists, one of whom writes: "Modern economic analysis has kept religion firmly outside the economic sphere and has thereby obscured the role it has played in the economic system." See Hirsch, *Social Limits to Growth*, 138.

16. See Stavenhagen, "Ethnodevelopment."

17. See Veiter, *Nationalitätenkonflikt und Volksgruppenrecht*.

18. On the relation between national states and ethnies in Europe see, among others, Héraud, *L'Europe des ethnies*; Petrella, *La renaissance des cultures régionales en Europe*; Minority Rights Group, *Co-existence*; and Krejci and Velimsky, *Ethnic and Political Nations in Europe*.

19. Cf. Carles Gispert and Josep Ma. Prats, *España: un estado plurinacional* (Barcelona, Editorial Blume, 1978); Bogdanor, *Devolution*.

20. Cf. Stavenhagen, *Social Classes*; Ake, *A Political Economy of Africa*.

21. Cf. Glazer and Moynihan, *Ethnicity*; Keyes, *Ethnic Change*; Anya Peterson Royce, *Ethnic Identity. Strategies of Diversity* (Bloomington, Indiana University Press, 1982); Rex, *Race and Ethnicity*.

22. Balandier, *Sociologie actuelle de l'Afrique Noire*, develops the concept of "colonial situation."

23. See Stavenhagen, "Classes, Colonialism and Acculturation"; González Casanova, "Internal Colonialism and National Development."

24. See Francis, *Interethnic Relations*, and Seton-Watson, *Nations and States*.

25. Claude, *National Minorities*; Azcárate y Flores, *League of Nations*. See also Capotorti, *Study on the Rights of Persons*.

26. See Stavenhagen, *Problems and Prospects of Multi-ethnic States*, United Nations University Annual Lecture Series no. 3 (Tokyo, United Nations University, 1986).

27. Horowitz, in chap. 1 of *Ethnic Groups*, distinguishes between ranked and unranked systems. Schermerhorn, *Comparative Ethnic Relations*, argues that ethnic pluralism and status stratification are independent variables that bear a dialectical relationship to each other – complementary rather than dichotomous (p. 261).

28. On the situation of blacks in the US, see Steinberg, *The Ethnic Myth*; Himes, *Racial Conflict*; Wilson, *The Declining Significance of Race*. For an alternative view, see Sowell, *The Economics and Politics of Race*.

29. Stavenhagen, *Social Classes*; for the chicanos in the US South-West, see Barrera, *Race and Class in the Southwest*; for Quebec, see Rioux, *La question du Québec*; and for the United Kingdom, see Hechter, *Internal Colonialism*.

30. Léon, *La conception matérialiste*. On Malaysia, see Nagata, *Malaysian Mosaic*. Cf. Shack

and Skinner, *Strangers in African Societies*.

31. The most brutal case, of course, is apartheid. But the phenomenon occurs in different parts of the world.

32. For a critical analysis of the use of ethnic categories in these two countries, see Amselle and M'Bokolo, *Au coeur de l'ethnie*.

33. See Adam and Giliomee, *Ethnic Power Mobilized*.

34. Cf. Bowser and Hunt, *Impacts of Racism*.

35. See, for example, Banton, *Racial and Ethnic Competition*.

36. Horowitz, in *Ethnic Groups*, warns against precisely this danger.

37. Isaacs, *Idols of the Tribe*.

CHAPTER 2

1. For a good sociological introduction to the origins of the modern State, see Poggi, *The Development of the Modern State*. Chapter 3 deals with the "polity of the Estates."

2. For a good introduction to this subject, see Akzin, *State and Nation*. An earlier, informative inventory is that by Hertz, *Nationality in History and Politics*.

3. Kedourie, *Nationalism*; Gellner, *Nations and Nationalism*. For a classical treatment, see Kohn, *The Idea of Nationalism*.

4. Kedourie, *Nationalism*, 68, 70.

5. See Jászi, *The Dissolution of the Habsburg Monarchy*. For a detailed historical analysis of the national question in the Habsburg monarchy, see Kann, *Das Nationalitätenproblem*.

6. Kedourie, *Nationalism*, 73.

7. Gellner, *Nations and Nationalism*, 53.

8. Ibid., 55.

9. Anderson, *Imagined Communities*, 15.

10. Anthony D. Smith, *The Ethnic Revival*.

11. Gellner, *Nations and Nationalism*, 48.

12. Smith, *The Ethnic Revival*, 133.

13. Ibid., 135

14. Anderson, *Imagined Communities*, chap. 5 *inter alia*.

15. Deutsch, *Nationalism and Social Communication*.

16. Breuilly, *Nationalism and the State*.

17. See Rothschild, *Ethnopolitics*.

18. Rothschild, *Ethnopolitics*, 2.

19. See Herod, *The Nation in the History of Marxian Thought*; Davis, *Nationalism and Socialism*; Idem, *Toward a Marxist Theory of Nationalism*; Marx and Engels, *La cuestión nacional*; Cummings, *Marx, Engels and National Movements*; Rosdolsky, *El problema de los pueblos*; Levin and Stone, "Nationalism."

20. Haupt, Lowy, and Weil, *Les marxistes*.

21. Luxemburg, *Textos sobre la cuestión nacional*; Aubet, *Rosa Luxemburg*; Lenin, *The Right of Nations*.

22. Bauer, *Die Nationalitätenfrage*; Kautsky, "Nacionalidad e internacionalidad."

23. Stalin, *Marxism*.

24. Lenin, *The Right of Nations*.
25. Connor, *The National Question*, provides an up-to-date, thoroughly documented study of the subject.
26. Davis, *Toward a Marxist Theory of Nationalism*; Amin, *Classe et nation*. For a strong Marxist argument that national struggle should be considered as a form of class struggle, see Blaut, *The National Question*.
27. M. Kim, *El pueblo soviético*; Glezerman, *Classes and Nations*; Giliov, *The Nationalities Question*; Yulian Bromley, *Major Ethnosocial Trends in the USSR* (Moscow, Progress Publishers, 1988).
28. For a critical analysis by outside observers on ethnic and national processes in the Soviet Union, see Karklins, *Ethnic Relations in the USSR*; Carrère d'Encausse, *L'Empire éclaté*; and Motyl, *Will the Non-Russians Rebel?*.

CHAPTER 3

1. On the relationships and the distinction between nationalism and Fascism, see Smith, *Nationalism in the Twentieth Century*.
2. On Western Europe, the following recent works can be usefully consulted: Elton Mayo, *The Roots of Identity*, who deals mainly with Bretons, Welsh, and Basques; Foster, *Nations Without a State*, in which a number of countries and different situations are covered; and Tiryakian and Rogowski, *New Nationalisms*, which includes theoretical discussions and a comparative analysis of contemporary nationalisms in Britain, Canada, and Spain.
3. Carrère d'Encausse, *L'Empire éclaté*; Motyl, *Will the Non-Russians Rebel?*; Dobrizheva, *The National Question*; Ruan, *Informe sobre las nacionalidades*; Gutiérrez Chong, *El destino de las minorías de China*. For a timely and well-documented volume on the national question in the Soviet Union, see Martha B. Olcott, ed., *The Soviet Multinational State. Readings and Documents* (Armonk, NY, M.E. Sharpe, Inc., 1990).
4. On minorities in the Middle East, see Esman and Rabinovich, *Ethnicity, Pluralism, and the State*, and Chabry and Chabry, *Politique et minorités*. For a discussion of Yugoslavia's nationalities' policy and situation in some other Eastern European countries, see Connor, *The National Question*.
5. Falk, *Human Rights*.
6. See Smith, *State and Nation*; Young, *The Politics of Cultural Pluralism*.
7. Okwudiba Nnoli, *Ethnic Politics in Africa* (Ibadan, Vantage Publishers, 1989) (African Association of Political Science). For a critical assessment of one such case, see Kengne Pokam, *La problématique*.
8. On this subject, see Asiwaju, *Partitioned Africans*.
9. For a critical review of the African situation, see Neuberger, *National Self-Determination*.
10. See Victor A. Olorunsola, ed., *The Politics of Cultural Sub-Nationalism in Africa* (Garden City, NY, Anchor Books, 1972).
11. See Kallen, *Ethnicity*, Nevitte and Kornberg, *Minorities*.
12. Benjamin B. Ringer and Elinor R. Lawless, *Race-Ethnicity and Society* (New York, Routledge, 1989), document the duality in the political-economic order of the

United States that has historically favoured the whites and discriminated against blacks and other non-white minorities.

13. McNeill, *Polyethnicity*.
14. Connor, *The National Question*.
15. For a pioneering analysis of this reality, see Nathan Glazer and Daniel P. Moynihan, *Beyond the Melting Pot* (Cambridge, Mass., the MIT Press, 1963). Also Michael Novak, *The Rise of the Unmeltable Ethnics* (New York, Macmillan, 1971); Richard Polenberg, *One Nation Divisible: Class, Race and Ethnicity in the United States since 1938* (Harmondsworth, Penguin, 1980).
16. Cf. Horowitz, *Ethnic Groups in Conflict*.
17. This point is made by Nnoli, *Ethnic Politics in Africa*.
18. Amin, *L'Accumulation*; Frank, *Dependent Accumulation*; Wallerstein, *The Modern World-System*, and other works by the same author.
19. Addo, *Imperialism*.
20. Cardoso and Falletto, *Dependencia*; Ake, *A Political Economy of Africa*.
21. González Casanova, "Internal Colonialism"; Stavenhagen, "Classes."
22. Blauner, *Racial Oppression*; Hechter, *Internal Colonialism*. For a reconsideration of the author's original position, see Hechter, "Internal Colonialism Revisited."
23. Smith, *The Ethnic Revival*.

CHAPTER 5

1. Asiwaju, *Partitioned Africans*.
2. Thornberry, *Minorities*.
3. Van Dyke, *Human Rights*, 6.
4. Eistenstadt, "Human Rights." Also, Jack Donnelly, *Universal Human Rights in Theory and Practice* (Ithaca, Cornell University Press, 1989).
5. Barth, *Ethnic Groups*.
6. Smith, *The Ethnic Revival*, 2. See also, by the same author, *The Ethnic Origins*.
7. Glazer and Moynihan, *Ethnicity*, 4.
8. Keyes, *Ethnic Change*, 5.
9. Bromley, *Theoretical Ethnography*, 8.
10. Brass, *Ethnic Groups*, 10–11.
11. Ibid., 9.
12. Smith, *The Ethnic Revival*, xii.
13. Anderson, *Imagined Communities*, 13.
14. See Smith, *The Ethnic Origins of Nations*.
15. Seton-Watson, *Nations and States*, 1.
16. McNeill, *Polyethnicity*.
17. Brass, *Ethnic Groups*, 3.
18. Capotorti, *The Rights of Persons*, par. 568.
19. In 1985, the Canadian member of the Sub-Commission, Jules Deschênes, submitted a slightly but not fundamentally different definition. He defines a minority as "a group of citizens of a State, constituting a numerical minority and in a non-dominant position in that State, endowed with ethnic, religious or linguistic characteristics which differ from those of the majority of the population, having a sense of solidarity

with one another, motivated, if only implicitly, by a collective will to survive and whose aim is to achieve equality with the majority in fact and in law" (UN Document E/CN.4/Sub.2/1985/31).

20. Thornberry, *Minorities*, 4.
21. Ermacora, *Der Minderheitenschutz*. See also Thornberry, *Minorities*.
22. Fei, "Ethnic Identification in China."
23. See Amselle and M'Bokolo, *Au coeur de l'ethnie*.
24. Van Dyke, *Human Rights*.
25. Tomuschat, "Status of Minorities."
26. The Convention on the Prevention and Punishment of the Crime of Genocide was adopted by the General Assembly on 9 December 1948. For a comparative analysis, see Kuper, *Genocide*; Horowitz, *Taking Lives*. For a more legal approach and an appeal for "humanitarian intervention" against genocide, see Harff, *Genocide and Human Rights*. On the genocide of the Jews, see, *inter alia*, Dawidowicz, *The War against the Jews*; Gordon, *Hitler*. On the genocide of the Armenians, see Chaliand and Ternon, *Le génocide des Arméniens*. On ethnocide, see the collective volume *De l'ethnocide* (Paris, Union Générale d'Editions, 1972); Jaulin, *La descivilizacion*; and Bonfil et al., *América Latina*.
27. See Connor, "Nation Building or Nation Destroying."
28. United Nations, *Human Rights*. See also, Thornberry, *Minorities*. The struggle for international instruments against racial discrimination has been a long one and not easy at that. At the Versailles Peace Conference in 1919, the Japanese government pleaded for a statement against racial discrimination and on the racial equality of all nations to be included in the Convenant of the League of Nations, but it was rebuffed by the Western powers, and particularly by President Wilson. See the illumination history of the policy and diplomacy of racial discrimination in Lauren, *Power and Prejudice*.
29. The "second generation" of human rights refers basically to economic, social, and cultural rights that require some kind of positive State involvement, as against the so-called "first generation" of human rights, the civil and political rights or fundamental individual liberties, which are usually invoked against the State.
30. General Assembly Resolution 637 (VII).
31. Cristescu, *Self-Determination*.
32. Gros Espiell, *El derecho a la libre determinación*.
33. Cristescu, *Self-Determination*, 31.
34. Ibid., 9.
35. Not everybody agrees that the right to self-determination should be considered a human right. For discussion of these issues, see Karl Joseph Partsch, "Les principes de base des droits de l'homme; l'autodétermination, l'égalité et la non-discrimination," in Vasak, *Les dimensions internationales des droits de l'homme*; Sieghart, *The International Law of Human Rights*; Guilhaudis, *Le droit des peuples*.
36. Cristescu, *Self-Determination*, 13, 22.
37. Casese, "The Right of Self-Determination."
38. Gros Espiell, *El derecho a la libre determinación*.
39. See Thornberry, *Minorities*, 5. For a broader discussion of these issues, see Crawford, *The Rights of Peoples*.
40. The "salt-water principle," according to which a stretch of ocean separating a metropolis from a colony gives the latter the right to exercise self-determination.

41. Obieta Chalbaud, *El derecho humano*. For a more philosophical analysis of the various facets of the idea of self-determination, see Ronen, *The Quest for Self-Determination*.
42. For a detailed study of specific applications of the right of self-determination in United Nations practice, see Gros Espiell, *El derecho a la libre determinación*.
43. See Stavenhagen, "The Indigenous Problematique."
44. Cf. Milne, *Politics*.
45. See, for example, Gellner, "Human Rights."

CHAPTER 6

1. The literature on modernization is vast. A well-known introduction within the functionalist-structuralist paradigm is Apter's *The Politics of Modernization*. An earlier, classic formulation is that of Deutsch, *Nationalism and Social Communication*. See also Rustow, *A World of Nations*.
2. A good example is provided by Blaut, *The National Question*, who reduces all kinds of "national struggles" to class struggles.
3. A valiant attempt at facilitating deep-rooted identity-driven conflict resolution has been developed by John W. Burton and his associates. See Burton, *Resolving Deep-Rooted Conflict*.
4. Rupesinghe, "Theories of Conflict Resolution."
5. Perhaps the best-known example of communal conflict in the world today is India. Though the secular Indian State stands steadfastly against manifestations of communalism, some observers consider that elements within the State frequently use communalism for political purposes. See Chandra, *Communalism in Modern India*.
6. See Brass, *Ethnic Groups*.
7. For an interesting analysis of three countries, Guyana, Malaysia, and Fiji, where ethnic conflicts and conflict management have occurred, see Milne, *Politics*.
8. See Stone, *Racial Conflict*. Though basically concerned with race relations rather than interethnic relations in general, Stone contends that "it is differences in *power*, and the dynamic change of power resources over time, that provide the key to an understanding of racial and ethnic conflict. . . " (p. 37).
9. On ethnic conflicts in unranked systems, see Horowitz, *Ethnic Groups in Conflict*. For an application of Rational Choice Theory to the field of interethnic relations, see Banton, *Racial and Ethnic Competition*. For a more formal methodological statement, see Schermerhorn, *Comparative Ethnic Relations*.
10. This is well expressed by Brass, "Ethnic Groups and the State" in Brass, *Ethnic Groups*.
11. See, *inter alia*, Kaur et al., *The Punjab Story*.
12. On the Basques, see Reinares, *Violencia y política*; on Northern Ireland, see Hadden and Boyle, "Northern Ireland: Conflict and Conflict Resolution," in Rupesinghe *Ethnic Conflict*.
13. For a good presentation of basic group identity and its expressions, see Isaacs, *Idols of the Tribe*.
14. See note 1, *supra*.
15. See Glazer and Moynihan, *Ethnicity*, Introduction, for an analysis of ethnic groups defined as interest groups.

16. See, for example, Banton, "Ethnic Groups," and the same author's *Racial and Ethnic Competition*. Also, Gordon, "Toward a General Theory of Racial and Ethnic Group Relations," Glazer and Moynihan, *Ethnicity*.

17. See Rothschild, *Ethnopolitics*. For a description of ethnopolitics in historical context in Europe, see Kloss, *Grundfragen*.

18. See chap. 9

19. Edward E. Azar, "Protracted International Conflict: Ten Propositions," writes: "The most useful unit of analysis in protracted social conflict situations is the identity group – racial, religious, ethnic, cultural and others. It is more powerful as a unit of analysis than the nation-state. The reason is that 'power' finally rests with the identity group." Cf. Azar and Burton, *International Conflict Resolution*, 31.

20. See Bonfil, *Utopía y Revolución*.

21. See Azcárate y Flores, *League of Nations*.

22. On this point, in the case of Malaysia, Nagata observes: "Obviously, there is an interplay between primordial sentiment and the more tangible requirements of the material situation. But the latter only plays upon and reworks sentiments already latently present and most dramatic effect when the issues and oppositions are sharpest." See Nagata, *Malaysian Mosaic*, 253.

23. See Haywood, *Negro Liberation*, for an early formulation. On the "new" black nationalism in the US see Cruse, *Rebellion or Revolution*, and Allen, *Black Awakening*; Robinson, *Black Marxism*; Marable, *Race, Reform and Rebellion*. For a pungent attack on black nationalists and other "ethnic chauvinists," see Patterson, *Ethnic Chauvinism*.

24. Cf. de Silva, *Managing Ethnic Tensions*; Committee for Rational Development, *Sri Lanka*; Rupesinghe, *Ethnic Conflict*; Tambiah, *Sri Lanka*.

25. See the articles on the ethnic conflict in Nicaragua by Manuel Ortega Hegg, Hazel Law Blanco, and Hans Petter Buvollen in Rupesinghe, *Ethnic Conflict*. Also, Schneider and Ohland, *Nationale Revolution*; and, for a different point of view, Dunbar Ortiz, *Indians of the Americas*. For a history of the "Miskito question," see Jenkins Molieri, *El desafío*. A balanced and objective analysis is provided by Vilas, *State, Class & Ethnicity*.

26. See Horowitz, *Ethnic Groups*; Boucher, Landis, and Arnold Clark, *Ethnic Conflict*.

CHAPTER 7

1. On the Green Revolution, see Pearse, *Seeds of Plenty*.

2. Bulgaria officially acknowledges the existence within its borders of an Islamic religious minority but refuses to recognize this same group as a Turkish ethnic or national minority.

3. Martínez Cobo, *Indigenous Populations*, par. 134.

4. Cf. Berting et al., *Human Rights*.

5. The Oxford Human Rights Institute held an international symposium on this subject in May 1987.

6. See, among others, the publications of the International Work Group for Indigenous Affairs (IWGIA), Copenhagen; Survival International, London; and Cultural Survival, Cambridge, Mass.

CHAPTER 8

1. Martínez Cobo, *Indigenous Populations*, pp. 1–2.
2. International Labour Office, *Indigenous Peoples*, p. III.
3. Ibid., 89.
4. Independent Commission on International Humanitarian Issues, *Indigenous Peoples*, 16, 17, 18.
5. Bodley, *Victims of Progress*.
6. Burger, *Report from the Frontier*, 17.
7. International Labour Conference, *Partial Revision*. Organización Internacional del Trabajo, *Convenio N⁰ 169*.
8. UN Document E/CN.4/Sub.2/1988/25. This information reflects the situation as of 1989.
9. International Labour Office, *Indigenous Peoples*, 23.
10. Unless all states that ratified Convention 107 also ratify Convention 169, there will in fact be two legally binding conventions of the ILO on indigenous and tribal peoples.
11. Martínez Cobo, *Indigenous Populations*, 28–29.
12. Margolis First, *La problemática indígena*.
13. Morse, *Aboriginal Peoples*, chap. 1.
14. Sandra Lovelace, a registered member of an Indian tribe, lost her membership according to Canadian law when she married a non-Indian. After her divorce she was refused the right to return to her tribe. The UN Human Rights Committee considered that Canada stood in violation of some of the articles of the International Covenant of Civil and Political Rights. See Sieghart, *The International Law of Human Rights*, 378.
15. Valdés, *El perfil demográfico*.
16. Cf. Stavenhagen, *Derecho indígena*.
17. Lynch, "Indigenous Rights."
18. Keyes, "Tribal Peoples," 24.
19. The Chilean government answered that it did not consider it necessary to revise the Convention, stating that in Chile there were no differences between indigenous and non-indigenous populations. Cf. International Labour Conference, *Partial Revision*, p. 4. On the discrimination against the Mapuche Indians in Chile, see Taylor, "The Mapuche Indians of Chile."
20. The United Nations University is establishing a computerized World Guide of Ethnic Minorities and Indigenous and Tribal Peoples, on the basis of existing ethnographic literature. It will take some years before the project is completed.
21. UN document E/CN.4/Sub.2/1988/25.
22. International Labour Conference, *Partial Revision*. Organización Internacional del Trabajo, *Convenio N⁰ 169*.
23. World Council of Indigenous Peoples, "Rights of Indigenous Peoples to the Earth," submission by the WCIP to the UN Working Group on Indigenous Populations, Geneva, 30 July 1985. Quoted in Burger, *Report from the Frontier*, 14.
24. Independent Commission on International Humanitarian Issues, *Indigenous Peoples*, 23.
25. Albert and Colchester, "Recent Developments."

26. Morse, "The Resolution of Land Claims," 680. See also Sanders, "Aboriginal Rights in Canada"; and Frideres, *Native Peoples in Canada*, chap. 4.
27. These issues have been thoroughly documented. Cf. Independent Commission on International Humanitarian Issues, *Indigenous Peoples*; Bodley, *Victims of Progress*; Burger, *Report from the Frontier*; various reports published by the International Work Group for Indigenous Affairs (Copenhagen), as well as by Survival International (London), and Cultural Survival (Cambridge, Mass.).
28. Independent Commission on International Humanitarian Issues, *Indigenous Peoples*, 45.
29. UN Document E/CN.4/Sub.2/1988/25.
30. Organización Internacional del Trabajo, *Convenio N° 169*.
31. For discussion of ethnicity and the military in South-East Asia, though not directly related to tribal areas, see Enloe, "When Ethnicity is Militarized." For a more general analysis of militarization and indigenous peoples, useful and illustrative reports appear in *Cultural Survival Quarterly*, vol. 11, nos. 3 and 4, 1987.
32. Lynch, "Indigenous Rights," 27.
33. Treece, *Bound in Misery and Iron*, 5.
34. Cf. Junqueira and Mindlin, *The Aripuana Park*, and Aspelin and Coelho dos Santos, *Indian Areas Threatened*.
35. Colchester, "Hydropower Projects in Central India," 23.
36. Personal communication by Smitu Kothari.
37. Anti-Slavery Society, *The Philippines*.
38. Paine, *Dam a River*.
39. Independent Commission on International Humanitarian Issues, *Indigenous Peoples*, 58.
40. World Bank, *Tribal Peoples*.
41. Treece, *Bound in Misery and Iron*, p. 30, considers that the World Bank's expressions of concern over tribal areas are "mere rhetoric, a cynical exercise in public relations intended as a cloak for the Bank's real policy. . . ."
42. Anti-Slavery Society, *The Chittagong Hill Tracts*. 27.
43. Survival International, *Genocide in Bangladesh*, 7.
44. Cf. Survival International, "Tribals in Indonesia," 1, and Suter, *West Irian*. See also Cultural Survival, *East Timor*.
45. Cf. Smith, *The Ethnic Revival*.
46. See, for example, Calvet, *La guerre des langues*; Laponce, *Languages*; Tortosa, *Política lingüística*; Aguirre Beltrán, *Lenguas vernáculas*.
47. Cf. Münzel, *The Aché Indians*, and by the same author, *The Aché*.
48. Martínez Cobo, *Indigenous Populations*, par. 121.
49. Ibid., pars. 122–123.
50. Ibid.
51. UN Document E/Cn.4/Sub.2/1988/25.
52. Argentina, Brazil, Guatemala, Nicaragua, Peru, among others. Cf. Stavenhagen, *Derecho indígena*.
53. Martínez Cobo, *Indigenous Populations*, pars. 89, 90.
54. Stoll, *Fishers of Men*; Hvalkof and Aaby, *Is God an American?*
55. See, for example, *Cultural Survival Quarterly*, vol. 6, no. 3 (Summer 1982).
56. UN Document E/Cn.4/Sub.2/1988/25, Article 8.

57. Martínez Cobo, *Indigenous Populations*, par. 134.
58. Ibid., par. 155.
59. Cf. Stavenhagen, *Derecho indígena*.
60. Resolution No. 20, reproduced in Ibid., p. 113.
61. Cf. Deloria and Lytle, *American Indians*.
62. Cf. Berger, *Village Journey*.
63. Frideres, Native peoples in Canada, p. 79.
64. Noel Lyon, "Constitutional Issues."
65. UN Document E/Cn.4/Sub.2/1988/24/Add.1.
66. Stavenhagen, *Derecho indígena*, 57–60; Vilas, *State, Class, and Ethnicity*, 170–181.
67. Eidheim, "Indigenous Peoples." For a more general analysis of Saami rights in the Scandinavian countries and other Northern Peoples, see International Work Group for Indigenous Affairs, *Self Determination and Indigenous Peoples*.
68. Dahl, "New Political Structure," and Petersen, "Home Rule."
69. Article 1 of the International Covenant on Economic, Social and Cultural Rights and that of the International Covenant on Civil and Political Rights are identical: "All peoples have the right to self-determination. By virtue of that right they freely determine their political status and freely pursue their economic, social and cultural development."
70. Quoted *in extenso* in Dunbar Ortiz, *Indians of the Americas*.

CHAPTER 9

1. See Gunatilleke, *Migration of Asian Workers*.
2. Power, *Migrant Workers*.
3. Barre, *Les immigrés*.
4. Conseil de l'Europe, *La culture immigrée*.
5. de Wenden, *Esprit*, 255.
6. Barre, *Les immigrés*, 36.
7. "Beurs" is the word "Arab" pronounced backwards, a form of social identity among young Arab immigrants in French cities. Rastafarian, originally a resistance movement from Jamaica, now identified the world over with reggae music and certain forms of dress and hair-styling. See Barrett, *The Rastafarians*. For a case-study in a British city, see Bryce, *Endless Pressure*. For the historical background of the Rastafarians, particularly in the Caribbean, see Campbell, *Rasta and Resistance*. In March 1989, the Rastafarians became Britian's newest officially recognized ethnic minority after an industrial tribunal victory by a man who claimed he was discriminated against at a job interview because he wore dreadlocks. Britain's Commission for Racial Equality backed the case and were able to show that Rastas had a long shared history and a cultural tradition normally linked to religious observance. Thus, Britain's 15,000 Rastafarians will have the same rights as Sikhs, Jews, and Gypsies, which had earlier been denied to them (*The Independent*, 31 March 1989). Similar cultural movements among young migrants occur in other contexts, for example, the "cholos" along the Mexican-US border, but unlike the Rastas, they do not claim a distinct ethnic identity.

8. European Parliament, *Committee of Inquiry.*
9. On the role of driving myths (*mythomoteurs*) in the formation of nations, see Smith, *The Ethnic Origins of Nations.*
10. Anderson, *Imagined Communities.*
11. Breuilly, *Nationalism and the State.*
12. On European attitudes towards non-European peoples, see V.G. Kiernan, "European Attitudes to the Outside World," and Winthrop D. Jordan, "First Impressions: Initial English Confrontations with Africans," in Charles Husband, ed., *'Race' in Britain, Continuity and Change* (London, Hutchinson, 1982).
13. Cf. Power, *Migrant Workers.*
14. The split labour market involves differentials in the price of labour between different ethnic groups as a correlate of ethnic and racial discrimination. See Bonacich, "A Theory of Ethnic Antagonism," 547–559.
15. The term "race" is here put in quotation marks because it corresponds to no real or scientifically definable object; it is merely a sociological or ideological category defined at will by whoever uses it. For a good critique of some current uses of "race," see Husband, *'Race' in Britain*, Introduction.
16. See Miles, *Racism and Migrant Labor.* For a more general discussion of race and racism, see the same author's *Racism.*
17. Cf. Rex, *Race Relations.*
18. The European Parliament reports: "Xenophobia . . . is on the increase, insofar as an increase in intolerance towards certain non-Community immigrant groups can be discerned. This intolerance is displayed in different degrees of intensity towards different immigrant groups. . . . The emergence of xenophobic tendencies certainly creates a fertile breeding ground for right-wing extremism and all formations that openly favour xenophobia. . . . A new type of spectre now haunts European politics: xenophobophilia. The term suits not only those who help stir up xenophobic feelings so as to exploit them politically, but also those who, while disapproving of the emergence of xenophobic tendencies, nonetheless try to derive political gain therefrom." Cf. European Parliament, *Committee of Inquiry*, 72. Also Baker, *The New Racism.*
19. Cf. Rex, *Race Relations.*
20. For a readable report of the situation in Britain, see Cashmore, *The Logic of Racism.* Also Centre for Contemporary Cultural Studies, *The Empire Strikes Back.* For a report on the situation in Germany, see Meinhardt, *Türken raus?* For a report on the situation in France, see Oriol, *Les immigrés.*
21. On these issues, the United Nations University, in collaboration with International Alert, organized an international seminar in 1987 on the new expressions of racism in Europe, the proceedings of which were published as SIM *New Expressions of Racism.*

CHAPTER 10

1. Cf. Palley, *Constitutional Law and Minorities.*
2. The comparative analysis of the legal situation and human rights of minorities in different parts of the world was undertaken for the UNU project by Dr. Patrick

Thornberry at the request of the Minority Rights Group. A preliminary publication of this material is to be found in Thornberry, *Minorities and Human Rights Law*, from which much of the material in this chapter is taken.

3. See Stavenhagen, *Derecho indígena*. For Brazil's recent constitutional changes, see Carneiro da Cunha, "A noçao de direito costumeiro," 263–273.
4. Minority Rights Group, *Uganda and Sudan*, 4.
5. Ismagilova, *Ethnic Problems*, 188.
6. Article 4 of the Constitution of the Republic of Somalia expresses a distinction between "nation" and "State" and establishes that "the Somali nation is one and Somali nationality is indivisible." Article 16 looks forward to the unification of Somali territories "under colonial occupation" – which means in this case fellow African States.
7. On the various uses of self-determination in post-colonial Africa, see Neuberger, *National Self-Determination*.
8. Cf. Kuper, *Genocide*.
9. Author's translation from French.
10. Territorial jurisdiction means that, subject to specified exceptions, the law of the State applies to all present on a particular territory; personality implies that to a degree, individuals carry their law with them – based, for example, on their membership of a particular religious community.
11. See Palley, *Constitutional Law and Minorities*.
12. See Minority Rights Group, *The Flemings and Walloons of Belgium*.
13. Minority Rights Group, *Cyprus*.
14. See Alcock, "The Swedish Community in Finland," 8.
15. See Van Dyke, *Human Rights*.
16. See Koulitchenko et al., *L'Etat Soviétique multinational*, who states: "L'épanouissement des nations et nationalités de l' URSS est indissolublement lié à leur rapprochement; il découle, en fait, de ce rapprochement. Ces processus qui s'interpénètrent, jouent un rôle immense dans la destinée du peuple en tant que communauté historique nouvelle" (p. 368). This official position has been overwhelmed by events in the Soviet Union in 1989 and 1990. For an alternative view, see Connor, *The National Question*.
17. Van Dyke, *Human Rights*.
18. Sigler, *Minority Rights*, 195–196.

CHAPTER 11

1. Unesco, *Cultural Rights*, 106.
2. Barre, Politiques culturelles."
3. On the Mexican situation, see Stavenhagen, "Linguistic Minorities and Language Policy in Latin America: The Case of Mexico," in Florian Coulmas, ed., *Linguistic Minorities and Literacy* (Berlin, Mouton, 1984), from which the preceding paragraphs are taken.
4. Unesco, *Etudes et documents, Sénégal*.
5. Unesco, *Etudes et documents, Tanzania*.

6. Srivastava, "Literacy Education for Minorities." Also Das Gupta, "Ethnicity."
7. Takdir Alisjahbana, "The Problem of Minority Languages."
8. See Kallen, *Ethnicity and Human Rights in Canada*, and Nevitte and Kornberg, *Minorities and the Canadian State*.
9. See Unesco reports on cultural policy for USSR, Byelorussia, Ethiopia, Viet Nam. For an analysis of the linguistic problem in the USSR, see Isayev, *National Languages in the USSR*. Also Connor, *The National Question*.
10. See Warwick and Cohen, "The Institutional Management of Cultural Diversity"; also Connor, *The National Question*.
11. Unesco report on cultural policy in Ethiopia (1982), cited in Barre, "Politiques culturelles."
12. Unesco report on cultural policy in Cameroon (1975), quoted in Barre, "Politiques culturelles."
13. Bonfil, *México Profundo*.
14. See Coulmas, "Linguistic Minorities."

References

Adam, Heribert, and Hermann Giliomee. 1979. *Ethnic power mobilized: Can South Africa change?* New Haven: Yale University Press.

Addo, Herb. 1986. *Imperialism: The permanent stage of capitalism.* Tokyo: The United Nations University Press.

Aguirre Beltrán, Gonzalo. 1983. *Lenguas vernáculas, su uso y desuso en la enseñanza: la experiencia de México.* México: Secretaría de Educación Pública, Ediciones de la Casa Chata 20.

Ake, Claude. 1981. *A political economy of Africa.* New York: Longman.

Akzin, Benjamin. 1964. *State and nation.* London: Hutchinson University Library.

Albert, Bruce, and Marcus Colchester. 1985. "Recent developments in the situation of the Yanomami." In Survival International, *An end to laughter? Tribal peoples and economic development.* London: Survival International.

Alcock, Anthony. 1986. "The Swedish community in Finland." In Minority Rights Group, *Co-existence in some plural European societies,* MRG Report No. 72. London.

Allen, Robert L. 1970. *Black awakening in capitalist America.* New York: Anchor Books.

Amin, Samir. 1971. *L'accumulation à l'echelle mondiale.* Paris: Anthropos.

———. 1979. *Classe et nation dans l'histoire et al crise contemporaine.* Paris: Les Editions de Minuit.

Amselle, Jean-Loup, and Elikia M'Bokolo (sous la direction de). 1985. *Au coeur de l'ethnie. Ethnies, tribalisme et état en Afrique.* Paris: Editions de la Decouverte.

Anderson, Benedict. 1983. *Imagined communities: Reflections on the origin and spread of nationalism.* London: Verso.

Anti-Slavery Society. 1983. *The Philippines: Authoritarian government, multinationals and ancestral lands.* London: Anti-Slavery Society.

———. 1984. *The Chittagong Hill Tracts: Militarization, oppression and the hill tribes.* London: Anti-Slavery Society.

Apter, David E. 1965. *The politics of modernization.* Chicago: The University of Chicago Press.

Asiwaju, A.I., ed. 1985. *Partitioned Africans: Ethnic relations across Africa's international boundaries, 1884–1984.* Lagos: University of Lagos Press.

Aspelin, Paul L., and Silvio Coelho dos Santos. 1981. *Indian areas threatened by hydroelectric projects in Brazil.* Copenhagen: International Work Group for Indigenous Affairs.

174

Aubet, María-José. 1977. *Rosa Luxemburg y la cuestión nacional*. Barcelona: Editorial Anagrama.

Azar, Edward E., and John W. Burton. 1986. *International conflict resolution: Theory and practice*. Sussex: Wheatsheaf Books.

Azcárate y Flores, Pablo de. 1945. *League of Nations and national minorities*. Washington, D.C.: Carnegie Endowment for International Peace.

Baker, Martin. 1981. *The new racism*. London: Junction Books.

Balandier, Georges. 1955. *Sociologie actuelle de l'Afrique Noire*. Paris: Presses Universitaires de France.

Banton, Michael. 1980. "Ethnic groups and the theory of rational choice." In Unesco, *Sociological theories: Race and colonialism*. Paris: Unesco.

———. 1983. *Racial and ethnic competition*. Cambridge: Cambridge University Press.

Barre, Marie-Chantal. 1986. "Les immigrés en Europe Occidentale." Unpublished report prepared for the United Nations University.

———. 1987. "Politiques culturelles et minorités ethniques." Unpublished report prepared for the United Nations University.

Barrera, Mario. 1979. *Race and class in the southwest, a theory of racial inequality*. Notre Dame: University of Notre Dame Press.

Barrett, Leonard. 1977. *The Rastafarians*. Boston: Beacon Press.

Barth, Frederick. 1969. *Ethnic groups and boundaries*. Oslo: Universitetsforlaget.

Bauer, Otto. 1924. *Die Nationalitätenfrage und die Sozialdemokratie*. Vienna: Verlag der Wiener Volksbuchhandlung.

Bellah, R.N. 1957. *Tokugawa religion*. Glencoe: The Free Press.

Berger, Thomas R. 1985. *Village journey*. New York: Hill and Wang.

Berting, Jan, et al., eds. 1990. *Human rights in a pluralist world: Individuals and collectivities*. Westport, Conn.: Meckler.

Blauner, Robert. 1972. *Racial oppression in America*. New York: Harper & Row.

Blaut, James M. 1987. *The national question: Decolonising the theory of nationalism*. London: Zed Books.

Bodley, John H. 1982. *Victims of progress*. Palo Alto: Mayfield Publishing Company.

Bogdanor, Vernon. 1979. *Devolution*. New York: Oxford University Press.

Bonacich, Edna. 1972. "A theory of ethnic antagonism: The split labor market." *American Sociological Review*, vol. 37 (October).

———. 1973. "A theory of middleman minorities." *American Sociological Review*, vol. 38 (October).

Bonfil, Guillermo, 1981. *Utopía y revolución*. Mexico: Ed. Nueva Imagen.

———. 1988. *México profundo*. Mexico: Secretaría de Educación Pública.

Bonfil, Guillermo et al. 1982. *América Latina: Etnodesarrollo y etnocidio*. San José (Costa Rica): FLACSO.

Boucher, Jerry, Dan Landis, and Karen Arnold Clark, eds. 1987. *Ethnic conflict: International perspectives*. Newbury Park, Calif.: Sage Publications.

Bowser, Benjamin P., and Raymond G. Hunt, eds. 1981. *Impacts of racism on white Americans*. Newbury Park, Calif.: Sage Publications.

Brass, Paul, ed. 1985. *Ethnic groups and the State*. London: Croom Helm.

Breton, Roland. 1981. *Les ethnies*. Paris: Presses Universitaires de France.

Breuilly, John. 1982. *Nationalism and the State*. Manchester: Manchester University Press.

Bromley, Yu. V. 1984. *Theoretical ethnography*. Moscow: Nauka Publishers.

Bryce, Ken. 1979. *Endless pressure*. Harmondsworth: Penguin Books.

Burger, Julian. 1987. *Report from the frontier: The state of the world's indigenous peoples*. London: Zed Books.

Burton, John W. 1987. *Resolving deep-rooted conflict: A handbook*. Lanham: University Press of America.

Buvollen, Hans Petter. 1988. "The Miskitu-Sandinista conflict: International concerns and outside actors." In Kumar Rupesinghe, ed., *Ethnic conflicts and human rights*. Oslo: Norwegian University Press, and Tokyo: United Nations University Press.

Calvet, Louis-Jean. 1987. *La guerre des langues et les politiques linguistiques*. Paris: Payot.

Campbell, Horace. 1987. *Rasta and resistance*. Trenton, N.J.: Africa World Press.

Capotorti, Francesco. 1979. *Study on the rights of persons belonging to ethnic, religious and linguistic minorities* (UN Document E/CN.4/Sub.2/384/Rev.1). New York: United Nations.

Cardoso, Fernando Henrique, and Enzo Falletto. 1969. *Dependencia y desarrollo en América Latina*. Mexico: Siglo XXI.

Carneiro da Cunha, Manuela. 1989. "A noçao de direito costumeiro e os direitos indígenas na nova Constituiçao do Brasil." *América Indígena*, vol. 49, no. 2, Mexico.

Carrère d'Encausse, Helène. 1978. *L'empire éclaté, la révolte des nations en URSS*. Paris: Flammarion.

Casese, Antonio. 1989. "The right of self-determination and non-State peoples." Paper presented at the Seminar on Minorities and the UN System, organized by the Harvard Law School and the International Center for Ethnic Studies, Oxford, April 1989.

Cashmore, E. Ellis. 1987. *The logic of racism*. London: Allen & Unwin.

Centre for Contemporary Cultural Studies. 1982. *The empire strikes back: Race and racism in 70s Britain*. London: Hutchinson.

Chabry, Laurent, and Annie Chabry. 1984. *Politique et minorités au Proche-Orient*. Paris: Maisonneuve et Larose.

Chaliand, Gerard, and Yves Ternon. 1980. *Le genocide des Arméniens*. Paris: Editions Complexe.

Chandra, Bipan. 1984. *Communalism in modern India*. New Delhi: Vikas.

Claude, Inis, Jr. 1955. *National minorities, an international problem*. Cambridge, Mass.: Harvard University Press.

Colchester, Marcus. 1985. "Hydropower projects in central India." In Survival International, *An end to laughter? Tribal peoples and economic development*. London: Survival International.

Committee for Rational Development. 1984. *Sri Lanka, the ethnic conflict: Myths, realities and perspectives*. New Delhi: Navrang.

Connor, Walker. 1972. "Nation building or nation destroying." *World Politics*, vol. 24, no. 3.

———. 1984. *The national question in Marxist-Leninist theory and strategy*. Princeton: Princeton University Press.

Conseil de l'Europe. 1983. *La culture immigrée dans une société en mutation. L'europe multiculturelle en l'an 2000*. Strasbourg. (Quoted by Marie-Chantal Barre, 1986).

Coulmas, Florian. 1984. "Linguistic minorities and literacy." In Florian Coulmas, ed., *Linguistic minorities and literacy*. Berlin: Mouton. (Papers of a United Nations University workshop on Minorities and Literacy, held in 1982).

Crawford, James, ed. 1988. *The rights of peoples*. Oxford: Clarendon.

Cristescu, Aurelio. 1981. *The right to self-determination* (E/CN.4/Sub.2/404/Rev.1). New York: United Nations.

Cruse, Harold. 1968. *Rebellion or revolution*. New York: William Morrow.

Cultural Survival. 1981. "East Timor: Five years after the Indonesian invasion" (Testimony presented at the Decolonization Committee of the United Nations General Assembly, October 1980). Cultural Survival Occasional Paper No. 2 (January 1981). Cambridge, Mass.

Cultural Survival Quarterly, vol. 11, nos. 3, 4, 1987; vol. 6, no. 3, 1982 (summer).

Cummings, Ian. 1980. *Marx, Engels and national movements*. London: Croom Helm.

Dahl, Jens. 1985. "New political structure and old non-fixed structural politics in Greenland." In Jens Brosted et al., eds., *Native power: The quest for autonomy and nationhood of indigenous peoples*. Bergen: Universitetsforlaget AS.

Das Gupta, Jyotirindra. 1975. "Ethnicity, language demands, and national development in India." In Nathan Glazer and Daniel P. Moynihan, eds., *Ethnicity: Theory and experience*. Cambridge, Mass.: Harvard University Press.

Davis, Horace B. 1967. *Nationalism and socialism: Marxist and labor theories of nationalism to 1917*. New York: Monthly Review Press.

———. 1978. *Toward a Marxist theory of nationalism*. New York: Monthly Review Press.

Dawidowicz, Lucy S. 1975. *The war against the Jews 1933–1945*. New York: Holt, Rinehart and Winston.

De l'ethnocide. 1972. Paris: Union Générale d'Editions.

Deloria, Vine, Jr., and Clifford M. Lytle. 1983. *American Indians, American justice*. Austin: University of Texas Press.

Deschênes, Jules. 1985. (UN Document E/CN.4/Sub.2/1985/31). New York: United Nations.

de Silva, K.M. 1986. *Managing ethnic tensions in multi-ethnic societies: Sri Lanka 1880–1985*. London: University Press of America.

Deutsch, Karl W. 1953. *Nationalism and social communication*. Cambridge, Mass.: Institute of Technology.

de Wenden, Catherine. 1985. *Esprit*, June, quoted in Marie-Chantal Barre, 1986.

Dobrizheva, L. 1985. "*The national question in the Soviet Union*." Unpublished report to the United Nations University.

Dunbar Ortiz, Roxanne. 1984. *Indians of the Americas: Self-determination and international human rights*. London: Zed Books.

Eidheim, Harald. 1985. "Indigenous peoples and the State: The Saami case in Norway." In Jens Brosted et al., eds., *Native power*. Bergen: Universitetsforlaget.

Eistenstadt, Shmuel. In press. "Human rights in comparative civilizational perspective." Paper prepared for the Nobel Symposium on Human Rights, Oslo, June 1988.

Eisenstadt, S.N., ed. 1968. *The protestant ethic and modernization*. New York: Basic Books.

Elton Mayo, Patricia. 1974. *The roots of identity: Three national movements in contemporary European politics*. London: Allen Lane.

Emerson, Rupert. 1960. *From empire to nation: The rise of self-assertion of Asian and African peoples*. Boston: Beacon Press.

Enloe, Cynthia H. 1987. "When ethnicity is militarized – The consequences for Southeast Asian communities." In Cultural Survival, *Southeast Asian Tribal Groups and Ethnic Minorities*. Cambridge, Mass.: Cultural Survival.

Ermacora, Felix. 1964. *Der Minderheitenschutz in der Arbeit der Vereinten Nationen*. Vienna-

Stuttgart, Wilhelm Braumüller.

Esman, Milton J., and Itamar Rabinovich, eds. 1988. *Ethnicity, pluralism, and the State in the Middle East*. Ithaca: Cornell University Press.

European Parliament. 1985. "Committee of Inquiry into the Rise of Fascism and Racism in Europe: Report on the findings of the inquiry." December 1985.

Falk, Richard. 1981. *Human rights and State sovereignty*. New York: Holmes and Meier Publishers.

Fei Hsiao Tung. 1981. "Ethnic identification in China." In Fei Hsiao Tung, *Toward a people's anthropology*. Beijing: New World Press.

Foster, Charles R., ed. 1980. *Nations without a State: Ethnic minorities in Western Europe*. New York: Praeger Publishers.

Francis, E.K. 1976. *Interethnic relations, an essay in sociological theory*. New York: Elsevier.

Frank, André G. 1979. *Dependent accumulation and underdevelopment*. New York: Monthly Review Press.

Frideres, James S. 1983. *Native peoples in Canada, contemporary conflicts*. Scarborough: Prentice-Hall.

Gellner, Ernest. 1983. *Nations and nationalism*. Ithaca: Cornell University Press.

————. 1988. "Human rights and the New Circle of Equity." Paper prepared for the Nobel Symposium on Human Rights, Oslo, June 1988.

Giliov, S. 1983. *The nationalities question: Lenin's approach (theory and practice in the USSR)*. Moscow: Progress Publishers.

Glazer, Nathan, and Daniel P. Moynihan, eds. 1975. *Ethnicity: Theory and experience*. Cambridge, Mass.: Harvard University Press.

Glezerman, G. 1979. *Classes and nations*. Moscow: Progress Publishers.

González Casanova, Pablo. 1965. "Internal colonialism and national development." *Studies in Comparative International Development* 1, no. 4.

Gordon, Milton M. 1975. "Toward a general theory of racial and ethnic group relations." In Nathan Glazer and Daniel P. Moynihan, eds., *Ethnicity: Theory and experience*, Cambridge, Mass.: Harvard University Press.

Gordon, Sarah. 1984. *Hitler, Germans, and the "Jewish" question*. Princeton: Princeton University Press.

Gros Espiell, Hector. 1979. *El derecho a la libre determinación* (E/CN.4/Sub.2/405/Rev.1). New York: United Nations.

Guilhaudis, J.F. 1976. *Le droit des peuples à disposer d'eux-mêmes*. Grenoble: Presses Universitaires de Grenoble.

Gunatilleke, Godfrey, ed. 1986. *Migration of Asian workers to the Arab world*. Tokyo: United Nations University Press.

Gutiérrez Chong, Natividad. 1986. "El destino de las minorías de China: Integración nacional o sobrevivencia étnica." Unpublished report to the United Nations University.

Hadden, Tom, and Kevin Boyle. 1988. "Northern Ireland: Conflict and conflict resolution." In Kumar Rupesinghe, ed., *Ethnic conflict and human rights*. Oslo: Norwegian University Press, and Tokyo: United Nations University Press. 1988

Harff, Barbara. 1984. *Genocide and human rights: International legal and political issues*. Denver: University of Denver.

Haupt, Georges, Michael Lowy, and Claudie Weil. 1974. *Les marxistes et la question nationale 1848–1914*. Paris: Maspero.

Haywood, Harry. 1948. *Negro liberation*. New York: International Publishers.

Hechter, Michael. 1975. *Internal colonialism: The Celtic fringe in British national development, 1536–1966*. London: Routledge and Kegan Paul.

——. 1985. "Internal colonialism revisted." In Edward A. Tiryakian and Ronald Rogowski, eds., *New nationalisms of the developed West*. Boston: Allen and Unwin.

Héraud, Guy. 1963. *L'Europe des ethnies*. Paris: Presses d'Europe.

Herod, Charles C. 1976. *The nation in the history of Marxian thought: The concept of nations with history and nations without history*. The Hague: Martinus Nijhoff.

Hertz, Frederick. 1944. *Nationality in history and politics*. New York: Oxford University Press.

Himes, Joseph S. 1973. *Racial conflict in American society*. Columbus, Charles E. Merrill.

Hirsch, Fred. 1976. *Social limits to growth*. Cambridge, Mass.: Harvard University Press.

Horowitz, Donald L. 1985. *Ethnic groups in conflict*. Berkeley: University of California Press.

Horowitz, Irving Louis. 1980. *Taking lives: Genocide and State power*. New Brunswick: Transaction Books.

Hvalkof, Soren, and Peter Aaby. 1981. *Is God an American?* Copenhagen: International Work Group for Indigenous Affairs, and London: Survival International.

Independent Commission on International Humanitarian Issues. *Indigenous peoples: A global quest for justice*. London: Zed Books.

International Labour Conference, 76th. Session 1988. *Partial revision of the Indigenous and Tribal Populations Convention (no. 107)*. Report 6(2). Geneva: International Labour Office.

International Labour Conference, 76th. Session 1989. *Partial revision of the Indigenous and Tribal Populations Convention, 1957 (no. 107)*. Report 4 (1). Geneva: International Labour Office.

International Labour Office. 1953. *Indigenous peoples*. Geneva: International Labour Office.

International Work Group for Indigenous Affairs. 1987. *Self-determination and indigenous peoples: Sámi rights and northern perspectives*. IWGIA Document No. 58. Copenhagen: International Work Group for Indigenous Affairs.

Isaacs, Harold R. 1975. *Idols of the tribe*. New York: Harper and Row.

Isayev, M.I. 1977. *National languages in the USSR: Problems and solutions*. Moscow: Progress Publishers.

Ismagilova, R.N. 1978. *Ethnic problems of tropical Africa*. Moscow: Progress Publishers.

Jacquard, Albert. 1982. "La science face au racisme." In *Racisme, science et pseudo-science*. Paris: Unesco Press.

Jászi, Oscar. 1929. *The dissolution of the Habsburg monarchy*. Chicago: The University of Chicago Press.

Jaulin, Robert. 1979. *La descivilización (política y práctica del etnocidio)*. Mexico: Editorial Nueva Imagen.

Jenkins Molieri, Jorge. 1986. *El desafío indígena en Nicaragua: El caso de los miskitos*. Mexico: Ed. Katún.

Jordan, Winthrop D. 1982. "First impressions: Initial English confrontations with Africans." In Charles Husband, ed., *"Race" in Britain, continuity and change*. London: Hutchinson.

Junqueira, Carmen, and Betty Mindlin. 1987. *The Aripuana Park and the Polonoroeste pro-*

gramme. IWGIA Document No. 59. Copenhagen: International Work Group for Indigenous Affairs.

Kallen, Evelyn. 1982. *Ethnicity and human rights in Canada*. Ottawa: Gage Educational Publishing Company.

Kann, Robert A. 1964. *Das Nationalitätenproblem der Habsburgermonarchie*. 2 vols. Graz-Cologne: Verlag Hermann Böhlaus.

Karklins, Rasma. 1986. *Ethnic relations in the USSR: The perspective from below*. Boston: Allen and Unwin.

Kaur, Amarjit et al. 1984. *The Punjab story*. New Delhi: Roli Books International.

Kautsky, Karl. 1978. "Nacionalidad e internacionalidad." In *La segunda internacional y el problema nacional y colonial*. Cuadernos de Pasado y Presente No. 74. Mexico: Siglo XXI.

Kedourie, Elie. 1970. *Nationalism in Africa and Asia*. New York: New American Library.

————. 1985. *Nationalism*. London: Hutchinson and Co.

Kengne Pokam, E. 1986. *La problématique de l'unité nationale au Cameroun*. Paris: L'Harmattan.

Keyes, Charles F. 1987. "Tribal peoples and the nation-state in mainland Southeast Asia." In Cultural Survival, *Southeast Asian tribal groups and ethnic minorities*. Cambridge, Mass.: Cultural Survival.

————, ed. 1981. *Ethnic change*. Seattle: University of Washington Press.

Kiernan, V.G. 1982. "European attitudes to the outside world." In Charles Husband, ed., *'Race' in Britain, continuity and change*. London: Hutchinson.

Kim, M. 1975. *El pueblo soviético, una nueva comunidad histórica*. Moscow: Progress Publishers.

Kloss, Heinz. 1969. *Grundfragen der Ethnopolitik im 20. Jahrhundert*. Vienna: Wilhelm Braumüller.

Kohn, Hans. 1948. *The idea of nationalism*. New York: The Macmillan Company.

Koulitchenko, M. et al. 1975. *L'etat soviétique multinational*. Moscow: Progress Publishers.

Krejci, Jaroslav, and Vitezslav Velimsky. 1981. *Ethnic and political nations in Europe*. London: Croom Helm.

Kuper, Leo. 1981. *Genocide*. Harmondsworth: Penguin Books.

————, ed. 1975. *Race, science and society*. Paris: Unesco Press.

Laponce, J.A. 1987. *Languages and their territories*. Toronto: University of Toronto Press.

Lauren, Paul Gordon. 1988. *Power and prejudice: The politics and diplomacy of racial discrimination*. Boulder: Westview Press.

Law Blanco, Hazel. 1988. "Indigenous rights and the Autonomy Project in Nicaragua." In Kumar Rupesinghe, ed., *Ethnic conflict and human rights*. Oslo: Norwegian University Press, and Tokyo: United Nations University Press.

Lenin, V.I. 1955. *The right of nations to self-determination*. New York: International Publishers.

Léon, Abraham. 1968. *La conception matérialiste de la question juive*. Paris: Etudes et Documentation Internationales.

Levin, Michael, and John Stone. 1985. "Nationalism, racism and the 'Marxist Question.'" In International Sociological Association, *Colloquium on Marxist perspectives on ethnicity and nationalism*. Belgrade.

Luxemburg, Rosa. 1977. *Textos sobre la cuestión nacional*. Madrid: Ediciones de la Torre.

Lynch, Owen J., Jr. 1987. "Indigenous rights in insular Southeast Asia." In Cultural Survival, *Southeast Asian tribal groups and ethnic minorities*. Cultural Survival Report 22.

Cambridge, Mass.: Cultural Survival.

Lyon, Noel. 1985. "Constitutional issues in native law." In Bradford W. Morse, ed., *Aboriginal peoples and the law*. Ottawa: Carleton University Press.

McNeill, William H. 1986. *Polyethnicity and national unity in world history*. Toronto: University of Toronto Press.

Marable, Manning. 1984. *Race, reform and rebellion*. London: Macmillan Publishers.

Margolis First, Ana. 1985. La problemática indígena en el mundo contemporáneo." Unpublished report presented to the United Nations University.

Martínez Cobo, José R. 1987. *Study of the problem of discrimination against indigenous populations*, vol.5: *Conclusions, Proposals and Recommendations*. New York: United Nations.

Marx, Karl, and Friedrich Engels. 1980. *La cuestión nacional y la formación de los estados*. Cuadernos de Pasado y Presente No. 69. Mexico: Siglo XXI.

Meinhardt, Rolf (Hg.). 1984. *Türken raus? oder Verteidigt den sozialen Frieden*. Hamburg: Rowohlt.

Miles, Robert. 1982. *Racism and migrant labour*. London: Routledge and Kegan Paul.

———. 1989. *Racism*. London: Routledge and Kegan Paul.

Milne, R.S. 1981. *Politics in ethnically bipolar States*. Vancouver: University of British Columbia Press.

Minority Rights Group. N.d. *Cyprus*. Report no. 30. London: Minority Rights Group.

———. N.d. *The Flemings and Walloons of Belgium*. Report no. 46. London: Minority Rights Group.

———. N.d. *Uganda and Sudan*. Report no. 66. London: Minority Rights Group.

———. N.d. *Co-existence in some plural European societies*. Report no. 72. London: Minority Rights Group.

Morse, Bradford W. 1985. "The resolution of land claims." In Bradford W. Morse, ed., *Aboriginal peoples and the law*. Ottawa: Carleton University Press.

Motyl, Alexander J. 1987. *Will the non-Russians rebel? State, ethnicity and stability in the USSR*. Ithaca: Cornell University Press.

Münzel, Mark. N.d. *The Aché: Genocide continues in Paraguay*. IWGIA Report No. 17. Copenhagen: International Work Group for Indigenous Affairs.

———. N.d. *The Aché Indians: Genocide in Paraguay*. IWGIA Report No. 11. Copenhagen: International Work Group for Indigenous Affairs.

Nagata, Judith. 1979. *Malaysian mosaic, perspectives from a poly-ethnic society*. Vancouver: University of British Columbia Press.

Neuberger, Benyamin. 1986. *National self-determination in postcolonial Africa*. Boulder: Lynne Rienner Publishers.

Nevitte, Neil, and Allan Kornberg, eds. 1985. *Minorities and the Canadian State*. Oakville, Ont.: Mosaic Press.

Obieta Chalbaud, José A. de. 1985. *El derecho humano de la autodeterminación de los pueblos*. Madrid: Tecnos.

Organización Internacional del Trabajo (Oficina Regional de la OIT para América Latina y el Caribe). 1989. *Convenio Nº 169*. Lima, OIT.

Oriol, Paul. 1985. *Les immigrés: Métèques ou citoyens?* Paris: Syros.

Ortega Hegg, Manuel. 1988. "The ethnic question in Nicaragua: Indigenous autonomy and ethnic plurality." In Kumar Rupesinghe, ed., *Ethnic conflict and human rights*. Oslo: Norwegian University Press, and Tokyo: United Nations University Press.

Paine, Robert. 1982. *Dam a river, damn a people?* IWGIA Document No. 45. Copenhagen:

International Work Group for Indigenous Affairs.

Palley, Claire. 1978. *Constitutional law and minorities*. Report no. 36. London: Minority Rights Group.

Patterson, Orlando. 1977. *Ethnic chauvinism, the reactionary impulse*. New York: Stein and Day.

Pearse, Andrew. 1980. *Seeds of plenty, seeds of want*. Geneva: United Nations Research Institute for Social Development.

Petersen, Robert. "Home rule in Greenland." In International Work Group for Indigenous Affairs, *Self-determination and indigenous peoples: Sámi rights and northern perspectives*. IWGIA Document No. 58. Copenhagen: International Work Group for Indigenous Affairs.

Petrella, Riccardo. 1978. *La renaissance des cultures régionales en Europe*. Paris: Editions Entente.

Poggi, Gianfranco. 1978. *The development of the modern State: A sociological introduction*. Stanford: Stanford University Press.

Power, Jonathan. 1978. *Western Europe's migrant workers*. Rev. ed. Report no. 28. London: Minority Rights Group.

Reinares, Fernando. 1984. *Violencia y política en Euskadi*. Bilbao: Desclée de Brouwer.

Rex, John. 1970. *Race relations in sociological theory*. London: Routledge and Kegan Paul.

Rioux, Marcel. 1969. *La question du Québec*. Paris: Editions Seghers.

Robinson, Cedric J. 1983. *Black Marxism: The making of the black radical tradition*. London: Zed Books.

Ronen, Dov. 1979. *The quest for self-determination*. New Haven: Yale University Press.

Rosdolsky, Roman. 1981. *El problema de los pueblos "sin historia."* Barcelona: Editorial Fontamara.

Rothschild, Joseph. 1981. *Ethnopolitics, a conceptual framework*. New York: Columbia University Press.

Ruan Xihu. 1985. "Informe sobre las nacionalidades minoritarias en China (Zhong Guo sha shu minzhu qingkuang baogao)." Unpublished report to the United Nations University.

Rupesinghe, Kumar. 1988. "Theories of conflict resolution and their applicability to protracted ethnic conflict." In Kumar Rupesinghe, ed., *Ethnic conflict and human rights*. Oslo: Norwegian University Press, and Tokyo: United Nations University Press.

Rustow, Dankwart A. 1967. *A world of nations: Problems of political modernization*. Washington, D.C.: The Brookings Institution.

Sanders, Douglas. 1987. "Aboriginal rights in Canada: An overview." In *Law and Anthropology*, no. 2.

Schermerhorn, R.A. 1970. *Comparative ethnic relations: A framework for theory and research*. New York: Random House.

Schneider, Robin, and Klaudine Ohland. 1982. *Nationale revolution und indianische Identität: Der Konflikt zwischen Sandinisten und Miskito-Indianer an Nicaraguas Atlantikküste*. Wuppertal: Edition Nahua.

Seton-Watson, Hugh. 1977. *Nations and States: An enquiry into the origins of nations and the politics of nationalism*. London: Methuen.

Shack, William A., and Elliot P. Skinner, eds. *Strangers in African societies*. Berkeley: University of California Press.

Shafer, Boyd C. 1972. *Faces of nationalism*. New York: Harcourt Brace.

Sieghart, Paul. 1983. *The international law of human rights*. Oxford: Clarendon Press.

Sigler, Jay A. 1983. *Minority rights, a comparative analysis*. Westport, Conn.: Greenwood Press.

SIM (Netherlands Institute of Human Rights). 1988. *New expressions of racism: Growing areas of conflict in Europe*. SIM special report no. 7. Utrecht: SIM.

Smith, Anthony D. 1979. *Nationalism in the twentieth century*. Oxford: Martin Robertson.

———. 1981. *The ethnic revival in the modern world*. Cambridge: Cambridge University Press.

———. 1983. *State and nation in the Third World: The Western State and African nationalism*. Brighton: Wheatsheaf Books.

———. 1986. *The ethnic origins of nations*. Oxford: Basil Blackwell.

Sombart, Werner. 1951. *The Jews and modern capitalism*. Glencoe: The Free Press.

Sowell, Thomas. 1983. *The economics and politics of race*. New York: William Morrow.

Srivastava, R.N. 1982. "Literacy education for minorities: A case study from India." In Florian Coulmas, ed., *Linguistic minorities and literacy*. (Papers of a United Nations University workshop on Linguistic Minorities and Literacy, Tokyo, 1982). Berlin: Mouton.

Stalin, Joseph. N.d. *Marxism and the national and colonial question*. (Marxist Library vol. 38). New York: International Publishers.

Stavenhagen, Rodolfo. 1965. "Classes, colonialism and acculturation." *Studies in Comparative International Development* 1, no. 6.

———. 1975. *Social classes in agrarian societies*. New York: Anchor Books.

———. 1984. "Linguistic minorities and language policy in Latin America: The case of Mexico." In Florian Coulmas, ed., *Linguistic minorities and literacy*. Berlin: Mouton.

———. 1985. "The indigenous problematique." *Dossiers de l'IFDA*, no. 50. Nyon: IFDA.

———. 1986. "Ethnodevelopment: A neglected dimension in development thinking." In Raymond Apthorpe and Andras Krahl, eds., *Development studies: Critique and renewal*. Leiden: E.J. Brill.

———. 1986. *Problems and prospects of multi-ethnic States*. United Nations University Annual Lecture Series, no. 3. Tokyo: United Nations University Press.

———. 1988. *Derecho indígena y derechos humanos en América Latina*. México: El Colegio de México and Instituto Interamericano de Derechos Humanos.

Steinberg, Stephen. 1981. *The ethnic myth, race, ethnicity and class in America*. Boston: Beacon Press.

Stoll, David. 1982. *Fishers of men or founders of empire?* London: Zed Books.

Stone, John. 1985. *Racial conflict in contemporary society*. London: Fontana Press.

Survival International. 1983. *Genocide in Bangladesh*. Survival International Annual Review No. 13. London: Survival International.

———. 1987. "Tribals in Indonesia." In *Development: Journal of the Society for International Development*, vol. 1.

Suter, Keith. 1979. *West Irian, East Timor and Indonesia*. Report no. 42. London: Minority Rights Group.

Takdir Alisjahbana, S. 1984. "The problem of minority languages in the overall linguistic problems of our time." In Florian Coulmas, ed., *Linguistic minorities and literacy*. Berlin: Mouton.

Tambiah, S.J. 1986. *Sri Lanka: Ethnic fratricide and the dismantling of democracy*. Delhi: Oxford University Press.

Taylor, Kenneth I. 1985. "Report on the situation of the Mapuche Indians of Chile." In Survival International, *An end to laughter? Tribal peoples and economic development*. London: Survival International.

Thornberry, Patrick. 1987. *Minorities and human rights law*. Report no. 73. London: Minority Rights Group.

Tiryakian, Edward A., and Ronald Rogowski, eds. 1985. *New nationalisms of the developed West*. Boston: Allen and Unwin.

Tomuschat, Christian. 1985. "Status of minorities under Article 27 of the United Nations Covenant on Civil and Political Rights." In Satish Chandra, ed., *Minorities in national and international laws*. New Delhi: Deep and Deep Publications.

Tortosa, José M. 1982. *Política lingüística y lenguas minoritarias*. Madrid: Editorial Tecnos.

Treece, Dave. 1987. *Bound in misery and iron: The impact of the Grande Carajás programme on the Indians of Brazil*. London: Survival International.

Unesco. 1970. *Cultural rights as human rights*. Paris: Unesco.

———. 1973. *Etudes et documents, Sénégal*. Paris: Unesco.

———. 1974. *Etudes et documents, Tanzania*. Paris: Unesco.

———. 1979. *Declaration on race and racial prejudice*. Paris: Unesco.

———. 1987. "Report on cultural policy in Cameroon (1975)." Quoted in Marie-Chantal Barre, "Politiques culturelles et minorités ethniques." Unpublished report prepared for the United Nations University.

———. 1987. "Report on cultural policy in Ethiopia (1982)." Cited in Marie-Chantal Barre, "Politiques culturelles et minorités ethniques." Unpublished report prepared for the United Nations University.

United Nations. 1984. *The United Nations and human rights*. New York: United Nations.

United Nations. 1988. Document E/CN. 4/Sub. 2/1988/24/Add. 1R.

———. 1988. Document E/CN. 4/Sub. 2/1988/25.

Valdés, Luz María. 1988. *El perfil demográfico de los indios mexicanos*. Mexico: Siglo XXI Editores.

Van Dyke, Vernon. 1985. *Human rights, ethnicity and discrimination*. Westport, Conn.: Greenwood Press.

Vasak, Karel. 1978. *Les dimensions internationales des droits de l'homme*. Paris: Unesco.

Veiter, Theodor. 1977. *Nationalitätenkonflikt und Volksgruppenrecht im 20. Jahrhundert*. Munich: Bayerische Landeszentrale für Politische Bildungsarbeit.

Vilas, Carlos M. 1989. *State, class and ethnicity in Nicaragua*. Boulder: Lynne Rienner.

Wallerstein, Immanuel. 1979. *The modern world-system*. New York: Academic Press.

Warwick, Paul V., and Lenard J. Cohen. 1985. "The institutional management of cultural diversity: An analysis of the Yugoslav experience." In Paul Brass, ed., *Ethnic groups and the State*. London: Croom Helm.

Weber, Max. 1958. *The religion of India: The sociology of Hinduism and Buddhism*. Glencoe: The Free Press.

Wilson, William Julius. 1978. *The declining significance of race: Blacks and changing American institutions*. Chicago: The University of Chicago Press.

World Bank. 1982. *Tribal peoples and economic development*. Washington, D.C.: World Bank.

World Council of Indigenous Peoples. 1987. "Rights of indigenous peoples to the Earth." Report by the WCIP to the UN Working Group on Indigenous Populations,

Geneva, 30 July 1985. Quoted in Julian Burger, *Report from the frontier*. London: Zed Books.

Young, Crawford. 1976. *The politics of cultural pluralism*. Madison: The University of Wisconsin Press.